Jim Britt's
Cracking the Rich Code⁵

Inspiring Stories, Insights and Strategies from Entrepreneurs Around the World

STAY IN TOUCH WITH JIM AND KEVIN

www.JimBritt.com

www.JimBrittCoaching.com

www.CrackingTheRichCode.com

www.KevinHarringtom.tv

For daily strategies and insights from top entrepreneurs, join us at

THE RICH CODE CLUB

FREE members site.

www.TheRichCodeClub.com

Cracking the Rich Code[5]

Jim Britt

All Rights Reserved

Copyright 2021

Cracking the Rich Code, LLC

10556 Combie Road, Suite 6205

Auburn, CA 95602

Jim Britt

Cracking the Rich Code[5]

ISBN: 978-1-64153-381-2

Co-authors from Around the World

Jim Britt

Kevin Harrington

Sara Sabin

Belinda Ellsworth

Moe Falah

Nadiya Manji

J.D. WildFlower

DrRon Jahner

Darren Christopher Rowland

Mike Weiss

Kevin T. Robertson

Pamela Bardhi

Joe Leone

Mato Gatnik

Marc Kaschke

Mark Yuzuik

Michael Nitti

Cindy May Grossman

Angeline Wehmeyer

Robin Bela

Mamie Valdez-Lamley

Brenda Jones

Chase Hughes

Michelle Guinn

Robert M. Curran

DEDICATION

Entrepreneurs will change the world. They always have and they always will.

To the entrepreneurial spirit that lives within each of us.

God Bless America!

Foreword by Kevin Harrington

You probably know me as one of the "Sharks" on the hit TV show Shark Tank, where I was an investor in many entrepreneurial ventures.

But my life and business wasn't always like that. I used to be your regular, everyday

guy patching cracked driveways to make money. I had hopes and dreams just like most, yet I worked around people who didn't support my dreams. But you know what? I not only found a way out, but I found a way to my dreams... and so can you.

Now, I wake up every morning excited about my day, and I surround with only the people I want in my life; entrepreneurs who really want something more than just getting by paycheck to paycheck.

Today we hear stories -- mostly from the mainstream media -- everyday about how bad things are, businesses are closing and jobs being lost, interest rates are on the rise, how the gap between rich and poor is growing and how you'll never make it on your own.

But here's what I know for sure. Entrepreneurs are going to change the world. We always have and we always will.

Forget the 1% vs the 99%. 100% of us entrepreneurs need answers. We need solutions. We need something more than what we're being told by those who don't have a clue. We need to start saying Yes! to opportunity and No! to all the noise.

The fact is that it's a new world and a new economy. The "proven" methods of doing business and investing that produced successful results, even two years ago, simply may not work anymore.

If you want to succeed (or even survive) in our new world, you need an entirely new set of skills and information.

You need to "reposition" yourself...often.

You need to revamp how you do business...often.

You need to change how you handle and invest your money...often.

Like any other situation, if you know WHAT to do and WHEN to do it, you'll not only be "safe"... you could easily skyrocket financially.

If you have the right knowledge for today, the right opportunities for today, the right strategies for today and most of all the right character and mindset for today, you can win — and you can win big!

What I've discovered in my over three-decade career as an entrepreneur, is that success in the face of financial adversity boils down to 3 things:

The right knowledge at the right time.

The right opportunities at the right time.

The right you... ALL the time.

The bottom line is this: you can no longer afford to rely on anyone else to navigate your financial future. You have to rely on your "self." The question is... do you have a "self" you can rely on? Unfortunately, when it comes to entrepreneurship and money, many people don't. They don't have the financial education, the mental toughness, the knowledge and the skills to build wealth... especially in an ever-changing marketplace. You need to get RE-educated. You need to REINVENT yourself for success in the new economy. You need to learn new strategies in the areas of business and career, finance and real estate that create wealth or at least financial freedom in today's new world. But that's not all...

Skills and strategies and all that profound new knowledge won't do you one bit of good if you don't have the CHARACTER, the HABITS and the MENTALITY it takes to get rich. If you have internal barriers, your road to success will be slow and full of pain and struggle. It's like driving with one foot on the gas and one foot on the brake and always wondering why you aren't getting anywhere. Your mind is working against you instead of for you.

I have seen business owners come to me with their business ready to go under — and have the next year be their best financial year ever. I've see others that had a business that should skyrocket, yet fail because they didn't have the mental toughness to go the distance. I have seen people stuck in dead-end, dreary jobs break out of their rut, get involved in a brand-new passion, and become wildly successful.

No matter what you do for a living...regardless of your education, level of business experience or current financial status…If you have a burning desire for financial change then you won't want to miss this rare opportunity to learn from the entrepreneurs within this book.

It will provide you with some of the same success strategies that Jim Britt and I have used personally and shared with tens of thousands of people who've had tremendous financial success…people just like you, who wanted to get out of the rat race and enjoy financial freedom.

In addition, you'll learn what others have done, mistakes they made and how you can avoid them. You'll discover strategies that could make your business into a major market leader. I always say, "Just one good idea can change everything."

Success is predictable if you know what determines it. This book offers some valuable tips, knowledge, insights, skill sets, that will challenge you to leap beyond your current comfort level. If you want to strengthen your life, your business and your effectiveness overall, you'll discover a great friend in this book. You'll probably want to recommend it to all your entrepreneurial friends.

Although I haven't followed Jim Britt's career over the last 40 years, but I do know that he is recognized as one of the top thought leaders in the world, helping millions of people create prosperous lives. He has authored 13 books and multiple programs showing people how to understand their hidden abilities to do more, become more and enjoy more in every area of life. I also want to recognize Joel Sauceda, our online business partner. He is the brains behind the many online PR, Marketing, Branding and Lead Generation strategies each entrepreneur coauthor and reader of the book will benefit from.

The principles, concepts and ideas within this book are sometimes simple, but can be profound to a person who is ready for that perfect message at the right time and is willing to take action to change. Maybe for one it's a chapter on leadership or mindset. For the next, it's a chapter on raising capital, or securing a business loan. Each chapter is like opening a surprise empowering gift.

The conclusion to me is an exciting one. You, me and every other human being are shaping our brains and bodies by our attitude, the decisions we make, the intentions we hold and the actions we take daily. Why is it exciting? Because we are in control of all these things and we can change as long as we have the intention, willingness and commitment to look inside, take charge of our lives and make the changes.

I want to congratulate Jim Britt for making this publication series available and for allowing me to write the foreword, a chapter in each book and be involved with the entrepreneurs within this book and series. I honor Jim and the coauthors within this book and the series for the lives they are changing.

As you enter these pages, do so slowly and with an open mind. Savor the wisdom you discover here, and then with interest and curiosity discover what rings true for you, and then take action toward the life you want.

So many people settle for less in life, but I can tell you from my experience that it doesn't have to be that way.

Be prepared…because your life and business, is about to change!

Jim Britt & Kevin Harrington

As co-creators of this book series Jim Britt and Kevin Harrington have devoted their lives to helping others to live a more prosperous, fulfilled and happy life. Over the years they have influenced millions of lives through their coaching, mentoring, business strategies and leading by example. They are committed to never ending self-improvement and an inspiration to all they touch. They are both a true example that all things are possible. If you get a chance to work with Kevin and Jim or becoming a coauthor in a future Cracking the Rich Code book, jump at the chance!

Table of Contents

Jim Britt

Jim Britt is an internationally recognized leader in the field of peak performance and personal empowerment training. He is author of 13 best-selling books, including *Rings of Truth; The Power of Letting Go; Freedom; Unleashing Your Authentic Power; Do This. Get Rich-For Entrepreneurs; The Entrepreneur; Directing the Movies of Your Subconscious Mind,* to name a few. He is the creator of a collaborative book series for entrepreneurs *Cracking the Rich Code.*

Jim has presented seminars throughout the world sharing his success principles and life-enhancing realizations with thousands of audiences, totaling over 1,500,000 people from all walks of life.

Jim has served as a success counselor to over 300 corporations worldwide. He was recently named as one of the world's top 20 success coaches, top 50 speakers and presented with the best of the best award out of the top 100 contributors of all time to the direct selling industry.

As an entrepreneur, Jim has launch 28 business ventures in the past 43 years and knows how to guide beginning and seasoned entrepreneurs toward a successful venture and avoid the classic mistakes made by the majority of new business launches.

Jim is more than aware of the challenges we all face in making adaptive changes for a sustainable future.

Think Like Superman

By Jim Britt

"Waking up to your true greatness in life requires letting go of who you imagine yourself to be."
--- Jim Britt

FACT: Becoming a millionaire is easier than it has ever been.

Many people have the notion that it's an impossible task to become a millionaire. Some say, "It's pure luck." Others say, "You have to be born into a rich family." For others, "You'll have to win the Lotto." And for many they say, "Your parents have to help you out a lot." That's the language of the poor.

A single mother with five children says, "I want to believe in what you're saying. However, I'm 45 years old and work long hours at two dead-end jobs. I barely earn enough to get by. What should I do?"

Another man said, "Well, if you work for the government, you cannot expect to become a millionaire. After all, you're on a fixed salary and there's little time for anything else. By the time you get home, you've got to play with the kids, eat dinner, and fall asleep watching TV."

Everyone has a story as to why they could never become a millionaire. But for every story, excuse really, there are other stories OR PEOPLE with worse circumstances, that have become rich.

The truth is that all of us can become as wealthy as we decide to be, and that's a mindset. None of us is excluded from wealth. If you have the desire to receive money, whatever the amount, you have all of the rights to do so like everyone else. There is no limit to how much you can earn for yourself. The only limitations are what you place on yourself.

Money is like the sun. It does not discriminate. It doesn't say, "I will not give light and warmth to this flower, tree, or person because I don't like them." Like the sun, money is abundantly available to all of us who truly believe that it is for us. No one is excluded.

There are, however, some major differences between rich and poor people. Here are some tips for becoming rich.

Change Your Thinking

You have to see the bigger picture. There are opportunities everywhere! The problem is that most people see just trees, when they should be looking at the entire forest. By doing so you will see that there are opportunities everywhere. The possibilities are endless.

You'll also have to go through plenty of self-discovery before you earn your first million. Knowing the truth about yourself isn't always the easiest task. Sometimes, you'll find that you are your biggest enemy—at least some days.

Learn from Millionaires

Most people are surrounded by what I like to call their, "default friends." These friends are acquaintances that we see at the gym, school, work, local happy hour, and other places. We naturally befriend these people because we are all in the same boat financially. However, in most cases, these people aren't millionaires and cannot help you become one either. In fact, if you tell them you are going to become a millionaire, some may even tell you that it's impossible and discourage you from even trying. They'll tell you that you're living in a fantasy world and why you'll never be able to make it happen. Instead, learn from millionaires. Let go of these relationships that pull you down when it comes to your money desires. It's okay to have friends that aren't millionaires. However, only take input from those that have accomplished what you want to accomplish. Hang out with those that will encourage and help you get to the next level. Don't give your raw diamonds to a brick layer to be cut.

Indulge in Wealth

To become wealthy, you must learn about wealth. This means that you'll have to put yourself in situations that you've never been in before.

ON OCCASION, DO SOME OF THESE:

Fly first class and see how it makes you feel.

Eat out at the finest restaurant and don't look at the price.

Take a limo instead of a cab or Uber. Watch how you feel.

Reserve a suite in a first-class hotel.

If you are used to drinking a $20 bottle of wine, go for the $100 and see how it tastes. It does taste different.

All I am saying is, try some of the things that wealthy people do and see how it makes you feel.

Believe it is Possible

If you believe that it is possible to become a millionaire, you can make it happen. However, if you've excluded yourself from this possibility and think and believe that it's for other people, you'll never become a millionaire.

Also, be sure to bless rich people when you can. Haters of money aren't likely to receive any of it either.

Read books that have been written by millionaires. By gaining a well-rounded education about earning large sums of money and staying inspired, you'll be able to learn the wealth secrets of the rich. I just saw a video on LinkedIn with my friend Kevin Harrington from the TV show Shark Tank. He said that one of his new companies just had a million-dollar day on Amazon.

Enlarge Your Service

Your material wealth is the sum of your total contribution to society. Your daily mantra should be, *'How do I deliver more value to more people in less time?'* Then, you'll know that you can always increase your quality and quantity of service. Enlarging your service is also about going the extra mile. When it comes to helping others, you must give it everything you have. You just plant the seeds and nature will take care of the rest.

Seize ALL Opportunities That Make Sense

You cannot say "No" to opportunities and expect to become a millionaire. You must seize every opportunity that has your name on it. It may just be an opportunity to connect with an influential person for no reason. Sometimes the monetary reward will not come immediately, but if you keep planting seeds, eventually you'll grow a fruitful crop. Money is the harvest of the service you provide and sometimes the connections you have. The more seeds you plant, the greater the harvest.

Have an Unstoppable Mindset

Want to know some of what my first mentor shared with me that took me from a broke factory worker, high school dropout, to millionaire?

First, he said, you have to start thinking like a wealthy, unstoppable person. You have to have a wealth mindset. He said that wealthy people think differently. He said, "I want you to start thinking like Superman!" Sounds crazy, right? Well, it's not. It's powerful and here's why. How you think will change your life.

Wealthy people think differently. They really do. And anyone can learn to think like the wealthy.

I'm not talking about positive thinking, Law of Attraction, or motivation. Let's get real. None of that stuff works anyway. Otherwise we would all be rich and happy already. I'm talking about thinking based in quantum physics science. Once you understand and apply it, it will change your life. You will become unstoppable!

If there was any person, fictional or real, whose qualities you could instantly possess, who would that person be? Think about it. Personally, I would say that Superman is the perfect person. Now, you are probably thinking I have lost it right? Just stick with me here. I think you will like what you are about to hear.

Superman is a fictional superhero widely considered to be one of the most famous and popular action hero and an American cultural icon. I remember watching Superman every Saturday morning when I was a kid. I couldn't get enough. He was my hero!

Let's look at Superman's traits:

Superman is indestructible.

He is a man of steel.

He can stop a locomotive in its tracks.

Bullets bounce off him.

He is faster than a speeding bullet.

No one can bring him down.

He can leap tall buildings in a single bound. Great powers to have in this day-and-age, wouldn't you say? What else would you need?

Now, for all you females, don't worry, we have not left you out. There is also a female version of Superman, named Superwoman. She has the same powers as Superman.

Now, this is where it gets interesting. Let's first look at the qualities that Superman possesses that you want to make your own. And to make it simple, I will refer to Superman for the rest of this message, and you can replace with Superwoman if you are female.

Again:

Superman is powerful and fearless.

Superman is virtually indestructible—except for kryptonite of course.

Superman can stop bullets.

Superman has supernatural powers. He can see through walls.

Superman can stop a speeding locomotive.

Superman can stop a bullet.

Superman jumps into immediate action when troubles arise.

Superman can crash through barriers.

Superman can even change clothes in a phone booth in seconds. Not too many of those around anymore. You'll have to duck behind a building to change.

So, you're thinking right now, *'Ok, I know that Superman has incredible supernatural powers, how can that help me? What good will it do me to think I am Superman, a fictional character?'*

Here is where science comes in. This is the part where you will be amazed when you learn about the supernatural powers that you already possess! NO, REALLY!

Your brain makes certain chemicals called neuro peptides. These are literally the molecules of emotion, like love, fear, joy, passion, and so on. These molecules of emotion are not only contained in your brain they actually circulate throughout your cellular structure. They send out a signal, a frequency much like a radio station sending out a signal. For example, you tune to 92.5 and you get jazz. Tune to 99.6 and you get rock. And if you are just one decimal off, you get static. The difference is that your signal goes both ways. You are a sender and a receiver.

You put out a signal, a mindset, of confidence about your financial success and people, circumstances, and opportunities show up to support your success. When you put out a signal of doubt and uncertainty and you receive support for your doubt and uncertainty. You've been around someone that you didn't trust, or you felt less than positive just being in their presence, right? You have also been around people that inspire you. That's what I'm talking about. You are projecting a frequency, looking to resonate with the frequency you are transmitting.

Anyway, the amazing part about these cells of emotion is that they are intelligent. They are thinking cells. These cells are constantly eavesdropping on the conversation that you are having with yourself. That's right. They are listening to you! And others are listening to your cells as well. Others feel what you feel when they are around you.

Your unconscious mind, your cells, are listening in, waiting to adjust your behavior based on what they hear from you, their master. So just imagine what would happen if you started to think like Superman...or like a millionaire.

Here are some of the thoughts you might have during the day:

"The challenges I face day today are easily overcome, after all I am Superman."

"I am indestructible."

"I have incredible strength."

"Nothing can stop me.....NOTHING."

"I have supernatural powers and can overcome anything."

"I can accomplish anything I want when I put my mind to it."

"I can break through any barrier."

"I can and I will do whatever it takes to accomplish my goal."

"I fear nothing."

The trillions of thinking cells in your body and brain listen, and they create exactly what you tell them to create. Their mission is to complete the picture of the you they see and hear when you talk to them. They must obey. It's their job!

Since you are Superman, you cannot fail. Why? Your thinking cells are now sending out the right signal, because you told them to. They are making you stronger, more successful, everyday! You have the ability to fight off all negativity, doubt, fear, and worry—nothing can stop you!

Superman has total confidence. So, your cells of emotion relating to confidence will now create more neuro peptide chemicals to promote feelings of power and confidence that others will feel in your presence.

Superman is fearless. So, your cells of emotion relating to fear will now create more neuro peptide chemicals to create feelings of courage. You are unstoppable!

And here's the key. Others will respond to you in the same way that you are talking to yourself.

If you are confident, others will have confidence in you.

You have thousands of thoughts every day. Make sure your thoughts are leading you in the direction you want to go. Make sure you are telling your cells a success story, and not a 'woe is me' story.

Most have been conditioned to think that creating wealth is difficult, or that it's only for the lucky few. What do you believe? It doesn't cost you any more to think like Superman; and it's much more inspiring!

Mediocrity cannot be an option if you decide to be wealthy and think like Superman.

Your decision, and communication with your cells, creates a mindset; that mindset influences how you show up.

None of that old type of thinking matters anymore…after all, you are Superman and you can accomplish anything.

If you want wealth, you have to stretch yourself. You have to do the things that unsuccessful people are not willing to do. You have to say "yes" to opportunity, then figure out how to get the job done.

Maybe you are uncomfortable selling and asking for money. If that's the case, then learn sales and learn to ask for money every day until you feel comfortable asking for it. You will never have money if you don't learn to ask for it.

I've learned a lot in the past 40+ years as an entrepreneur. I've learned that in order to have more, you have to become more. I've also learned that if you are comfortable, you are not growing. I learned that I couldn't go from a nervous rookie speaker with minimal self-confidence to hosting TV shows and speaking in front of 5,000 people overnight. I simply wasn't ready. I grew into that, one speaking engagement at a time. Every time I finished a speaking engagement, I would ask myself, "How did I do, and how could I do it better?" I still do that today.

And I've learned from the hundreds of thousands of people I've trained, coached, and mentored that none of us can do something we don't believe is possible. It's not going to happen if you're not ready to step out of your comfort zone and stretch yourself.

This has led me to understand the single most important principle of wealth-building, that has meant the difference between poverty and riches for people since humans first traded for pelts.

Are you ready?

Come in just a little closer. Listen up!

Every income level requires a different you, a different mindset! If you think that $10,000 a month is a lot of money, then $100,000 a month will be completely out of reach. If you believe that having $5,000 in the bank would make you rich, then $50,000 won't miraculously appear. You will never earn more money than you believe is "a lot" of money.

What you do as a business is only a small part of becoming rich. In fact, there are thousands, if not tens of thousands, of ways to make money—and lots of it. What I've learned over the years is that, by focusing on who you want to become instead of what you need to do, you're going to multiply your chances of getting rich a hundred-fold.

Ask anyone who's found a way to make a large sum of money legally, and he or she will tell you that it's not hard once you crack the code. And cracking the code starts with you and your mindset. The "code" to which I refer isn't a secret rite or ancient scroll. It's not even a secret. It's a certain way of thinking and believing in which you've trained your mind to see money-making ideas.

That's where you see a need in the marketplace, and you jump on the idea quickly. It might involve creating a new product; or, it may just be teaching others a special technique you've learned. It may even require raising capital to start a company or to market a product or idea on social media.

Don't Hold Back. You Have to Take Action to Change.

Start right now to imagine yourself as already having wealth. How would your life be? How would your day unfold? Start to own your wealth mindset now! The subconscious mind is unable to differentiate between actual fact and mere visualization. So, by imagining that you already have it, you're encouraging your subconscious mind to seek the ways and means to transform your imaginary feelings into the real thing.

Find yourself some mentors. Nobody has all the answers. Surround yourself with people that will support, inspire, and provide you with answers that keep you moving in the right direction. If you truly want to attain wealth, have a thriving business, or reach the top of your game in any endeavor, having a qualified mentor is essential.

Okay, lets come in for a landing …

It is absolutely essential to have a crystal-clear picture of what you want to accomplish before you begin. If you want to attain wealth, you must learn to operate without fear and with a sharply defined mental image of the outcome you want to attain. This comes from thinking like a wealthy person, (like Superman) making decisions like a wealthy person and being fearless (like Superman) when it comes to stepping out of your comfort zone. Look at the end result as something you're already prepared to do, you just haven't done it yet.

Think about this. Your success is something that you have been preventing; it's not something you have to struggle to make happen. The key is to not let fear, doubt, other people, or mind chatter push your success away. You'll find that the solutions taking you toward your goals will come to you in the most unexpected and sudden ways. You don't need the *perfect* plan first. What you need is a perfectly clear decision about your success, the right mindset, the right mentoring, and the ideal way to get you there will materialize.

The greatest transfer of wealth in the history of the human race is happening right now. Are you positioned to get your share?

Remember, in order to get a different result, you must do something different. In order to do something different you must know something different to do. And in order to know something different, you have to first suspect that your present methods need improving.

THEN, YOU HAVE TO BE WILLING TO DO SOMETHING ABOUT IT.

***

For more information on Jim's work:

www.JimBritt.com

http://JimBrittCoaching.com

www.facebook.com/jimbrittonline

www.linkedin.com/in/jim-britt

For free audio series www.RichCode1.com and www.RichCode2.com

To find out how to crack the rich code and change your subconscious programming regarding money: www.CrackingTheRichCode.com

Kevin Harrington

Kevin Harrington is an original shark from the hit TV show *Shark Tank* and a successful entrepreneur for more than forty years. He's the co-founding board member of the Entrepreneurs' Organization and co-founder of the Electronic Retailing Association. He also invented the infomercial. He helped make "But wait... There's more!" part of our cultural history. He's one of the pioneers behind the *As Seen on TV* brand, has heard more than 50,000 pitches, and launched more than 500 products generating more than $5 Billion in global sales. Twenty of his companies have generated more than $100 million in revenue each. He's also the founder of the *Secrets of Closing the Sale Master Class* inspired by the Master of sales—Zig Ziglar. He's the author of several bestselling books including *Act Now: How I Turn Ideas into Million Dollar Products, Key Person of Influence,* and *Put a Shark in Your Tank.*

Becoming A KPI

By Kevin Harrington

The Key Person of Influence (KPI) in any given industry is the leader. It is the leader of the business world, the leader of automobile dealerships, the leader of selling hats—you name it. In other words, being the KPI means being the go-to person. The crazy thing? Anyone can be a Key Person of Influence. Any entrepreneur can be a KPI, a doctor, a salesperson, anyone. Just follow five steps and you will be well on your way. What comes with being a Key Person of Influence is value, ideally a massive amount of money, and being the leader in your field. The KPI is the person who comes up in conversations when it relates to a certain product, business, company, industry, or field. This is the person others seek out, the go-to person. Being the Key Person of Influence is how I got on *Shark Tank*.

Here's the story: I got a phone call from Mark Burnett's company. Mark Burnett is a television producer. He produced shows like *Survivor* and *The Voice*. His office called to set up an appointment. Mark was starting up a new show and wanted me to go out to Los Angeles to talk business. I was curious as to how Mark Burnett's company found me, and why they reached out for my services. They told me it was because I was a Key Person of Influence. I was all over the internet as a result of everything I was doing. It was 2008, and I had been in the business for 25 years. I had created huge brands. I helped build Tony Little. I helped build Jack Lalanne. I helped build Food Saver. We did the NuWave Oven. We worked with people like George Foreman and countless others. The problem was, everybody knew the brands, which was good for business, but did nothing for my personal brand. Consumers knew about the Food Saver, they knew about Tony Little, and they knew about Jack Lalanne, but not everyone knew I was the guy behind all of these people. Nobody knew me.

At that point, I made a conscious effort to build my brand. I wanted to become the go-to person so I could get the hot products and the phone calls. I helped build Tony Little's business, but everyone called him; they weren't calling me. What's wrong with that picture? Well, for one, I invested millions and millions of dollars of my own capital into Tony Little, and then he got all the phone calls. Shame on me for doing that, right? So, I decided to build my brand, and that's when I came out with my book, *Key Person of Influence*. I promoted myself by doing radio talk shows, TV shows, trade journals, speeches, etc. This is how I got on *Shark Tank*.

If I hadn't met Daniel Priestley, my book could have become *How To Become The Go-To Guy* because that's what I was looking to do, but Daniel very eloquently created this five-step system called the "Key Person of Influence." Realizing we were on to something, we co-authored and launched *Key Person of Influence*. Let's look now at the necessary steps to become a KPI.

Obtaining Customers

In 1984, I started a business of obtaining customers on TV. One evening, I was watching the Discovery Channel and suddenly the channel went dark for about six hours. I then called the cable company just in case there was a problem. They told me there wasn't a problem, that the Discovery Channel was an 18-hour network. That's when the light bulb went off. This was downtime. They put no value on those six down hours. Instead of showing something during this time, bars were put up on the screen. I started thinking about what I could put in place of that downtime, to sell something, obtain customers, and make money. I'm like the Rembrandt TV guy. I created and invented the whole concept of going to TV stations and buying huge blocks of remnant downtime. In all these years of me doing this, no one has challenged the idea that I was the person who did it, created it, and invented 30-minute infomercial blocks.

I was buying big blocks of time. Why? Because I wanted to obtain customers. How do you obtain customers? A lot of ways, but you ultimately have to get some form of media. How does it start? There are two metrics you have to look at when obtaining customers. What does it cost to obtain the customer? That is called the Cost Per Order (CPO). What is your Average Lifetime Revenue Value (ALRV), or Average Order Value (AOV)? The cost to obtain the customer obviously has to be less than the cost you are going to receive in income from the customer. The bottom line in obtaining customers: you have to set up a system. You have to set up testing. You have to set up as many sources for obtaining customers as possible. Even though I was in the TV business, I didn't just get customers through TV. Customers came through TV, radio, the internet, retail stores, international distribution, home shopping channels, etc. The first step is to make a laundry list of every possible resource for attracting these customers.

Today, some people who are into the digital space are basically just getting customers on the internet. Some of the areas I mentioned above have become very expensive. It's tougher to make money on TV. While we started on TV, the cost to get customers has become too high; so we now have made the switch to digital. When you talk about internet, there's many different ways to obtain customers, from Google AdWords to Facebook ads to social media, etc. You can also attain customers with public relations and influencers. You have to decide what works best with your product. The bottom line is a lot of people do not realize they have to be sophisticated, from a business analysis standpoint, to set up a business. You need a marketing plan to obtain customers.

First, focus on two numbers: your Customer Acquisition Cost (CAT) and Average Order Value (AOV). Those numbers have to work. Customer service is crucial in the business world as well. A business can't have bad customer service and retain customers This is especially true in this day-and-age.

Raising Capital

I had a 50-million-dollar-a-year business, making $5 million a year in profit. Feeling confident, I met with seven banks to get some financing. I thought it was going to be easy because I had a very profitable business. Unfortunately, bank after bank after bank turned me down. I had great credit and all of that. The only asset I had was the business. Part of the problem was I didn't know how to approach the banks. I was a young entrepreneur in my twenties. I had no real credibility in the banking world; I was walking in and just showing my numbers from the year before.

So, what did I do to get the capital? Well, I ran into a mentor who was a former bank president, and he said, "Kevin, you went about it all wrong. I come from the banking business, and if you walked into my office and said, 'I need 5 million bucks,' I would have told you to turn around and get the hell out of my office. What do you have to do? You have to sell them on the future. What you did last year is well and good, but they are giving you money because they know that you are still going to be in business three years from now repaying their loans. You need projections. You need your forward business plan. You need your five-year master plan. You need to talk the talk and walk the walk, otherwise they aren't even interested."

I hired my mentor as a consultant to the company. I brought him in on the ground floor as part of my dream team. To make a long story short, we went back to re-pitch some of the same banks. We didn't get 5 million dollars, but we got a 3-million-dollar line of credit. It was all in how we talked to the banks. We had the same business, but it was all in the presentation. It's all in how you talk and how prepared you are. Raising capital is mental. It's in the pitch. It's in the relationships you build, etc.

One of the biggest challenges with any business is having enough capital to do the things you want to do. You have to have a successful business plan if you want to raise money. Here are the elements of a successful business plan.

> (1) You need an executive summary (one page summarizing the whole plan). You need an industry overview, defining the problem you are solving and an overview of the market.
> (2) You need a description of your product or the service. How does it serve as a solution?
> (3) You need a competitive analysis. What/who is your competition?
> (4) You need a sales and marketing plan.

(5) You need to identify your target customer and proof for your concept.

(6) What is your method of operations?

(7) Who's on your management team, your board of advisers, your dream team?

(8) What are your financial projections?

(9) You need to outline your risk analysis and appendix.

If you are going to raise capital, you don't just talk to an investor. I get people all the time that come to me saying they have an idea, and boom… it's on a napkin. They tell me that they just need $100K for 10 percent. I ask if they can send me their business plan. They then ask me what I mean when I say, 'business plan.' If they don't have one, that means I am going to end up giving them 100K and never see it again.

One of the most important parts of raising capital is coming up with a reasonable ask, and then explaining how the proceeds will be used. Many entrepreneurs don't understand this. For example, a guy came on *Shark Tank* saying he needed 150K for 10 percent of his company. I asked what he was going to use the 150K for?

His response was essentially this, "Well, I am going to use the money as a down payment for a piece of real estate where we are going to build a building, then launch the business."

"Okay, so you are going to build the building and then equip the building with furniture. Where is that money going to come from?" I asked. He said once he got the real estate, then they would figure out that batch of money at that time. I told him, "$150K dollars doesn't get you in business. $150K dollars gets you a piece of land. How are you going to build the business, generate revenue, and pay me back?" This guy told me he thought I would have more money for him after that. I said, "Well, no. You are not going to get the first batch of money based on the answers you are giving me."

Instead, he should have said he was going to lease a small office and start generating massive amounts of revenue with the money I gave them. Then, pay me back all of my money, plus a huge return on my investment, and then build it into a global business. That's what I wanted to hear. I want to know that people have a successful business plan, a successful marketing plan, and then I will talk about how to go about raising the capital, how to call on investors, and what the sweet spots are for the investors.

The bottom line on raising capital is, you can't just go build yourself a huge global business without thinking about how you're going to finance it. In the old days, I thought if I built a successful business, money was going to be easy. It's not, unless you know how to do it. There's an art to raising capital. Part of it involves making sure you are prepared and know how to pitch your business properly.

The Perfect Pitch

While the actual product or service you are trying to sell is a critical part of the process, it is just as important to sell the customer on yourself, your services, and your business. Even though I have made thousands upon thousands of pitches, have spoken to thousands of people, and have seen a great amount of success, I still pitch myself and my businesses. No matter who you are, or what you do, you have to be ready to drop the perfect pitch. It doesn't matter if you are going to make this perfect pitch in front of a crowd of thousands, or a crowd of one. To help with the concept of a perfect pitch, I have created a 10-step system.

Before you can start perfecting the perfect pitch, you have to ask yourself a couple of questions. What are you pitching? In other words, what product, business, or service are you trying to sell? Next, what do you want to get out of this pitch? More customers? More sales? Nonetheless, these questions are for you to answer, and you need to answer them before devising your perfect pitch. The perfect pitch can be broken down into these 10 steps:

(1) The **Tease** is your hook; the period of time when you plant the seed. This is when you reveal a problem. You have to explain to your customers why you are giving the pitch. You also have to use showmanship, which sets the pace for the rest of the pitch. If your showmanship skills are demonstrated in the Tease portion of your pitch, then you will have your audience (or your customer) hooked from the very beginning.

(2) Next up is **Please**. In this part of the perfect pitch, you are telling your customer how your product or service can solve the problem you mapped out in the first step. Ideally, your product or service will solve this stated problem in the most efficient, elegant, and cost-effective way. You have to relay to your customer that your solution is the best solution, and it will solve the problem better than anything (or anyone) else. It is important to also show off your features and benefits, and to display the magical transformation that will take place.

(3) The third step to the perfect pitch is **Demonstration/Multi-functionality**. First, you have to ask yourself if you can demonstrate your product, your service and your value. This is the key to any successful pitch, and it brings multi-functionality to the forefront. It shows it off. Think of this step as an added value. Ideally, your service or product is multifunctional. If you can show this off to your customer, then you just brought bonus points to the table.

(4) But Wait There's More! is the fourth step, and it's not just for infomercials on TV. This is the step where you give more value to your product or service by showing and adding more to the pitch—maybe added bonus items or "buy 2 get 1 free if you act now" incentives. At this point, your customer should already be biting, but now is the time to really win them over. So, show them what else you have to offer.

(5) Testimonials are the fifth step to creating the perfect pitch. You are now using someone else to do the pitching. In other words, who says so besides you? This is the proof behind your business, product, or service. Testimonials can include consumers (actual users of the product or service), professionals (leaders in your industry), editorial (articles, experts, press, journals, trade publications, magazines, newspapers), etc. Testimonials can also feature celebrities. Celebrity testimonials can be very powerful for the simple fact that people love celebrities. Then there are documented testimonials, which can include clinical studies, labs tests, and science. Once again, this is one of the most important areas for creating the perfect pitch.

(6) Another important step is **Research and Competitive Analysis**. For this step, you should be asking yourself if you have done your research. If so, then this is the portion of the perfect pitch when you show off all of that information. This can include information on the industry, market and competitors. It can also be facts, figures, and statistics. This research should show off the fact that you, your company, and your product/service is unique.

(7) The seventh step is **Your Team.** In this step, you are bringing the credibility of your team and putting it right there on the metaphorical table. Who makes up your team? It could be advisers, management, directors, and strategic partners. Your team will help scale, open connections, add on the knowledge factor, and so much more.

(8) Why? is the eighth step. Why are you pitching? How will the person in front of you help? This step will change based on who you are actually pitching to. For example, if you are looking for funds, then this is a big section, and you need to incorporate many talking points.

(9) The ninth step is **Marketing Plan.** You have done your pitch and given out all your information. Now, how will you make everything happen? For instance, you need to know your marketing and distribution plan. As is the case throughout your entire pitch, it is essential that you show confidence. Sell whoever you are pitching on your product or service, and yourself as well. People invest in people all the time.

(10) The 10th and final step is **Seize**. You laid everything out, now ask! What are you trying to accomplish? Ask it! Being the final step, this is the time to present the final call to action.

Remember, each pitch will be different. Some pitches last for over an hour and others last only a few seconds or minutes. It just depends on how much time you are given or how much time you need. That is why you need to craft your pitches accordingly. Practice, practice, and more practice.

***

To contact Kevin:

www.KevinHarrington.tv

Chase Hughes

Chase Hughes is CEO of Applied Behavior Research and #1 bestselling author of five books on influence and behavior skills.

Chase develops and teaches advanced skills in persuasion, influence, interrogation, and behavior profiling. Referred to by Entrepreneur Magazine as the 'Jason Bourne of psychology,' Chase teaches not only the public, but elite intelligence agencies around the world. He was named with Mark Zuckerberg in the top 40-under-40 CEO's of the year, and was called the 'best of the best' by Dr. Phil.

After 20 years of service in the US military, Chase developed the '6MX behavior profiling system for intelligence agencies, now known as the gold standard in tradecraft. Chase is also a trial consultant, assisting in jury selection and courtroom strategy. He's the *only* trial consultant in the world to offer a 300% money-back guarantee.

Chase is also the creator of the PEACE-4A system for police de-escalation, and violence-prediction to save both the lives of officers and the public.

Chase focuses his time now on teaching behavior skills to the public, and enhancing the way we all connect, communicate, and influence the world around us. Chase's company motto reflects all that he does in business: 'We rise by lifting others.'

Your New Butler

By Chase Hughes

By the time you read this, you've already become someone new.

Almost every problem in our lives comes from a *single* source, and all of our success comes from the *same* source: Time-traveling priorities. I promise I'll unpack this in a sec…

Lots of people tell you they have the secret to success; some will tell you they will change your life. This chapter will.

Imagine waking up in a pristine bedroom. You feel amazing as you sit up in bed and see that your clothes have been laid out for you. Even your shoes are in the perfect spot; laid out so that you need minimal effort to put them on.

When you go downstairs, the coffee or tea is already set up, and your kitchen is clean and welcoming. The stuff you need for work is laid out near the door as you exit. All your to-do lists, books you need, and the phone charger that you've been promising yourself you'd bring to work one day – it's all laid out for you. As you climb into your car, you see that it's full of gas.

You deserve this. You've lived long enough without it.

One more scenario:

Imagine that for the past six months, you've been enjoying the lavish benefits of having a butler. Your butler has been taking good care of you; setting everything you need up for you, and even forcing you to eat the right food. The butler even paid all your bills on time, kept in touch with old friends, and helped you get those Christmas cards all sent out. They did everything just for you. What would your life look like? What would YOU look like?

How many times have you woken up late for something because you stayed up too late the night before? How many hundreds of decisions left you pissed off at your past-tense self?

Most of our life's issues stem from this single failure: putting the needs of your present-tense self above your future-self. We might think something like, 'I can stay up all night…I'll figure it out tomorrow.'

YOU AREN'T THE PROBLEM, BUT YOU USED TO BE

People do stupid things. I'm no exception.

I hear it from clients all the time:
- I need to lose weight
- I have no discipline
- I'm massively in debt
- I can't get it all done
- I'm overwhelmed
- I can't get to the gym
- I can't lose weight
- Somehow, I can't stop smoking
- I can't stop overeating
- I can't stop losing my cool with people at work
- I'm always late
- I never have things planned well

These are only a few. Chances are you've uttered similar statements. There are books and training courses for all these things. 'How to Get Organized,' 'How to lose weight super-fast,' 'how to have self-discipline.' They all have a technique that worked for *some* people…sometimes.

There's a shocking secret I'd like to share with you; all those problems above stem from the *exact* same issue.

Would a butler be able to help you with lots of these things? All of them, perhaps? Absolutely!

Here's the major issue:

Your *current* behavior is not the problem. Your *past* behavior is.

Let me unpack this and show you how it's true:

Over the course of your life, you've accumulated a lot of habits. The problems never came from a choice to smoke, drink too much, stay up too late, ignore the teachers in school, or eat an entire bag of Cheetos.

Our issues stem from one central thinking pattern: a failure to prioritize the benefits of your *future-self*. Our success or failure is a result of how much priority we assign to our future-self *over* our present-self. All the decisions we regret have their roots in this lack of future-self prioritization.

The past-tense 'you' didn't give a sh*t about the present-tense 'you.' They only cared for themselves. After twenty years of study in human behavior, success, influence, and persuasion, I discovered that successful people do a lot of things. People tend to analyze what they do in the present instead of what they did in the past, to become successful. They may have common habits or morning routines we can spend weeks dissecting and analyzing, but there's one thing they all have in common that got them to where they are now:

They all prioritized their future-self over their present-self. Let me show you a few examples:
1. A world-leading surgeon applied to college; his friends wanted to party instead while he went to classes he didn't even enjoy.
2. A champion boxer who's called an 'overnight success' decided to train daily for twenty years while his friends chose to use drugs or 'relax.'
3. A 75-year-old man who's in amazing shape spent a lifetime eating nutritious foods and exercising attends the funeral of a friend who ate like a king.
4. The successful CEO, for decades, opted out when his friends would skip class, miss work, or collect unemployment because it was easy.

Look at anyone who's successful; you'll find this quality. Their lives are a product of foregoing present-tense gratification in favor of *future enjoyment* and benefit. In an ideal world, the person who has lived with this butler in their lives feels three things throughout their day:
1. Gratitude for the decisions of their **past**-self.
2. Discipline toward the **present**-tense self.
3. Deep concern for the welfare of their *future*-self.

We've been pissed off at our past-tense self way too often. We stayed up too late when there was an exam or a big meeting the next day. We ate a plate-full of crap when we knew we'd regret it. We drank too much at a party knowing our future-self would suffer. We decided to head out with friends instead of finishing that task from work; letting our future-self bear the burden of punishment.

This shows up in every aspect of your life no matter who you are. Your future-self deserves better, and your present-self deserves a freaking butler. Life's about to change.

QUIET ENJOYMENT

We all know these people; they are the friends we had in high school who showed up late to the party because they were finishing an English paper. They always had the clean bedroom growing up that we secretly envied. They cancelled on plans because a task came up that you thought was ridiculous considering how boring and trivial it was. Who says no to a night out for something like cleaning out a closet? Seriously?

The single *present-tense* quality that successful people all share is 'quiet enjoyment.' This (seemingly) innate ability to calmly get things done that other people would put off, neglect, or ignore.

We imagine them happily sifting through thousands of pages at their kitchen table to get their taxes done, or whistling gleefully as they fold their laundry, placing it neatly into their drawers as little birds fly around the house like a Disney movie.

This isn't the case.

While they are sitting there at the kitchen table, or placing that folded shirt into their drawer, it's not a scene from a musical. Often, they are **not** enjoying the moment. In reality, they are *quietly enjoying* something else as these tasks are getting completed. Their butler is completing this task for them while they are focused on the future; the benefit they will get from doing this, or the moment itself. It's not the *task* that brings them enjoyment, it's the *benefit*, the act of doing it, the sheer completion of it.

If you look through your yearbook and find that popular kid who also managed to get into Yale somehow, you'll probably remember that they had this quality. They had Quiet Enjoyment running in the background of all their mental programs. They still showed up to the parties, but *after* they completed their tasks at home (which we didn't see). They still socialized and got into mischief, but quietly, in the background, they completed things that others didn't.

These people can quietly enjoy doing things that others put off or ignore.

We're going to bring this into your life, and it's going to be kickass. The benefit that you'll have over these other people is that your butler is going to be doing all these things for you. The butler will focus on the future, not the moment.

Would a complete devotion to the welfare of a future-self have stopped someone from smoking, drinking too much, staying out too late, spending too much money? You bet. The issue is that so many 'coaches' address the symptoms of this problem, instead of the cause. It all goes back to prioritizing your future self.

When you absolutely crush this (and you will!), it has a snowball effect that will make it incredibly addictive.

Success is a result of tiny tasks, quietly completed, that others chose not to do.

Discipline is the ability to prioritize the needs of your future-self over your own.

Be your own butler.

WHAT NO ONE TALKS ABOUT

Social media has given us a lot. But we tend to only see the top 1% of people's lives; assuming that all these other people are perfect, living in flawless houses and never having bad days.

When we see people who go to the gym every day, it's admirable. You might think to yourself, 'Wow. I wish I had that level of discipline!'

The truth is that you *do*. And here's the secret that none of them will tell you. **What you're seeing there is not discipline, it's habit.** These people only needed about a teaspoon of discipline to start going to the gym regularly. After a few days, it was a habit. This 'magic' ability they possess to eat healthy, work out, and stay in great shape is all habit formed with a few drops of discipline.

Discipline is an expendable resource. Think of discipline like a hundred bucks. Every day, you get a hundred dollars when you wake up. Having to pick out clothes, decide what to eat, make coffee, check the gas tank, and force yourself to go for that quick run on your lunch break, all costs money. Each one costs a lot at first.

Let's assume each task costs twenty dollars. Picking out clothes, deciding what to eat, making coffee, struggling to find your car keys, rushing to add gas to your tank...these would quickly burn through that hundred bucks. By the time lunch rolls around, the break room with free bags of chips might seem a lot more tempting than going for a run and having to shower.

When we start new habits, it costs more. The more often they are *repeated*, the less they cost. They move gradually from requiring discipline to 'just part of the day.'

When you make a list of new-year's resolutions a mile long, what happens? It takes too much discipline to do them all at once. This 'money' is spent so trying to 'fund' all these new activities so it's easy to burn out.

What would all this mean in a summarized list?
- You only need a little discipline to start and form a habit
- The more you set your future-self up for success, the more discipline you have the following day
- The repetition of these life-changing tasks diminishes the effort required to complete them over time

MAKING IT ALL WORK

If you met yourself in 30 years, would they be upset with you, or would they hug you and thank you? What habits would you plead with your younger self to adopt or *drop*?

The more you're able to prioritize the welfare of your future-self, the more you will be focused on them. I want you to care for your future self like they are the most important person in your life, because they are!

Implement a system to force yourself to think of your future self. Here's a one-month breakdown of how you could bring all of this into your life:

Week 1:

Download one of those apps that makes you look 40 years older. Print a few photos of your older self and put them where they will be relevant and keep you 'thinking forward.' For instance, you might place them on the fridge, the desk, in the car, or anywhere else they will impact your judgment in the moment. This will get your brain to start rewiring itself – focusing its awareness away from you and onto the 'you' in the future.

Week 2:

Start doing little favors for future-you! Before you go to bed, get the coffee ready for them. As you enter your bedroom at night, set out an outfit for them. I want you to say to yourself (out loud) 'They will love this!' Make a dinner ahead of time, order your future-self a gift that won't arrive immediately. These small acts will reprogram your brain a little more – getting it to tie future-thinking with reward and enjoyment.

Week 3:

Continue putting things in your life that make you future focused. This reward process you're setting up will become addictive very soon. You're now into the 21-day mark! That (according to some people) means you're in HABIT territory! This week do a few things that are a little further in the future. Think of things that your future-self will absolutely love. You could open a savings account that is hidden from sight for them to find later, like a little money time capsule. You could set a few calendar reminders on your phone for way in the future to congratulate yourself or remind them that you were thinking of them way back then (now). Get creative. They (you) will thank you.

Week 4:

Make a two-part list of what you'd like in the future:

Part one: The daily activities and tasks that you will perform for your future self. Like setting up coffee, building to-do lists for the following day, or making sure there's plenty of healthy food ready to go for tomorrow's 'you.'

Part two: The one-year list. What would you need to start doing now to 'build' the ideal you, and the ideal life for you? Leave a sticky note where you will find it later in the future that simply says, 'I was thinking of you.'

What would happen in a year if you only worked for the welfare of future-you? How would your life look? How would your health, finances, relationships, and even happiness change? It took me twenty years to discover this single method to fast-track success. I want you to have in in twenty minutes.

Holly: Past self does not define you – helped you become you – today's self can help you for future

Whatever your past-self did, forgive them. It's no longer *you*. Until you feel massive gratitude for your past-self setting you up for enjoyment and success, send them forgiveness. Your new way of life is to **take care of that person you will never meet but will always be contributing to**:

future-you.

You absolutely can do this. Not only do you deserve it, just imagine how thankful and proud the future-you will be. One more time; you *can* do this!

***

To contact Chase

Chase's website: www.ChaseHughes.com

Mark Yuzuik

Mark Yuzuik was raised in a family where he was one of 4 boys and one sister. He witnessed his parents struggle through many hard times and swore to himself he would find a way to become wealthy so he could take care of his family. As time passed his thirst for creating wealth turned into a passion for helping people.

Mark is an author, speaker, transformational coach and businessman. His true love of helping others succeed and preforming since 1991 all over the world with his funny and powerful hypnosis shows. With over 10,000 shows, and over 8 million people worldwide he still says he too can find the fun and humor in preforming. Nothing beats the smile of an audience when looking out from stage, watching thousands of people forgetting their problems and enjoying the moment.

Mark touches the lives of people everywhere he goes. Mark is an avid student, surrounding himself with mentors and people that hold him accountable to the standards he needs to live by in order to maximize his talents.

Mark conducts multi-day seminars along with his partners in the areas of Real Estate Investing, business, Personal Growth, and Hypnosis. He teaches his students that simply having the knowledge is not enough...setting your mind up to take consistent actions is the key to success.

Mark's passion for making a difference shines through in his words and presence.

Can't Hypnotize Me, I'm Smart and Strong Willed.

LOL, Yeah Right

By Mark Yuzuik

Can you remember a time when you did something, met someone or happened to be at an event, that your life would be forever different than you thought? Maybe it was a new opportunity or relationship you created just by showing up somewhere and a different path was born. We plan our lives as we feel would be the best decisions and turned out that one small event changed everything. That's exactly what happened to me. It was in the Fall of 1985 when I saw something at the fair in Phoenix, Arizona that would change my life forever. It was not a ride or anything I ate. It was mind blowing, unbelievable and no possible way that what I saw was real! Oh, was I wrong! There I was sitting in the audience of a hypnotist show, that's right, a hypnosis show. I am, what I would say, "an intelligent strong minded individual and not at all gullible". There was no way I was going to buy into that stuff. The hypnotist was famous all over the US and Canada. His name is Terry Stokes, and what a show he did. He is the best entertainer I've ever seen, even to this day.

So how is this story going to help YOU create more in your life? More of what you want! What if the answer was more of what YOU wanted and have strived for your entire life to achieve and just haven't been able to quite get it or master that skill (if indeed it is a skill), then this is what I'm talking about. More on how you will be able to achieve what you want is a bit further in this chapter.

After seeing what I saw and experienced, I developed a friendship with Terry and asked him if he would teach me how to become a hypnotist. He said no I won't teach you that, however you go to a school that teaches you how to hypnotize people, I will teach you how to become an entertainer using hypnosis. I asked him what was the difference? He said "*anyone can learn how to hypnotize people, however it's what do you do with someone after they are in hypnosis. Are you wanting to become an entertainer or hypnotherapist"?* I said entertainer. He told me that first, understand how the mind works and know that you are about to embark on a very powerful tool. This will allow you to entertain as well as empower people to make great changes in their lives, when used properly. I will only train you if you are ethical and moral. Your intentions, and what you pay attention to when dealing with people while using hypnosis, will be life changing for you and those you influence. Whether it's an audience of thousands or helping someone personally. That's why you MUST go to school first, then we can talk. And so I did, and he kept his word, Terry Stokes taught me how to become the best entertainer I can be. Over 10,000 shows in front of over 8 million people so far. I've traveled all over the world making people laugh as well as teaching people how to use the gift of hypnosis to make changes in peoples' behaviors. Working with so many artist and influencers has been more than a blessing. I have also had the privilege of teaching others the art of stage hypnosis as well, both in a group as well as spending a month with me on tour and practicing daily getting experience.

Let's get right down to the point of this chapter and how it will affect you personally.

Do you know anyone that procrastinates, has fear and has not yet reached their potential or goals? Maybe focuses on things that they don't even want to think about or focuses on the wrong things only to feel the way they don't want to feel? Does that person have any resemblance to you or look like you? LOL.

I love it when I hear the statement *"NO ONE CAN HYPNOTIZE ME. I TOO SMART AND STRONG WILLED, HYPNOSIS IS FOR WEAK MINDED PEOPLE"*

Are you thinking the same thing? Are you now or have you procrastinated in the past? Have you ever been influenced by fear before? Why is that? Why would you or anyone for that matter have a mission, goal or desire to succeed, get the knowledge, information, and even get excited only to let that slip away? Or put it off until the "time is right"? "I can't be hypnotized "and yet you still comply and do things you don't want to do (like procrastinate and have fear). I want to give you my definition of what "hypnosis" really is, and then you tell me if you have ever been hypnotized. Or maybe you are being hypnotized and don't even realize it. "Oh no, not me, I too strong willed". Yeah…ok…

Hypnosis: someone says something to you, you see, feel, hear or experience something and believe it to be true and then react to it… It is nothing more than a program on our minds that we received from a past event or experience that we are responding to today. Think of it like this. Imagine your computer, and the hard drive on that computer; is it possible that you could pick up a program, or virus on your computer that is not allowing you to receive the best results you want, without you even noticing that you have a small virus or program? That is possible, right? Well, what would happen if you didn't fix that problem or even worse just pretended that your computer is just fine the way it is? Does that make the problem go away? No, it does not. Not only that, guess what else will happen? It will continue down the road and will proceed to pick up even more viruses without you knowing it. However before long, BOOM, you notice that your computer is not responding as you need it to. Right? You need a different program on your computer to clean out your hard drive. Are you getting the picture? Sounds familiar? Do you see what I am saying? So, ask yourself "is it possible that you could have some programs on your mind that are not giving you the results you currently want? Is it possible that you or someone you know is focusing on things they don't want to focus on to feel a way they don't want to feel, and they do it anyway? Why is that??? Is it really that easy to be influenced? Is all this really a story that other people want you to believe? Is this reality or an illusion? What do you think? Isn't reality nothing more than your story or even someone else's story, that you start to believe? Maybe you yourself have created a story and believe it, and because you believe it your actions will confirm that the story is the truth, and that now becomes your truth. But if all stories can be created from an illusion and all illusions become reality for us, then can't we create our own story? What if you forgot the story you've been telling yourself and you had an opportunity to create a new story, what would that be? What if you created a story that became reality, where would you be in life? Imagine that your entire life is a story that you tell yourself of what is real and what is not. Do you know that your mind does not know the difference between reality and imagination? That is true. Have you ever imagined that you wanted something, and you got it? You didn't know how it was going to happen, but you were absolutely convinced that it was if fact going to happen and it just did. Hmmm, interesting. Or someone was going to call you and they did? Just as they called you, you probably said, "I was just thinking about you," right? Is that just a coincidence or what? Whatever you think it was, you're right. It's like a movie, that's how powerful your mind is. So that being the case, why don't you start now, creating your own illusion (reality) and stop living in other people's movie that you really don't even want to be in, let alone be the star in it? This thing called life has many chapters and sequels to it. Here is where it becomes immensely powerful! You are now the writer, director, creator and editor of this movie. How do you want it to be? Who do you want in our new life (movie) and who do you cut out of it? Maybe now is the time to get new people in your life so your movie (and your mind) is exactly what you decide it to be! Imagine right now you are in full control of everything, everything you ever wanted to do, have and be? What does that look like now? What books are you reading? What events are you attending? Who is your new influencer of peers, mentors and friends? Listen to people that want more for you and that invite you into their circle of true friends and peers so you will be *creating the life you want*. (That is also the name of my book, you can receive it as a gift for reading this chapter. Just go to my website at www.successcombination.com).

As you can see by now being "strong minded" or stubborn as I like to say, will only prevent you from having an open mind. Being open minded is what offers you the opportunity to have the life and lifestyle you were unable to create for yourself before. The power of "hypnosis" is all about being influenced to have an open mind, so you do attract and control the things you want in life. It's not about losing control but being in control of the right programs you respond to. Are you now open to take control of our life and create a new program that will allow you to attract the things in life that you always wanted and knew you deserved? Knowing what is going in your mind and who you allow to influence you is what takes you to the next step. This is not only possible but very do-able. Just because someone tells you *"you can't do that"* or *"that's not possible"* that is THEIR belief and story, not yours. That is only their limitations of what they cannot do and will never achieve. Trust me, some people will try to lower your abilities and beliefs, so they don't have to raise their own. If you only knew how many people, I got a "divorce" from in order for me to achieve more, you would be surprised or maybe not. You can still have them as friends and family, just not as influencers. Remember this, no one can influence you unless you allow them to. No one can. If you start to believe *"their limitation"* then that now becomes your limitation too. Rewrite the story where you become the leader and let them catch up.

"But what if I can't stop thinking about my past and "I'm not getting ahead"? Do you feel stuck at times and you really are trying and you just keep hitting a wall? I get it. I remember one time when I was studying for my Total Transformation event I was doing (3-day event) and as so many of the mentors I learn from, my wife Yolanda Martinez, who is a powerful coach for women with her *21 days with Yolanda* program (**www.21DaysWithYolanda.com**). Yolanda is writing her own chapter for the next book. Jim Britt, Michael Stevenson, Michael Nitti, Bob Proctor, Chase Hughes, Michael Silvers, Mamie Lamley, Tony Robbins and so many more than this stuck with me. It was Tony Robbins that said:

"Your limitations are not based on what you can achieve, it's based on what you feel you deserve. Society will also convince you that it's not your fault and allow events to create your meanings and limitations in life, instead of looking for the empowering messages from your past. Everything you have in life is based on what you feel you deserve not what you can accomplish".

Wow. I started thinking about why people are still stuck and have pain; maybe, just maybe, people tend to focus on what they are not getting instead of how they can give back. We cannot change events, I get that, however that one thing we are in control of is what things and events mean to us. That is how we get rid of the pain. We are in control of what we say to ourselves, not anyone else. We are also in control of what things mean to us. Never allow anyone to try to convince you otherwise. Ask yourself this: Who is in charge of your mind? You are, right? Who is in charge of what we say to ourselves? Once again, you are! Unless we give that power to someone or a past event that is not happening currently. Right? Why we still have pain in our life is simply that we are focused on what we are not getting, instead of what we are not giving. This is our mind being in survival. The pain is there because we haven't got the lesson. How you take events, and never ever give the power to someone or something else, is to look for, and find the empowering meaning in it. I am not saying that what happened in the past is ok at all, it is not. What is not ok is to still allow the past to keep influencing us in a negative way.

Why is it that some people that are given everything and have the "perfect upbringing", financially successful parents, that seem to buy them everything they want, the best college, cars for their high school graduations or birthday, or whatever they want they get…etc. They really do not have anything to worry about, some seem to have more problems than others? I am not saying that everyone is like that, some grow up and do make a huge difference in other lives as well. Let's also face the fact that some may have alcohol abuse and addictions, drug problems, cheating, workaholics or whatever that "distraction" is for them. They had it all, so we thought. And yet on the other hand we have those that have been abused mentally, physically, spiritually, sexually and other ways of being violated. However, some of them grow up to become super achievers in life too. That is because we say, ***"Never again will I ever let anyone or anything take my mind, body, freedom or life from me again, never"***. The difference is that we took our pain and found a way to channel it, so we help others avoid that same pain we had endured. I'm not saying that the events that happened were good in any way, what I am saying is that when you find a way to look for the empowering meaning in that event, and that situation, you take your power back and no one will ever control your mind again, ever. Look at some of the super achievers out there and what they did. Oprah, Tony Robbins, Nelson Mandela and now, even you, that's if you decide that's the way it is. Not someone else, you! Remember this, our brains are designed for one thing, "Survival", that is just the way it is. So, when we see, hear, feel or experience something that sticks in our mind we will react to it. Now here is the difference, you decide what story you are going to tell yourself and how you are part of the solution, and by you helping others that may have gone through what you may have experienced in the past.

The reason that people still have pain from their past, is because they have not got the lesson. The lesson will empower you and others to have a very compelling future and be in control of the way you want to feel and create the actions you desire to take.

In my 3-day Total Transformation event we teach you even more on how to change the story and create an impelling future. Plus, I teach you how to hypnotize others as well. That is so much fun seeing everyone learning this skill properly.

I remember one event in particular where we had this young girl (Morgan) just 13 years old, during one of the sessions we have people break through a board, we do this as a metaphor that when you follow through in life, you get the results you want. Sometimes doing some things in life are a lot easier than you imagined. Have you had that experience before? Remember, our imagination can work for us or can create an illusion that something is not possible. I remember that my wife, Yolanda was working with Morgan, who was very shy when she began the event, had realized by the 2nd day, she was the one inspiring others, and when she broke through the board she just started crying with joy. You should have seen her parents, they cried even more. I share this short memory because of two reasons. First, Morgan is an immensely powerful young lady today and is no longer shy. More importantly, her mom Michelle Quinn became a motivational speaker and is also in this book with her chapter. If it were not for Yolanda, mentoring Morgan and Morgan deciding that she really wanted more in life, where would her mom be? When you think that you don't have anything to share because no one is watching you, you are wrong. You are an influence on more people than you ever thought and by pretending you're not, you are just lying to yourself and hurting those that love you and who really need YOU NOW!!! Now is the time to take your life back and make some differences in other peoples lives as well. Pay it forward, empower others and yourself, YOU deserve it.

Get my "Love & Wealth" program (8 audios & 2 PDF workbooks) for reading this chapter for only $47.00! This is over 90% off ($597.00 value). Go to www.successcombination.com and put in the code "family" and I will also have you and a guest at my Total Transformation live event ($997.00 value). See you at our next event!

***

To contact Mark:
https://www.facebook.com/Hypnotistmark
https://youtube.com/c/MarkYuzuik
https://www.linkedin.com/in/markyuzuik
https://www.instagram.com/markyuzuik/

Michael Nitti

Michael Nitti has been touching peoples' lives, as well as their hearts, for over 3 decades.

As a Full-time coach for the past 15 years, Michael has worked with both budding entrepreneurs and the leaders of multi-billion-dollar corporations (including the President of one of the largest entertainment companies on the planet); drawing from over thirty-five years of intensive Transformational course work & study, both as a student and as an acclaimed teacher & course leader.

Having held Executive-level positions in several industries, Michael found his way to the top of self-help field in 1997, when he was recruited by Robbins Research in San Diego. Where, for the next eight years, he was privileged to serve as a member of Tony Robbins' Executive Team, which not only allowed him to travel the world in support of Robbins' extraordinary events, he was able to evolve his coaching skills while working directly with Tony, serving as a Vice President for RRI before transitioning into coaching full-time in 2005.

Since then, Michael has been coaching an average of 60 - 80 clients per month, which allowed him to refine and perfect his signature teaching, "The Trophy Effect" (which was published in book form in 2009). Today, Michael continues to coach both privately and for Robbins, specializing in coaching business leaders & other high-profile professionals, with a focus on 'Mastery,' Relationships, Entrepreneurship, & Supreme Certainty! All of which lead him to being featured on the 'EXTRA' television series "The Masters" in 2017.

Supreme Certainty

By Michael Nitti

"The first step toward believing that you can is to acknowledge that you've been brainwashed into believing that you can't. When you upgrade your beliefs, you upgrade your life. Fortunately, what you believe is totally up to you. Believe wisely..." ~Michael Nitti

Here's a question for you… What does it actually mean to be an entrepreneur?

Well, and from both a practical and a *conscious* perspective, it's very much about 'owning' that *you* are fully in charge of what you're up to, rather than having to check in with anyone else before showing up as the 'creator of magic' you were born to be!

And yet, it has absolutely nothing to do with being 'the Lone Ranger,' as the surest way to sabotage any success is to resist any input from your fellow 'magicians' in favor of going it alone. In fact, if you truly intend to show up as the superstar you deserve to be, it's critical that you remain open to anything & everything the universe is sending in your direction…

Still, and even though being an entrepreneur has nothing to do with going it alone, it does require that *you* take full responsibility for your own success, which is a result of 'knowing yourSelf' as the ultimate creator of everything you say and do!

To which end, I invite you to fully embrace the following three critical aspects of taking full control over *who you are* and *how you're showing up* in every moment:
  1. Bringing both your 'Full Intention' & 'Supreme Certainty' to everything you do!
  2. Allowing your Intention & Certainty to override your 'survival mind' & your 'limiting beliefs'
  3. Taking full ownership of 'who' you are, by both knowing yourself as the creator of your life and forever showing up *on Purpose!* (versus simply 'going along for the ride')

So, now that you know *what* needs to be done, how do you begin to put it all into practice?

Well, the *first* step is to actually do away with your 'need to know how' in the first place! In fact, your belief that you need to know 'how' in order to *feel more certain* about whatever it is you're doing, is simply *your mind* looking to justify its position, once it starts screaming at you to give up! When, in actuality, your ability to show up as 'fully intentional' has nothing at all to do with knowing *how*...

Given which, I invite you to replace your minds' belief that you need to know 'how' to show up in a 'supremely certain state,' with an actual 'knowing' that it's already fully within you to bring confidence & certainty along for the ride... which you have every ability to unleash *at will!*

Which means, if ever you're doubting that you have this ability, it's simply because 'doubt,' itself, is a *limiting belief*, and not because you're lacking this ability! (again, you were *born* with this ability!)

Of course, just because you own this ability doesn't mean that you're actually living from it (given that most of us are *not*), yet the good news is that this is precisely what the rest of this chapter is all about! Which, as you're about to discover, will not only allow you to take ownership of the 'Five Key Elements of Supreme Certainty,' but to actually become a master at putting them into practice!

Which, and although we'll be focusing on all five elements very soon, the very *first thing* we'll be doing is a little 'invasive surgery' on your *limiting beliefs*...

In other words, we're about to do a little digging into your relationship with your *Survival Mind*... which, as you're about to see, is simply being honest about what it *is* and what it *isn't*...

> *"The ability to know yourSelf as fully worthy isn't something you attain from outside yourself, nor is it going to magically show up once you accumulate enough proof. You were born worthy! Begin there."* ~Michael Nitti

Question: When was the last time you even thought about doing anything the slightest bit risky without having any second thoughts before you took action (or, you actually allowed those 'second thoughts' to stop you from taking action)?

In fact, and even though the 'default setting' of *entrepreneur* is to 'go for it,' given that the 'default setting' of *being human* is to avoid taking any risk at all, it's totally normal for your survival mind to 'dig in its heels' the moment you start thinking about doing anything even the slightest bit entrepreneurial; suggesting instead that you go find yourself a really nice job.

Which, of course, you likely have no intention of doing or you wouldn't be reading this book! Although, it most definitely *will* serve you to not only understand 'why' your mind is always screaming at you to rethink your plans, but 'how' to ignore it and stay your course in spite of the screaming!

And yet, in response to you trying to override it, you'll find that your mind instinctively beefs up its defenses, by way of reminding you of all your fears & 'limiting beliefs'… which, although none of them are true, given that you're forever being reminded of them, they still *feel* like they're true – which is why they tend to stop you in your tracks, even *before* you get started!

Even so, it's not that your mind is opposed to your success, it that it's simply doing 'its' job' in order to keep you from failing (which, in fact, is its *default concern*, based upon what it knows about your biology, your history, and your limiting beliefs).

In light of which, and in support of you ultimately ignoring your biology & your beliefs, the first thing you need to know is that even though you can't turn your mind off, you can *override* it. And, although this is precisely where we're going next, there are still a few things you need to know first…

1) Limiting beliefs are *not* 'real' (which is why they're called 'beliefs', not 'truths')

2) You have every ability to totally disregard them, on the way to creating the life of your dreams!

3) 'Supreme Certainty' is not only the 'intention' behind you overriding your mind, it's fully within you to bring forth, simply by taking ownership of the following distinctions...

First of all, and no matter what you or I are holding onto from the past, whenever we're inspired to finally take action is support of achieving something we desire, there are still only two options available to any of us in any given moment, which are; 1) we go for it, or, 2) we don't!

And, whenever we choose 'number 2' (and I invite you to appreciate the metaphor), it's pretty much tied to one reason, and one reason only... *our limiting beliefs!*

And yet, as debilitating as our 'limiting beliefs' tend to be, it's never our beliefs themselves that stop us (after all, they're simply *thoughts*), it's that you & I have been allowing them to rob us of our certainty! When, in fact, given that they are 'simply thoughts,' they have absolutely no inherent power over how any of us show up in any given moment... except when we allow them to!

Which means, whenever you and I are *not* showing up in a state of Supreme Certainty, it's never because we don't have it within us to do so, it's because we are living 'in reaction' to our belief that we don't have it within us to do so!

Which is why, instead of stepping into our power and taking action in favor of whatever it is we want, we're inclined to live *in reaction* to whatever our *mind* is whispering (or screaming) in our ear!

Given which, the first step to overriding your 'limiting beliefs' is to own the fact that 'being human' includes the inclination to allow *the memory* of any situation where you've fallen short in the past, to live within your mind as a limiting belief!

In other words, your limiting beliefs are never proof that there's anything *wrong* with you, they're simply proof that you 'think' there is...

News Flash! Not only are our *limiting beliefs* nothing other than *memories,* given that our memories are really nothing more than our thoughts about how things 'use to be,' in actuality, our 'memories' are really nothing more than that; 'thoughts!'

Which means, you & I have every ability to simply disregard them as *background noise;* knowing that all that's really been going on is that instead of us owning the fact that 'life' includes *having memories,* we've been walking around unconsciously allowing our memories *to have us!*

Which also means, once you stop focusing on your rear-view mirror, you'll realize that it's never been about whether you've considered them to be 'thoughts' or 'limiting beliefs' that's the problem, it's that you've been *allowing* them to rob you of your certainty, *that's the problem!*

Given which, even as you continue to have similar thoughts, you must never forget that they are not your *'personal thoughts'!* Remember, it's simply your *survival mind*, tapping you on the shoulder, and screaming anything it possibly can in your ear – hoping that you'll reconsider doing anything that you're about to do that might get you into trouble…

And yet, now that you know *the truth* – even as your mind is imploring you to play small – given that you are *not your mind,* you must never forget that its forever within you to take much bigger steps!

Hence, the question… are you willing to start taking bigger steps, or waiting for more certainty?

Hence, the following question: When would now be a good time to give up waiting for something to show up that's already fully within you?

Well, assuming that you answered 'now' to the second question, are you willing to see that *overriding* your limiting beliefs, *showing up* as absolutely certain, and *honoring* your intention to create whatever it is you intend to create, pretty much go hand-in-hand?

Of course, they do! And not only do they go 'hand in hand,' it's the actual marriage of these forces, which not only inspires us to ultimately learn all that we need to learn in order to become *masters* at what we're doing, the underlying intention, which actually enables you & I to show up this way in the first place, is not only the source of 'supreme certainty,' it *is supreme certainty!*

And yet, with regard to actually having knowledge of anything to the degree that we feel 'fully certain' about our level of expertise about it, all of us are inclined to appreciate that we 'need' to have not only been practicing it long enough to consider ourselves a 'master' of this ability, but for others to accept that we're masters as well...

Which is why, with regard to you speaking about anything that actually requires you to have a specific level of expertise, no matter how much certainty you're bringing to the party, unless you actually own that skill or talent, you can talk until the cows come home, and it's still going to show up as hot air!

However, with regard to our ability to intentionally 'bring forth' *a State of Supreme Certainty,* which, energetically, is based solely upon how we are 'showing up' and how we are 'being' (versus our degree of expertise with regard to how much we actually 'know' about a specific topic), our ability to show up as 'absolutely certain' in any given moment is governed by nothing more than our *willful intention* to fully 'own it' and 'declare it' into the universe!

(which, by the way, has nothing at all to do with 'faking it until you make it,' but with 'being it' until you make it, which means causing something powerful to show up, which likely wouldn't have shown up in the absence of your certainty)!

And yet, no matter the level of 'energy' from which you're declaring whatever it is you're putting out there, nor how confident you are with regard to whatever it is you're certain about, unless what you're declaring is in full alignment with 'the truth' *and* in service of something beyond whatever's 'in it' for you (even though you surely deserve to benefit), it's likely going to show up as 'hot air' as well...

However, to the degree that whatever you are putting out there is born of your willingness to step beyond your conditioning and your limiting beliefs, while, as the same time, allowing 'the truth' of what you're saying to 'flow through you,' you will know in your heart that everything you're saying is born solely of your 'intention' – rather than as a function of 'knowing *how*'…

Which, and in support of you actually *becoming* a 'master' of 'supreme certainty,' brings us to the aforementioned 'Five Master Steps' to showing up in an Absolutely Certain state, which are:

1) Owning that You truly *are* the Creator of your Life. In other words, knowing that it's fully up to you to show up as Absolutely Certain in any given moment! Which has nothing at all to do with 'ego,' and *everything* to do with your intention to remain humble & respectful of others!

In fact, one of the primary reasons that so many of us tend to *resist* showing up as supremely certain, is because of our aversion to showing up as 'too full of ourselves'… Which, of course, is a good thing – yet it's just as critical to know that showing up as Absolutely Certain is no way an expression of arrogance, unless you've forgotten to leave your *ego* at home…

2) Knowing that even if you've been playing small or have a history of being uncertain, this is in no way proof that you're somehow devoid of the ability to show up as 'Supremely Certain' – but simply proof that you 'didn't even know you didn't know' that you actually have it within you to do so!

Which, in fact, is because *nobody* knows it until they know it! Which, in actuality, is because Absolute Certainty is never a function of figuring out 'how' to show up this way, it's a function of 'being certain' simply because it's within you to do so!

3) Letting go of the belief that you're a fraud when you're showing up Absolutely Certain without any supporting evidence or 'proof' that it's 'warranted.' When, in fact, the *actual* fraud is the one you're mind has been running in the background, convincing you that you'll be 'faking it' if you show up as supremely certain without a reason – even though 'supreme certainty' is never about 'faking it until you make it,' it's about showing up in full alignment with who you *already* are!

And yet, the ability to show up in a Supremely Certain State is not a skill (although you will find that it does get 'easier' over time), it's simply the willingness to show up in alignment with who you truly are, yet which has been hidden beneath your fears and limiting beliefs! Which, by the way, includes the biggest limiting belief of all, which is the belief that your limiting beliefs are actually true! Which, of course, they are *not!*

4) Stepping into your ability to 'show up' and 'BE' Absolutely Certain, simply because you can – rather than waiting until you 'know how.' Which, by the way, is a function of simply giving up the belief that you need to know how in order to know how! Which, paradoxically, is function of being willing to give up this belief, even without knowing *how!* (think about it)…

Again, the culture has conditioned us to believe that we need to know how in order to be able to do something we don't already know how to do (which, with regard to the practice of a 'specific skill' is obviously true!). And yet, since showing up in a Supremely Certain state is not a skill, but an *intention*, when would now be a good time to give up believing that you need to know how?

And Finally, #5) Giving up the belief that Supreme Certainty is an 'ability' that can only be mastered over time (and again, with respect to mastering an actual skill or talent, is clearly the way it is).

However, since SUPREME CERTAINTY *is not a skill* (which I believe I've mentioned previously), I invite you to simply bring it with you wherever you go, *because you can!*

And yet, even though it's not a skill – or even a 'feeling' – might you be inclined to feel even *more* confident in your ability to bring it to the party, the *more* you bring it to the party?

Well, like anything else you practice long enough, you'll likely find that you *are* showing up *more* certain, the *more* you 'practice it.' However, it since the pathway to confirming whether this is true is paved with you simply doing so, when would *now* be a good time to start paving?

Finally, I invite you not only embrace all Five Key Elements, but to be willing to immediately put them into practice! Knowing, however, that it's never a function of 'how,' but a function of simply stepping into your truth and then doing so! After all, and at the end of the day, the only one who's ever really in charge of you, is *you!*

"Happiness is a function of accepting what is. Success is function of desiring more and refusing not to have it. Mastery is a function of knowing that life is a game and being grateful for every opportunity to play. Bliss is a function of igniting the fire in your heart and sharing your Love & your Light with the universe! If you want to wake up on fire, be the flame!" ~Michael Nitti

* * *

To Contact Michael:

Cell: 858-354-8014

HM: 702-483-6564

Website: www.intentionquest.com

Social Media:

Facebook; Michael Nitti, Las Vegas

Instagram: CoachNitti

Mamie Valdez-Lamley

Mamie is committed to moving global impact leaders from "Invisible to INVINCIBLE!" She stands for culture & tradition while integrating innovation, industry disruptive technology, Personality & Emotional Intelligence to build trust, create lasting relationships, and shape a people-focused and profit-driven community.

Today, Mamie skillfully masterminds and trains with corporations, business owners, and entrepreneurs. She provides strategic step-by-step processes to implement responsible and ethical artificial intelligence to decipher client buying behavior, elevate sales revenue, mitigate budget risks, and close more sales in less time!

Mamie's mission is to ignite, inspire, and influence 21 million Influencers to lead with integrity and strengthen their communications to generate intentional support, money, and reputation. As the founder of Empowerment on Fire and a Founding Partner at Heroic Voice Academy, Mamie's focus is to help businesses clearly define their mission, vision, values, and vows while delivering their message with precision, mastery & connection!

Hawaii Special Olympics honored her as a Hall of Fame Inductee. Codebreaker Technologies® recognizes her as its Nurturing Icon in its Global Community. Women Economic Forum named her an International Award-Winning Speaker and an "Iconic Woman Making a Difference in the World."

Moving from Invisible to Invincible

Creating Presentation ROI

By Mamie Valdez-Lamley

How to move from Invisible to Invincible

"You never know how strong you are, until being strong is your only choice."

~Bob Marley

My dear friend Jason Tyne once told me, "I honestly believe that you are a living breathing miracle, predestined for greatness, and I believe in you!" I stood in awe of this man as he continued, "You have more power than you realize, and it all starts with the words you use and the meaning behind them!"

The impact of Jason's words rattled me to the core. Why, because he saw in me what I could not put into words. He voiced what I felt inside of me and would never say for myself. Playing small and hiding behind the fear of "not being good enough!" I was on the road to Nowhere Ville. Good enough to run a 10,000 people event. Not good enough, so I thought, to get on stage and own it.

With over fourteen years of service with the largest global event organizer, and working alongside some of the leading experts in personal development such as Tony Robbins, T. Harv Eker, Cheri Tree, Jim Britt, Mark Yuzuik, Michael Nitti, Robert Kiyosaki, Nick Vujicic, and Gary Vaynerchuk, I finally decided to take responsibility and make a change. I went from being invisible at the back of the room to declaring my path to invincible on the stage as an assistant trainer for Warrior Training Camp, created by T. Harv Eker.

The shift to become invincible took another turn when 97 women raised their hands to learn how to speak their passion into existence. In April 2018, after a year of coaching, Juliette Willoughby and Jeanne Zierhoffer, along with 17 of the 97 women, gathered at

Newark Airport to make the trek to New Delhi, India, for the Women Economic Forum. For some, it was the first time for many things. First time out of the country away from family. Visits to the Taj Mahal, presenting on stage in front of 2000 people and streaming video to over 150 countries. When the excitement settled, all seventeen women returned home to the USA as International Award-Winning Speakers.

I am no longer invisible. Leadership starts with me. My life's focus is to sustain a system that will help build a community of influencers and empowered leaders. The experts I need for self-mastery, growth, and learning surround me. I am a top trainer and Director of Coaching for Codebreaker Technologies, the Owner and Founder of Empowerment on Fire, and a full Partner at Heroic Voice Academy.

"We are BIGGER than me," and teams can do more than individuals. We now connect continents, countries, and communities; by helping, leaders amplify their voices to support their global impact mission. These teams have been instrumental in generating millions in sales revenue while changing people's lives and companies worldwide. T. Harv Eker says, "Success leaves clues!" Here's a clue for you. Put on your life-long learner hat. The curtains are going to lift. In this chapter, I'll share tips and strategies you can use on your journey to invincible through incorporating a concept we use at Heroic Voice Academy called Presentation ROI.

"Let your audience determine your Presentation!"

~Tony Robbins

Return on Investment (ROI)

How do you look at Return on Investment (ROI)? Are you looking at it as only money?

If your answer is yes, you may be missing a significant business generator. Presentations help grow your revenue, relationships, trust and expand your quality reputation. ROI is NOT just about the MONEY!

As leaders, influencers, entrepreneurs, business owners, or corporate executives, this could be the time for you to generate a new ROI Equation. An equation that steps out of the ROI norm of money and incorporates additional business assets: Money, Support, and Reputation. Referred to as Presentation ROI.

"An Investment in knowledge pays the best interest."

~Ben Franklin

What is Presentation ROI?

Presentation Return on Investment (ROI) is the ability for successful leaders, entrepreneurs, business owners, and executives to consistently convert their high-stakes speaking opportunities into business assets: money, support, and reputation.

The significance of public speaking or becoming a trainer has never been higher. The demand for presentations is no longer just for information. Audiences expect more. Communication mastery is a measurement of competency, self-assuredness, connection, and relatability, and, more importantly, your ability to read your audience.

Are you prepared? Have you done your research? Are you ready to take on conversations with investors, be a keynote speaker, run a town hall meeting, podcasts, or media interview on the last-minute request? If your answer is anything, then "yes," read on to learn more about expanding your ROI equation.

Elements of your Presentation ROI Equation

To achieve more than money in your ROI, you will need to add two more business assets to your equation. Your new ROI equation is:

Money + Support + Reputation = Presentation ROI

MONEY ASSET

Money is an essential business asset. Train yourself to "think outside of the box" and develop different strategies. One thing for sure, "Money comes from other people," such as significant clients, investors, donors, sponsors, products and services, online, at live events, and more.

There are abundant opportunities when someone is open to listening. Business 101 is to identify a problem and provide a solution to a problem. You can increase your Money ROI when you creatively offer a solution to a problem.

Remember: ***Money*** *+ Support + Reputation = Presentation ROI*

Here are some tips on up-leveling your money assets:

1. Know yourself. How do you make buying decisions? How do you sell? If you don't know, here's a website where you can learn more: https://crackmycode.com/EmpowerYou
2. Know your avatar and how they make buying decisions? Do you know their preferences, needs, buying behaviors, and sales cycles?
3. Know your audience. Tailor your talks with your audience in mind to help you generate ROI.
4. Know your business indicators. Keep in mind, information is power, and data drives informed decisions.

Money Strategy – Think "outside" the box

Do not discount your product or services. Use an alternative option that maintains the value of your services called "Mixed Currency." Below is an example of this strategy.

Option one: Payment in full.

Option two: Mixed-Currency. The client can designate a percentage, up to 25%, of their contract in a value exchange. The value of the contract is $20,000 for six hours of consulting. They pay $15,000 in cash and elect to do $5000 in mix-currency. Their mix-currency agreement introduces our team to their top five clients. We recorded three podcast interviews to post to their membership site with (40K members) and their recruitment site.

Do you think we gained more than $5000 in other revenue? What opportunities can you think of to up-level your MONEY asset in your new ROI Equation?

> *"Support and encouragement are found in the most unlikely places."*
>
> ~Raquel Cepeda

SUPPORT ASSET

Support is the next essential business asset. When you are committed to making a global impact, people are interested in what you stand for and who you are. They want you to demonstrate that you have clear and concise answers and can articulate it with "ease and grace."

There are three types of support. One, people who will lend you support. Two, those who will join your team. Three, celebrity endorsements, sponsors, and business partners. All these collaborations will help build a community that brings attention to your cause, product, or service. Like all business assets, have a well-defined plan for who and what type of support you look for and expect to attain.

*Remember: Money + **Support** + Reputation = Presentation ROI*

Here are some tips to gain support:
1. Know yourself and the support you want from others. Be logical and organized. Note, we are great at offering help - Don't be afraid to ask for help.
2. Know your personality code – click here https://crackmycode.com/EmpowerYou
3. Know your prospect's code. Look for common ground. Be willing to learn about what other people do, how they do it, and when it aligns with your mission and vision, find a way to support each other.

Support Strategy – Servant Leadership

With loyal clients, we gift complimentary training to a qualified charity or non-profit organization of their choice. It fulfills a need by the charity and builds community rapport. Together, we earn trust, create "raving fans" and a substantial referral base. It is amazing how sometimes when you lead with your heart, oppose your need for money, your clients or audience will resonate with you and create even more significant opportunities.

Your business is not a "one-size" fits all. What are you doing to gain support? Who can you align with to collaboratively take your goals to the next level?

"Your brand name is only as good as your reputation."

~Sir Richard Branson

REPUTATION ASSET

The last element to support your ROI equation is reputation. How many of you have heard the saying, "People do business with those they know, like, and trust." The reaction to that is a resounding "YES!" A positive reputation elevates trust, distinguishes you from your competitors, and intellectually sets you apart. Be prepared. Do your research. Doing your homework will increase your value, leverages speaking opportunities, and increase collaboration. Here are a few outcomes from having a stellar reputation: media interviews, podcasts, industry-related panels, and conferences. These engagements can expand your industry footprint.

When you derive most of your business from the internet, here are some statistics to keep in mind. According to The Local Consumer Review Survey, "90% of consumers trust online reviews as much as personal recommendations." Reputationx.com found that "58% of Fortune 500 executives believe reputation management should be a core part of every organization's marketing and branding strategy."

*Remember: Money + Support + **Reputation** = Presentation ROI*

Here are some tips to help build your reputation:
1. Know the value proposition. When you make a promise, deliver on that promise!
2. Know what people are saying about you online and through word of mouth. Be visible.
3. Know what your client wants. Use social media to build content to be an expert.

MONEY + SUPPORT + REPUTATION = PRESENTATION ROI

Reflection Exercise

Defining your Presentation ROI:
1. Who is your Audience?
2. What is your desired ROI for your presentations?
   a. Money – (Sales goals, registration goals, etc.)
   b. Support – (Referral, volunteers, etc.)

    c. Reputation – (Building brand, Connections, etc.)

3. How will this ROI contribute to the growth of your business or organization?

For more information on Presentation ROI, visit us at https://www.HeroicVoiceacademy.com.

For Business, Emotional, and Personality Intelligence visit: https://codebreakertech.com/EmpowerYou

How to Lead, Teach, and Inspire

"The function of leadership is to produce more leaders, not more followers!"

~Ralph Nader

Master influencers know how to lead, teach, and inspire their audience, and excellent presentations connect the presenter, audience, and message. Whether you are speaking to one or 10,000, you must create a connection. Connection to your message demonstrates your passion for your vision. When you connect with your audience, you build trust and rapport. When the audience connects with your message, they will give you their support.

Powerful conversations happen when you connect your audience's hearts and minds. Storytelling is a perfect tool for your audience to experience this connection and serve as an inspiration to support your vision.

Precision in your presentation creates a learning experience for the audience. Successful presenters are masters at choosing the fewest words for maximum impact, optimizing the content for audience retention, comprehension, and your presentation delivery is memorable and engaging.

Personal development is your responsibility. Self-Mastery of this responsibility starts with leading yourself. Below are skillsets you want to focus on and learn.

Emotional Intelligence (EI)

Emotional intelligence is essential when you take the stage or have a high-stakes conversation. EI, coupled with empathy, is the ability to recognize your emotions, understand what they are telling you, and realize how your emotions impact others. It considers others' perceptions and feelings and allows you to engage your audience through excitement, predictable structure, expertise, logic, and authenticity. In the next section on Personality Intelligence (PI), you will learn how understanding EI and PI can make your presentations and conversation even more powerful.

Relatability

Relatability strengthens the connection with your audience. It assists in identifying shared values that communicate you care about the same things. It is crucial to include audience research as part of your preparation to provide quality content and integrate what is important to each audience member.

- **Motivation:** Motivate yourself for achievement with a clearly defined "WHY," a positive attitude, and commitment that aligns with your vision and mission. Be ready to act on opportunities.
- **Self-Awareness**: Developing self-awareness gives you the ability to recognize an emotion as it happens and be in tune with your true feelings. Self-confidence and emotional awareness help you to evaluate and manage your reactions as events happen.
- **Social Skills:** Good interpersonal skills bring on success in your life and career. "People Skills" are even more critical because they can influence others through clear communication. Initiating and managing change makes you a change catalyst and adds to the inspiration and leadership qualities others are looking to achieve. Collaboration and cooperation enhance team capabilities and create synergy in pursuing collective goals.

Reflection Exercise

You are the key to unlocking the future for yourself and others. Create time to recognize your leadership and empowerment skills. Decide how you want to show up. Reflect upon the following questions:

1. Who inspired you to be the leader you are today? Write what they taught you.
2. List Leadership skills you want to practice growing more leaders?
3. How will you create an environment where people can thrive?
4. Which of the above skillsets do you need more practice? What three actions can you commit to accomplishing?

To book an appointment with
Mamie: https://my.timetrade.com/book/PBPCN

Cracking the Rich Code using BANKCODE™

Connection | Opportunity |Structure | Self-Mastery

One of the most successful presentation tools that I use to up-level my Presentation ROI is a values-based methodology called BANKCODE®. Over 9-years ago, I met Cheri Tree, Founder & Chairperson for Codebreaker Technologies, while running a personal development workshop out in Palm Desert. Although personality typing has been around for thousands of years, none that I have worked with (DISC, MBTI, etc.) have ever told me why people buy or how they decide to say "yes" during the sales process.

More remarkable is the fact that Cheri reverse-engineered the science of personality types, and San Francisco State University scientifically validated that the B.A.N.K.® methodology predicts buying behavior in less than 90 seconds.

This section shows how powerful this toolset can be in closing more sales in less time from the stage. Learning these four profiles will fine-tune your delivery and create relatability with high emotional intelligence to each member of your audience. As you read through each of the characteristics, have a pen and paper ready to write up a list of people you see as a match for each personality.

Personality Intelligence

Blueprint Personality

People with a Blueprint Personality expects everyone to follow the rules and be on time. Blueprints place high value on organization, time management, explicit details, and predictable systems with no risk. You gain their trust through proven authority. Blueprints tend to see through the lens of right and wrong and run an agenda-driven meeting with efficiency, structure, and responsibility.

Action Personality

Action personality types are optimistic and act on instinct. They live for "the sizzle," and unlike the Blueprint, they do not like details. They want the bottom line, and in bullet point fashion! They are:

- Profit-driven and love freedom
- Open to opportunity and enjoy the competition
- Flexible, fun, and spontaneous
- Hands-on learners
- Risk takers

Actions resonate with Presentation ROI because it is a way to measure and celebrate their success by generating money, support, and reputation contributing to the bottom line.

Nurturing Personality

Nurturing personalities are primarily kind, generous, and diplomatic people. They have a tremendous love for community and relationships, often putting other's needs first. The values important to a Nurturing person are:

- Authenticity and Significance
- Contribution and Teamwork
- Personal growth and high emotional intelligence
- Ethics, morality, and harmony

Nurturing personalities live for connection and believe in supporting and empowering others to be their best. Because their currency is people, you want to incorporate it into your presentations and conversations.

Knowledge

The Knowledge personality type trusts logic and reason above all. Being the smartest people in the room, they love to debate and question your competence and expertise. Science, data, proof are what they live for, and if you do not make sense, they will challenge you. They map out a strategy at a macro level and are precise in speech, and notices contradictions. The knowledge person thrives on seeing the big picture, long-term results, and universal truths. They pride themselves on self-mastery, intelligence, and accuracy.

To learn more about Codebreaker Technologies, go to https://codebreakertech.com/EmpowerYou

Elevate your conversational Leadership Skills

As a global impact leader, make your primary objective to connect with your audience. Invest the time to learn and master these four personalities. Level-up your presentation ROI and always be authentic with your audience. The vision I hold for you is to ignite, inspire, and influence. Lead with integrity and strengthen your communications to generate intentional support, money, and reputation. Empower people to define their vision, values, and vows to align their mission with clarity, purpose, precision, mastery, and connection.

Special thanks to my mindset transformation partner and friends, Mark Yuzuik, and Yolanda Martinez. For my Heroic Voice Ohana, Anthony Lee, Sean Adams, and Ruth Uribe Mahalo! Shout out to Jeanne Zierhoffer & Juliette Willoughby for your support and guidance and all the people in my international family who believed in me!

***

For more information on Consulting, Training, Masterclasses, Coaching, or Mastermind Groups:

Email: Mamie@HeroicVoice.com

HeroicVoice.com | EmpowermentOnFire.com |
Codebreakertech.com/EmpowerYou |
Crackmycode.com/EmpowerYou

Social media:

Facebook:
Mamie Lamley: https://www.facebook.com/mamie.lamley
Mamie's Events: https://www.facebook.com/MamiesEvents
Powerful Communicators:
https://www.facebook.com/PowerfulCommunicators

LinkedIn:
Mamie   Lamley: www.linkedin.com/in/mamie-jean-lamley-a4892058
Heroic Voice: https://www.linkedin.com/company/heroicvoice/
Twitter:
 https://twitter.com/MamieLamley
Instagram:
https://www.instagram.com/empowermentonfire
Website Links & Video Links
https://www.heroicvoice.com/
https://www.empowermentonfire.com

Founder, Empowerment On Fire & Partner, Heroic Voice Academy

(710) 210-7588

Mamie@EmpowermentOnFire.com

Pamela Bardhi

Pamela Bardhi immigrated to the U.S when she was 5 Years old from Albania with her family. She started in small business at her family pizza shop in Boston when she was 10 years old. Pamela started two restaurants by the time she was 21 and shortly thereafter bought her first single family home to flip. She fell in love with real estate since then.

She's been featured in Time Magazine, Forbes, and among other major media outlets highlighting her 9-figure real estate career and achievements. Her educational background includes Stonehill College, Babson College & Harvard Business School.

Pamela is a serial entrepreneur and the founder of the Mosché Group, a real estate company comprising development, construction and brokerage based in Boston, MA. She has recently released a podcast called "Underdog" which hit Apple Podcasts' New and Noteworthy within 30 days of launching catapulting her show into the top 1% of podcasts. Pamela interviews guests from all walks of life to share their Underdog Story. Pamela is deeply passionate about helping empower others to follow their dreams and breaking through their Underdog Challenge.

The Underdog

By Pamela Bardhi

Part 1: Landing

It was a cold winter night in Massachusetts when we touched down at Logan Airport. I was 5 years old and my little brother was a baby. It was my first time being on a flight for so long. My brother would not stop crying and I was angry that I could not understand what anyone was saying to me because I did not understand English. I kept asking "Baba, why are we here?" My parents kept telling us that we were going to a new place that will provide opportunities that we would never have in Italy or Albania. I kicked and screamed that this place was too far away, and I did not like it.

We finally landed after 11 hours of flight time. We were picked up by a family friend that we had never met before. We were taken to their 3-bedroom apartment in Roslindale with 8 of us living there at the same time. Here we were as a family of 4: my parents, myself and my screaming little brother. Nonetheless, they welcomed us in with open arms and helped us get on our feet. They helped my parents find an apartment and jobs. Within a few months, we were able to move out and venture out on our own.

We pulled up to this red brick apartment building with the ugliest maroon awning in existence that had "70 Lafayette" printed on it in white lettering. We met the property manager who walked us into our apartment. The hallways were dark, smelled of strange foods and the neighbors did not seem friendly. Walking through those hallways, I said to my Dad, "Hey Baba, this place feels like prison. I want to go back to Italy where people are friendly." He looked at me and said in Albanian, "It's the best we can do right now Baba, it is only temporary." The property manager opened our apartment door, Apartment #20 at 70 Lafayette Avenue in Chelsea. So, the journey began.

Part 2: Hustle

Months passed by and I barely saw my Dad. I kept asking my Mom where Dad is. She always told me that he was working 3 jobs so my brother and I could have a better life. I kept telling her that I don't need money, I just wanted to see my Dad. I would stay up late just to see him in between his shifts for all 3 of his jobs. He did roofing, put away photos at Kodak and eventually became introduced to a friend who owned an Italian restaurant. His job options were limited because he could not speak English. My Mom had to stay home with my brother and me. She was fortunate to get a job working from home painting unique crafts.

Since both my parents were working all the time, our only day off was Sunday and we did not go far. I would always go to the park across the street from our red brick apartment building. The park was a hill full of green grass, cement stairs and open bench seating. Behind the park, at the very top of the hill, there was a massive water tower that was checkered in Red and White with the words "Soldiers Home" since it was a rehab facility for Veterans who served our country. I would always walk up the cement stairs to the top, take a right and look at the view of the city of Boston. It was a perfect bird's eye view of the city. At the time, it seemed like a whole big world of its own. I vowed and dreamed to myself that one day, I would run that city and that my parents would not ever have to work a day in their life again.

One evening, I was exploring our apartment building and went to the very top floor. I discovered a small hallway window that had the view of the city of Boston. Although not as nice of a view as the park, it was still a beautiful view. This was the greatest discovery because I could not go to the park every day since my parents were always working and would not allow me to go by myself. I stared off at that view for what seemed like hours most days and just dreamed vividly.

I dreamed of being on a stage with the world listening. I dreamed of making people laugh and smile. I dreamed of a life where my parents did not ever need to worry about a single thing. Here I was, 7 years old, staring out of this narrow window at the marveling city of large buildings and bright lights. It was at that time I made a promise to myself looking at that view that I would become a millionaire by 30 and that the whole world would one day know my name.

Part 3: Dreams

"Your Dad is buying a restaurant business." my Mom told me one day. I asked her how and why. She explained that Dad's mentor in the restaurant business advised him to buy a business. I asked again, "Why?" She said, "Dad is buying a business so he can own something in his name because owning businesses and real estate in the United States is the way to build wealth." My response was "Oh, that's great Mama. So, does that mean when he makes a lot of money, he doesn't have to work as much and can stay home with us?" She smiled and laughed, "Yes, one day."

Dad then bought his restaurant business 3 years after moving to the United States in the year 2000. In Summer 2000, I was 9 years old, bored at home in this red brick apartment building, intrigued by this idea of a business so I asked my Dad if I could go with him. He kept saying no because it would be a very long day for me. Nonetheless, I persisted, and I did not take no for an answer.

There the journey began when I was 9 years old; the day I walked through those black glass doors for the very first time. As soon I walked in, there was a green and white old school tile counter with a grey Pepsi menu board that had manual blue letters on it. The store smelled of mouth-watering fresh pizza coming out of the oven. My job was to stay at the counter and say hello to everyone that came in. Who knew this would be the start of my Underdog story?

At 16 years old, I got my first car from my parents under the stipulation that I would deliver pizzas when I wasn't in high school or playing sports. I then started waitressing at my cousin's restaurant, Arcadia, during breakfast hours on weekend mornings. I would waitress in the morning then deliver pizzas starting in the afternoon. After those 15 hour workdays, I would ride around in my black 1996 Nissan Sentra, the first thing my family ever owned in the United States, with the music blasting and windows down, dreaming I was in a black Lamborghini. I envisioned myself in a badass black blazer sitting in q large conference room table as CEO in huge glass office building. My dream was to grow up to be one of the most powerful women in business. That dream has become so vivid...

Part 4: Fate

"You were just too ambitious." This sentence changed my entire life trajectory. I was told these words by my Supervisor after I spent an entire semester interning at a major corporate events and sports venue and received a B minus. I was 19 and it was my junior year in college. My goal was to get hired by this company when I graduated college and then start my own business down the line. My entire world felt like it was crushed. My master plan had fallen apart and I felt like a failure for about 4 minutes.

After I walked out of the threshold of those office doors, I realized that a corporate setting with cubicles is prison to me and that my ambition will serve me well on my own. I walked out of those office doors that day, called my parents and told them I was starting a business. I vowed to them that I would never work for anyone but myself. My parents were terrified, but I was well on my way to starting my first venture.

After speaking with my father, we discovered that his tenant was closing his jewelry store next to my father's restaurant. I told my Father that I was going to create the most delicious dessert and gelato café in the US. Since I was born in Albania and lived in Rome, I wanted to bring in flavors of my culture to my Boston community. My father asked me to put together a business plan and get started! So I did.

A few months later, I got an email from my previous boss from a company I used to intern for. He asked me to become his business partner for a restaurant business located at the Charles River Esplanade at the Hatchshell in downtown Boston. Of course, I said yes! I never turned down opportunity. I just always found a way to make it happen.

Here I was, 20 years old, in my senior year of college, with two restaurants about to open up within the same year. I faced doubts from many people. They said I was too young and inexperienced, and I would not make it. In my mind, having two restaurants by 21 was insane, but I was ready.

Part 5: Diversify

Fast forward about a year with both restaurants under my belt, I somehow found myself bored and unhappy with my decision. I was shocked that after all this effort and hustle that I did not have a sense of fulfillment. I had my teams laid out for both restaurants and I did not need to physically be present at either location. In my mind, that time created space for a new opportunity. An opportunity to learn and diversify my revenue streams. At the time, all my eggs were in all one basket: the restaurant industry.

All I ever knew since I was 9 years old was the restaurant industry and it was time to take on a new challenge. Whenever anyone mentioned diversification, real estate was always what everyone pointed to as the industry that creates the most millionaires. In my mind, I had nothing to lose by trying.

I hired my first mentor to teach me all about real estate development in late 2013. Within months, I purchased my first single family home to flip and I absolutely fell in love with it. Shortly thereafter, I received my real estate salespersons license simply so that I could understand my investment markets.

Then, the brokerage side of my business took on a life of its own through residential sales. I was then headhunted by a firm that ultimately brought me into the commercial real estate world. After 4 years, I got my real estate broker's license then went on to get my unrestricted construction supervisor license (General Contractor's License) as one of the youngest females in Massachusetts' history at 25 years old. By 27, I was magically accepted into Harvard Business School to study Real Estate Development as one of the youngest females in program history.

Fast forward to today where I have sold, developed or acquired over $100 million in real estate assets in and around the Boston, MA market. I am the Underdog and living proof that hustle beats talent any day of the week.

However, I would be lying to you if everything I just told you came easy and flowed with grace. I used to max out credit cards and would have severe anxiety that would consume me. Most days, I did not know how I was going to be able to afford payroll. I put my entire soul and my family's only source of wealth on the line just to chase my dream.

That dream that I would one day be that boss lady CEO sitting at those fine conference tables in those gorgeous glass office buildings. That dream that my parents would look at me and proudly say their sacrifices in life coming to America was worth it. That dream that my family and my future family would not ever have to worry about a single bill in their life. That dream that fueled me to be the Underdog in such a fearless way. That dream that empowered me to tell my story so I can empower the world. That dream is what pulled me through the darkest moments of doubt and fear. That dream is what created this Underdog.

Part 6: The Underdog Lessons

Many people come to me seeking advice on how I made it from a young, in debt Underdog to a Top Dog earning 7 figures in Real Estate. Here are the top 5 lessons of wisdom that got me to where I am today:

1. **ENERGY is KEY!**
   a. You could have the best business strategy in the world. However, if you have a negative thought process, you will exert negative energy which will repel the relationships and opportunities you seek. Train your mind to think positive thoughts which will affect your energy positively in order to attract your dream relationships and opportunities.

2. **RELATIONSHIPS BEFORE MONEY**
   a. NEVER put money before a relationship. You should ALWAYS seek to add value to everyone in your life.
      i. For example, say you go to pitch to a potential client, do NOT sell them on your product or service. Get to know them first by hearing their story, their triumphs and challenges. Once you do that, offer how you may be of value only if it is a genuine fit. People will love and appreciate you that much more by taking a human approach and

taking the time to build that rapport. This approach will skyrocket your word-of-mouth referrals.

b. The minute you put money over a relationship is when you decide that you will stay a small fish. Big fish are always givers. Be a giver.

3. Hustle out beats talent every day of the week.

a. You do not need to know it all. You just have to be willing to learn it. Remember, I knew nothing in construction but yet I bought my first real estate flip and jumped right in.

4. Coaches are key. INVEST IN THEM

a. Would you rather make expensive mistakes on your own or pay a coach to provide you the blueprint to succeed and avoid costly mistakes? Choose wisely.

5. BE KIND

a. Everyone you meet is always going through a struggle that you know nothing about. One of the most critical elements as to how I have built outstanding relationships is by having empathy. What is my definition of empathy? Treating another human being with dignity, respect and pure love.

b. When you come across a client or friend, ask them how they are genuinely doing. Compliment them. Support them in their endeavors. If they have kids, ask about their kids. Ask them what they like to do on their spare time. Empower them. Take the human approach and show that love to them to brighten their day even the slightest. You may never know how much it may mean to someone who is having a tough time.

Part 7: The Underdog Mentality

Everyone in the world dreams of crushing it in their career, being financially free, finding true happiness and living freely to do as they wish. These dreams are entirely possible. I know because I've been to the top but I have also experienced the bottom. I've drowned in debt before, hit rock bottom and struggled to see the bright light at the end of the tunnel. The following formula contains the Underdog qualities that enabled me to go from in debt Underdog to Top Dog earning 7 figures in real estate. I call it the **FACTS formula**:

F- Fearlessness

A- Adaptability

C- Compassion

T- Trust your gut

S- Self Confidence

1.) **Fearlessness** is simple. Think of being on a diving board. You don't look down; you just jump because you know you will not sink, and you will float back up. When you want to follow your dreams, don't think about it, just do it. The universe will always make sure you float back up.

2.) **Adaptability** is critical in business and just life in general. If you do not have the ability to adapt and are constantly reacting to your world, you will never find true happiness and success. Whenever a problem arises, all you need to do is think of a solution. DO NOT react, just problem solve. It will help you get in the flow and make adapting easy.

3.) **Compassion** is key to all successful relationships in your life. Put yourself in other people's shoes. You must ALWAYS remember that someone is fighting a battle you know nothing about. Be kind and show love to every person you come across in your life.

4.) **Trusting your gut because it never lies.** Every single time I chose not to listen to my instincts, I have been wrong. Remember, energy never lies. Trust yourself.

5.) **Self Confidence-** How are you going to win if you are not right within? Who will buy your product and/or service if you are not confident over your competition? Love thyself, build your confidence and watch every aspect of your life flourish.

For a free consultation with me, please book an introductory call at www.meetwithpamela.com. Let's explore how we can add value to one another and inspire the Underdog in you.

***

To contact Pamela:

pamela@themoschegroup.com

617-259-7732

www.pamelabardhi.com

Check out my Podcast:

www.theunderdogshow.com

Sara Sabin

Sara Sabin is a qualified accountant, former start-up founder, and a transformational coach. Having been through many transformations herself over the years, it wasn't until the most recent transformation that she really cracked it! Sara loves to work with entrepreneurs and leaders, who have a grand vision and want to make a big impact on the world around them, through their business. She helps them to develop 'future intelligence', so they remain competitive in the years to come. Sara uses neuroscience, positive psychology and cutting edge transformative coaching techniques, to coach leaders, to become more self-aware and emotionally intelligent, and to approach leadership and business challenges in a more creative way, so that they become more influential, effective and profitable, ultimately increasing their business and bottom line impact. https://sarasabin.com

Becoming an Unshakeable, Purpose Driven Entrepreneur

By Sara Sabin

"Knowing when to walk away, is Wisdom. Being able to, is Courage. Walking away with Grace, and your held head high, is Dignity" – Ritu Ghatourey

As I strode through Heathrow airport, on my way to catch a flight to Istanbul, my mobile phone rang. "We did it." The voice on the other end of the line said. My start-up co-founder. "He's going to invest into the business. Just wanted to let you know." My heart sank.

I am an entrepreneur. When I left the corporate world five years ago, I knew that I was done with it. What I hadn't factored in, when I entered it with rose coloured glasses, was just how hard it could be. Chasing the glory, the success, the money – it's not enough to sustainably get you through the lows. You can push through it, with willpower and sheer grit. I've done that. But long term, it burns you out and doesn't bring happiness or satisfaction.

And after all, why are we entrepreneurs, if not to forge our own path and live our dreams?

The few months prior to that phone call, I had started to regain my sanity, after more than two years of chronic stress, anxiety and near burnout. The phone call was a jolt to my system. It meant that if we took the investment, I was tied to my start-up for the next few years, and I quite simply could not bear the thought of it.

A month after that phone call, I shut down my business.

Other people found it hard to understand. They said, "but you've put so much time and money into this, it's a shame to not carry on". "You're doing well, you're gaining traction." I didn't listen, because I could no longer deny what my intuition told me was the right decision to make. I knew that if I continued, I was headed down a dark tunnel.

I had founded two start-ups by that point in my life – the first one, although successful, I walked away from retaining a small shareholding, after my relationship with my co-founder broke down; and then, I decided to start a tech start-up on my own, determined to prove that I could do it. And, like many decisions in my life, up until that point, it was done for all of the wrong reasons.

I am a fan of grit and determination and perseverance. Ask anyone who knows me and words like resilience, perseverance and tenacity come up again and again. What I've learned is when something is really worth the pain and when it's time to call it a day.

What makes the difference? Purpose.

The reasons why we do the things we do (if we're honest enough to admit it), give us some indication if what we're choosing to do is sustainable.

Up until that point, every decision in my career was about proving something.

Ever since I remember, I was always trying to prove something to someone. If someone told me I couldn't achieve a certain grade, or get into a certain school, or act in a certain play; I would go to tremendous lengths to prove them wrong. Most of the time, I did indeed prove them wrong, through sheer force of will. I took great satisfaction in doing so.

I didn't realise how much I took that conditioning forward – everything became about proving to myself and other people that I COULD do something. Whether I really wanted to do it was not something I stopped to consider.

That kind of fighter spirit does take you to a certain level of success, it helps you get things done. However, because it feels like you're always fighting against something, it eventually means that you become exhausted by it all, and it can stop you from reaching the next level of success. Real, sustainable success.

I founded my own start-up. Just to prove I could. I told myself at the time that it was my passion. It wasn't. It was my ego. If I think back to why I went down the start-up route, it was because I had a glamourised ideal of it in my mind. Nothing about that business was authentic to me.

And everything in my life suffered – my relationships with my partner, friends' and family. I barely had time for any of them, and when I did have time, I was irritable and tired. My constant unhappiness and anxiety became my new 'normal', my constant companion. That is not my definition of success.

The truth is that, sometimes, maximum effort does not equal maximum output

The 'always on' hustle culture that we live in says that, if we're not getting the results we want, we need to try harder. In fact, constant 'busyness' is worn like a badge of honour. It's the only addiction that people actually celebrate.

Let's face it, if we let it, our To Do list might be endless. There is always something we could be doing. And if you have an obsessive personality, everything needs to be done NOW.

What is often not conveyed is that by living and working like this, we don't always generate the output we want. Rather than working even harder, we should look at the reasons WHY we're not getting the results we want. Often, that involves taking a step back from doing (especially, if you are an action- oriented person, that does even more to get through the pain). It involves a reflective process, going deep within ourselves, to understand what is really going on and how we are holding ourselves back. The answer always lies there. It can be raw and painful. But if we are really committed to achieving our full potential and dreams and living a fulfilled life, we need to go there, nonetheless.

My start-up, when I was running it, built up real traction at various points. But were these results commensurate with the effort put in? Probably not.

I never stopped to ask myself why that was. I stayed on the constant treadmill. That's what everyone else does, I told myself. In fact, every time things seemed to pick up, they then slowed down again. That could be attributable to business cycles, sure. But I also think I was sabotaging myself all along and slowing myself down because my heart just wasn't in it.

My heart just wasn't in my tech start-up

I did it to prove I could, I did it for the prestige, I did it to make money, I did it because other people I knew had done it.

None of those reasons are good reasons.

In retrospect, the way I talked about it, should have been a clue for me. I was always one foot in, one foot out. "Oh, I'll try and make it work." "Most tech start-ups fail in the first few years."

When I found my purpose and started my coaching business, I was in a state of flow and love, and wonderfully, with minimal effort (which hardly felt like effort at all), I got great results. It has had usual ups and downs of business ever since. And what I have done is turn inwards, to get through the lows. Something I never would have done before I came across transformational coaching.

I'm not saying that if your heart is in a project, that it will be 100% smooth sailing. It likely won't be. But at least, you will always know your WHY. And that powerful why, can carry you through the hard times. That WHY is the reason for pushing through. When you're all in, you're committed. And when you're really committed to something, you'll overcome what's blocking you (internal or external) and always find a way to make it happen.

For example, I have never missed a flight in my life. I always talk about flights, in terms of "I'm getting that flight to XXX". I'll never say, "I'll try my best to be on that flight." And sometimes, there was a close shave, but I have never missed a flight.

Sometimes you need to let go and walk away.

Whether that be the job you hate, the business that saps the life out of you and feels misaligned, or your failures.

Letting go is hard. Especially for people who like to be in control.

However, if we truly realised all the wonderful things that await us on the other side of 'letting go', perhaps, it wouldn't seem so bad. It wouldn't seem like giving up or failure.

By letting go, we allow something better to come into our lives. Something better suited to us. Otherwise, we stay where we are.

After I shut down my start-up, I forced myself to take a break from starting anything new. I shut out (mostly) the voice in my head and allowed myself time and space for my innate intelligence to come through – that intuitive voice, usually drowned out by all the noise. For the first time in years, I had time to breathe. Around that time, I came across my calling, transformational coaching, and I knew. I knew the message I wanted to share with the world and how I wanted to impact it.

At any moment, our lives can change. At any moment, we can re-create ourselves. Sometimes, it's slow and painful, involving lots of experimentation. Sometimes, our lives can transform in a very short space of time.

For faster transformation, we need to be more discerning about the experiments we try

I do not regret anything that I have done in my life. As Brene Brown says: "There is no innovation and creativity without failure. Period."

And in order to compete as a business now, we need to be innovative, adaptive and creative.

However, we can be more discerning about our experiments.

If I describe this in a dating context. You go on a date. From that, you get a gut feeling if this person might be for you. You then proceed to make a series of mini-commitments – more dates, exclusivity, moving in together, marriage, children. Relatively few people in the Western world would jump straight to marriage and babies, without the experimentation phase along the way. At some point, you may decide to just stop dating or break up, because it's not working. So why in business are we not more open to experimenting?

How many of you have gone against your gut feeling and tried experiments that ultimately didn't work out? Or listened to other people, when you felt instinctively, it was wrong?

Having that initial sign off from your gut, allows you to be more discerning in your business experiments. The neuroscientific evidence is there. There are two neural pathways going from the gut to the brain and only one from the brain to the gut. It also contains some 100m neurons, more than the spinal cord. Our gut is a natural decision maker: we get a feeling and then if we listen to it, we send it up to the brain for processing.

In business, you should actively question everything you know and try things out: if they work, great. If they don't, cut them off quickly. We work best by contrast and finding out what doesn't work. Staying with the tried and tested and doing what everyone else does will not lead to you or your business standing out or being unique.

Purpose before profit? Purpose = Profit.

How many people think that purpose and profit are mutually exclusive of each other? Not only are they inextricably linked but they increase the likelihood that you will be around in years to come (both you and your business) and that you will generate the financial abundance as well, as a result of the value that you are providing.

Studies show that actually there is a link between purpose and high growth.

If you think of this in terms of a car – imagine getting in a car, with no destination (no Purpose) at all in mind. You might have a plan or a vague direction but there is no guiding light or North Star to direct where you are going. You are more likely to take a long time, only to end up in a place you never really wanted to visit.

It makes sense logically. Having a clear intention helps you succeed in actualising those ambitions.

Going back to the car analogy – you don't need to plan out every step of the way on your route. Just plug your Purpose into your GPS system and let things take their course. Try as we might, we can never be certain about what the future holds. We are driving in the dark, and we can only see clearly each metre of the path as it unfolds in front of us. If we encounter obstacles, the GPS simply reroutes us, and we have the option whether to follow it or not. The final destination remains unchanged. However, we allow ourselves the flexibility to change and pivot.

This agility is demanded of us more and more (as we have seen with Covid-19). We have to be able to adapt quickly to survive and thrive in business. The best laid plans are always subject to change. The key is to build the connection to Purpose and the entrepreneurial mindset to deal with these changes.

Purpose and Brand Messaging

The decision to buy or not is often an emotional one. We make decisions emotionally, before we start to analyse it. So, help people 'feel' you!

People love being part of a story and a Purpose. It makes them feel good about themselves.

And from a marketing perspective, if you can successfully integrate your Purpose into everything that your brand and your company's brand does and says, that makes your raison d'etre stronger. It attracts the employees you want to work for you and the customers that you want to work with. In other words, it speaks to the people that resonate with your message.

And the reality is that many companies are falling short. In the Deloitte Millennial Survey 2018, 40% of respondents believed that the goal of businesses should be to 'improve society'. In the Deloitte Survey 2020, barely half of millennials felt that business was a force for good.

That, of course, means that there is a real opportunity for businesses to appeal to this younger, purpose driven generation, by actively showing their commitment to Purpose. Data actually shows that customers are more loyal to purpose driven brands.

For example, the shoe-maker TOMS. For every pair of shoes, you buy, a pair of shoes goes to a child in need. All things being equal, would you rather buy that style of shoe from TOMS or an equivalent brand that does not have the feel-good factor?

When you've found your Purpose, Fight for It. And Filter out the Noise.

If you're lucky enough to have got crystal clear on your Purpose, then fight for it.

Personality tests telling you that you'd be a great entrepreneur are no measure of whether or not you can do it. Get out there, do it. But pick your battles. Your personality is not a box, a finite measure. It evolves, strengthens and grows over time. If you choose.

As Seth Godin says in the book The Dip: "Quit or be exceptional. Average is for losers." "To be a superstar, you must do something exceptional. Not just survive the Dip but use the Dip as an opportunity to create something so extraordinary that people can't help but talk about it, recommend it, and, yes, choose it."

In a nutshell, quit when it's right. Stick it out when it's right. And if you're sticking it out, be sure why you're doing it, and don't settle for being average. Be the best.

I find so many people, including myself sometimes, just want to be told what to do. By their board of advisors, investors, consultants. Follow this magic 7 step formula for success, follow this marketing method I tried that worked for me, follow this, follow that. A quick fix to success. The noise becomes endless. And yes, some advice is great advice, worth listening to!

However, until you develop your own inner wisdom and guidance system, you will not be discerning enough to determine which people you should listen to and which people to ignore. Or understand whether you're being led by your ego.

Yes, it's harder to find your own way. But I ask the question, did anyone ever become exceptional, by following someone else's exact formula? They learned from various teachers, gurus, coaches and inspiring people. Then, they used their discernment to filter out what to listen to, what to try, what to leave. They used their learnings to forge their own path.

My final message is...

I've been there myself. The successes you've achieved feel like the tip of the iceberg. High performers know that development is never done. If you want to be the best, you and your business need to constantly be challenged.

The answers lie within you. I can help bring them out.

If you're ready to do the work, to connect with your own and your business's purpose, so you can smash those invisible ceilings you've set up for yourself, so you can live your purpose, and so that purpose can filter through to everything you do in your life and business and translate into more abundance than you ever dreamed possible, contact me.

I work with purpose driven entrepreneurs, who want to get crystal clear on their Purpose, develop an authentic, influential leadership style, and a killer mindset, so that they can put an action plan and KPI's in place, to build thriving teams and businesses that make a big impact and profit!

To contact Sara:

Visit https://sarasabin.com/ and book your Discovery Call.

Connect with me on https://www.linkedin.com/in/sara-sabin/ or drop me an email at sara@sarasabin.com

Angeline Wehmeyer

Angeline Wehmeyer is an accomplished entrepreneur, investor, and national speaker on the topic of mastering your finances. For the last decade, Angeline has made it her mission to help others achieve their financial dreams using her simple and attainable wealth blueprint.

At a young age, Angeline knew she wanted to be an entrepreneur and investor. From humble beginnings in China to amassing a multi-million-dollar empire in the USA, Angeline has spent countless hours studying the secrets of the financial industry. After amassing a sizable real estate portfolio of over 1,000 housing units, Angeline shifted her focus to expanding her income streams through investing. After many years of success, she founded the "Financial Genius Academy" to teach people how to master their finances. Angeline is also the owner and CEO of "Abundant Heart Financial" a financial services company that helps clients invest their money following the same principles that led to her success. Her passion is to empower people with the knowledge and mindset they need to create an even stronger financial foundation for their family. One that can weather any storm in life.

From Living in a Barber Shop to a Multi-Million-Dollar Empire

By Angeline Wehmeyer

SACRIFICE

I was born in Zhangpu China, a very small rural town in the South. I didn't grow up with a silver spoon, or even a wooden spoon for that matter! I had very humble beginnings. My parents were born in Vietnam, and due to the war, they relocated to China. They had no money and were living off of government support. With basically the shirts on their backs they decided to open a humble barbershop. We couldn't afford our own home. We all had to live in the back area of the shop.

Most of my young childhood was spent at their barbershop. I slept behind a curtain while they worked in the front. I learned to live with a servants' heart while watching my parents take loving care of their customers. After approximately five years of having steady customers, my mother had a realization and a vision.

My mother realized she would never be able to pay for my college. The income from their barbershop kept them in constant financial stress and living paycheck to paycheck. She had a vision for more than that. She wanted enough financial stability to provide the life for me that I deserved. She could have stayed where she was. Instead, she took a risk for her family.

My childhood was far from normal. My parents left our village and went far away to make more income. I stayed back and lived with my grandparents. Many nights I would cry in the shower, wondering where they were, and would they ever come back? Even as I write this chapter, the tears come back to my eyes. I never experienced love or joy with my parents like most kids. I was very lonely and insecure. I never experienced the feeling of my parents holding me in their arms or showing affection. Our reunions were always about checking in on me and making sure I had everything I needed. That was it, no fancy dinners or celebrations.

Even through all this pain, I learned a lot of valuable life lessons. I learned at a very young age how to take care of myself. I matured very quickly. Because of my parents' sacrifice, I was ultimately able to attend college. It was an exciting moment for me. Life still hadn't changed that much though. I remember the first day of school at the dorms. Everyone's parents were there helping them get set up. They were all so excited and proud to see their kids start this new and exciting chapter of their lives. I was the only person whose parents weren't there. I really admired what they had. In spite of this, I continued on.

I let go of the disappointment and focused on getting the job done. I made a commitment to myself. I told myself every day to study extra hard. I wanted to make my parents proud. More importantly, I didn't want their sacrifice to be in vain. My non-negotiable promise was to get straight A's. I never missed a class, I always showed up early, and always sat in the front row. I would even stay after class and talk to my professors to make sure I understood all the content and got my assignments done. Not tolerating anything less than my vision became my new mindset.

My hard work paid off. To my surprise, I won the school's Golden Key award: a prize reserved only for the top student of the whole graduating class! On top of this prestigious honor, I was chosen to give the commencement speech in front of the whole class. This was one of the proudest moments of my entire life. I never aspired to be top of my class. I just focused on my vision and the result came. Even with all this joy, the reality of my life set in again. My parents were too busy working to attend this special moment in my life. They couldn't afford to make the trip to see me give the speech and accept the award. At this point in my life, I believed that in order to be successful, I needed to sacrifice. I thought that the way my parents lived was the only way to make a good living, and making money was hard. My beliefs all changed when I came to America.

MINDSET SHIFT

I had the opportunity to come to America to pursue my financial dreams. My mother's voice was still in my head, "In order to have a good life, you need to study hard and get a good job!" Up until this point, I followed her blueprint of financial success. After graduating in China, I enrolled in Fairleigh Dickinson University in New Jersey. It was here that I got my master's degree in business. After I received my degree, I was so excited to get a good job, and make some real money! However just like my life in China, reality set in yet again. The reality was, that even with an MBA, it was hard to find a good job with a decent salary.

During this time, something drew me to read the book, *Rich Dad, Poor Dad* by Robert Kiyosaki. After reading the book, I had a mindset shift. I realized very quickly that working a 9-5 job was all about trading time for money and a "Rat Race" that never ends. I didn't see any hope of financial freedom if I continued with this path. All of a sudden, a light bulb went off and I had an "Aha" moment. I realized that I could be my own boss and become an entrepreneur and investor. This was something that I never heard, or learned about, from school or my own parents. I was so excited to adopt this new belief system and start taking action based on what the book was teaching me.

My new belief was to have money working hard for me, versus me working hard for money. I was focused on earning a strong income and investing. In the book, Robert Kiyosaki mentioned real estate as the best way to create lasting wealth. After my husband and I moved to Texas, I had a strong intuition to invest in real estate. The only problem was I had zero real estate knowledge or experience, and I had no money to invest. At that point I was facing many obstacles. After graduating and moving from New Jersey, I was faced with making a choice of finding a job for a paycheck or following my dreams of becoming an entrepreneur and investor.

I had a conversation with my husband, and I told him I wanted to invest in real estate. The first thing that came out of his mouth was "No way, it's too risky!" He was concerned that the market could shift and that I had little to no experience. Even though he kept saying no, I was determined.

I shut out the naysayers in my head and became unstoppable in finding my first investment property. I took massive action and looked at more than 20 houses per week. I did this for months, until one day I found the right property. I made the decision I was going to make this deal happen. I talked to my husband and I wasn't going to take no for an answer.

After we closed on the first property, I gained a lot of momentum. I kept the same ferocious search going and eventually closed on another deal shortly thereafter. I started generating positive cash flow after I rented them out. I still remember the day my husband's tone shifted. Instead of trying to stop me he said, "We should buy more of these, they're great!" It felt great to have my gut intuition validated. I continued to buy more properties. All the properties had great cash flow and were rapidly appreciating in value. Eventually the value shot up so much we decided to sell them. In the end, we made on average a 300% return on our investments. At that moment I really experienced the power of having money work FOR me. I realized that through investing I could change my life.

After all that success, I started to get greedy. I tried to speed up the profits by flipping properties. The first deal I bought seemed like it was going to be a homerun. Then just as we were finishing the rehab work, we discovered foundation and other unforeseen issues. I ended up losing $50,000 on that deal. I felt so ashamed and filled with doubt. From this experience I realized that investing has risk as well. You can lose money as easily as you can make it. I learned it wasn't about how much you make, rather it was how much you can keep. Unfortunately, we usually are only taught about how amazing certain investments are, we rarely learn about the risk and how to minimize it. After this I decided to go back and educate myself more about investing and personal improvement.

I eventually found my own niche of investing in apartments. I sold all of my single-family homes and invested in over a thousand apartment units. However, the income from these investments still wasn't enough to reach my financial goals. I was asset rich but cash flow poor.

INVESTMENT BREAKTHROUGH

Many people have limiting beliefs about investing. I used to think some of the same things too. I got trapped in the idea that we need to make all of our money from one thing. This was the mindset I had with real estate until I had an epiphany. I realized that building wealth wasn't about a silver bullet. It was about a well-diversified strategy and blueprint. I became even more passionate about studying all the different ways to make and invest money. I was determined to grow multiple streams of income through investments.

Throughout this process I was introduced to the financial services industry. As I dug deeper, I realized so many people didn't understand how investing works, including myself. I thought because of my real estate success that I knew everything. I was opened up to a whole new world of investing: one where you have multiple streams of investment income. I realized building wealth was like building a house. We can't just focus on one part of it. In order to have a strong house you need a strong foundation along with sturdy walls, a roof, and many other components. If not, the house would eventually crumble.

Let me share a story with you of what I mean by this. One day, my husband and I visited his grandparents in the nursing home. I saw how much care they needed and what it was costing. I also realized that there wasn't any way for them to earn income. It made me start thinking about myself. What if all of the sudden I lost my ability to be actively involved in real estate. All of my money would be trapped in the assets. Where would I get the income to support myself?

I spent more time studying the financial industry and speaking to my mentors. I came to the realization that the top one percent of wealthy individuals were given access to all the tools and products to truly leverage their financial resources. The rest of the population have knowledge of a small variety of either mutual funds or stocks and bonds. Most people weren't introduced to all the tax efficient and risk adverse solutions available in the market. I discovered the secret sauce and made it my mission to share the recipe with the masses. I opened my own financial services company and began working with clients to empower them with the knowledge I had learned.

I believe that if we want to crack the *Rich Code*, there are three key ingredients for success:

First, it's important to have the right investment strategy. We don't get rich by doing certain things. We get rich by doing things a certain way. The sequence of investing is just as important as what we are investing in. Unfortunately, this is not something they teach us in school. Worst yet, if we try and research online there is a maze of information and most of it is misleading.

Second, we need to have different vehicles to grow our money. The more investments we have in different asset classes the more protected our money is from loss. When I sit down with people to develop their investment strategy, I realize different people have different needs. It's never a one size fits all solution. By sitting down with a professional they are able to come up with a proper plan to diversify their income streams.

Lastly, to speed up your financial success, it's important to have the right mentor. Do you believe one person can change your life? I had a lot of trial and error in the beginning. I really wasted a lot of time and money. It wasn't until I started working with my mentors that I developed my own personalized investment strategy and vehicles. I applied what I learned and developed a multi-million-dollar investment portfolio.

We have two choices, we can choose to either figure things out on our own and make mistakes, or we can choose to accelerate our success and follow someone who has been there and done that. What choice would you make?

TURNING DREAMS INTO REALITY

You may wonder how to find the right mentor? When you are ready the right mentor will appear. In other words, when the student is ready, the teacher will appear. Over the years I've had so many different mentors. Each unique in their own way and each adding value in a different way. One mentor in particular really gave me a significant boost. He was very patient with me and was genuinely committed to my success. Under his guidance I was able to turn my yearly income into a monthly income. We were on a mission together. He believed in the same cause of helping people reach their financial dreams as me.

Although he has now passed away, I will continue on this journey of mentoring others to create even more financial success in their life. I work with a lot of younger people. I teach them the principles of investing and help them develop a good habit of setting aside a few hundred dollars per month to create millions in their retirement. Imagine if we can teach our kids and young adults all of these principles, how much better off they would be in the future. I also work with people who have significant assets. Surprisingly, when they come to me, they don't even understand what investments they have or how they work. I spend time with them to mentor and educate them on the most tax efficient and wealth building solutions that help them meet their needs. I still remember the smiles and relief they have after our sessions. It makes me feel so fulfilled and energizes me to serve more.

You have the power to turn your dreams into reality. Ask yourself, what are your dreams? If you could live life without limits, what would you really want? Would you like to travel more freely with your family and see beautiful places around the world? Or maybe it's just more time freedom you seek? You may just want to have more financial success so you can help others and fulfill your life purpose. My friend, these are the questions I asked myself. The answers led me to the path I chose.

Financial freedom is not a dream, it's a priority. Just like when we pay attention to eating right and working out, we end up with a healthy body. People are able to get to the next level in their financial journey by focusing on their goals. They have cracked the *Rich Code*. They've shifted their beliefs about investing like I have and put their focus into massive action. My life's purpose is helping countless people achieve their financial goals. I am honored to mentor people and be their financial guide. I encourage you to focus on your dreams, regardless of what your current situation is. Develop healthy financial habits and continue to expand your wealth mindset. I believe in the power of you! I believe all you need is within you now!

***

To contact Angeline:

Email: angeline@angelinewehmeyer.com

www.angelinewehmeyer.com

Nadiya Manji

Nadiya Manji is a sought-after leadership and emotional intelligence expert who helps clients break through their personal, professional and social vulnerabilities. She develops self-awareness in professionals of all levels, producing balanced, emotionally intelligent, and resilient leaders in both life and business. Nadiya has lived and practiced in three continents, where she developed a love for helping people identify and overcome their inner blocks and barriers that prevent them from optimizing their human potential.

Nadiya is a transformational master coach, registered clinical hypnotherapist, board certified master NLP, international TEDx speaker, and author of the self-help book titled, "Searching for Balance". She has spent over 20 years honing her skills in science, spirituality and intuition. Now, Nadiya offers a wide range of coaching programs and services including in-person coaching, corporate workshops, training sessions and on-board consultations.

Crack the Code of Life and Business

By Nadiya Manji

"Become uncomfortable to create the comfortable life you always wanted." – NM

Where are you going?

As you work towards cracking the rich code, have you asked yourself what that actually looks like?

How do you define it, and what do you visualize in your mind, to know that you've made it?

Close your eyes, or gaze off into the distance, and take a few deep breaths. Begin to create an image of the state in which you feel truly successful; what do you see? We're likely to first identify the items that align with consumerist ideals such as cars, a large home, financial wealth, and travel. Or perhaps a cabin in the woods, affording you with all the privacy your money can buy you.

Regardless of what your wealth goals are, ideally, you aren't reaching these goals on your own. As you visualize this moment of "making it", how do you imagine your:

- Close relationships?
- State of mind?
- Physical health?

We will inevitably experience ebbs and flows with our business ventures, therefore we need to establish other positive spaces to keep us committed, engaged, and motivated. When we solely focus on dollars and asset accumulation, we can get frustrated and lose sight of our dreams, especially when these goal posts are not met fast enough to meet our expectations. This is why cracking the code for both life and business is necessary. Ensure that you cultivate your relationships in tandem with your work, so that you don't reach your pinnacle alone.

There is a myth of success, that success automatically yields happiness. Wherein lies the fallacy. Success can provide validation, and even luxury, but like an asymptote, it can only get you so close to happiness. Defining the parameters of what makes you happy and fulfilled (as we cannot expect to experience happiness all the time), allows you to understand the levels at which your business and personal relationships can contribute to that sense of fulfillment.

As you visualize a more holistic view of your success picture, you can create a game plan that incorporates all areas of your life. Business professionals who allow themselves to be all consumed in a singular goal can risk losing key support systems and social networks that can aid in making their goals a reality. Emphasizing dedication to one's business *and* life ensures that an individual can draw inspiration and support from either area.

Now that you know where you want to be, let's start cracking the code to get you the fuller picture!

Where are you now, and why are you not there yet?

To unlock your code, you need to first understand what your specific code is. Your code is a combination of your life history, alignment with your values and goals, and lastly, the specific vision you have for your business. This is critical as understanding yourself allows you to maintain the success you achieve along the way. It also informs how you approach success and work; you see, as you understand yourself, you'll recognize your code, and enable yourself to crack it.

So, what has brought you to this point? If you are reading this book, you are looking to create a different reality than the one you are living in now. So how did you get here, and what has prevented you from moving forward towards your goals?

Perhaps this question is making you cringe a little, or slightly flush with embarrassment. Who wants to be asked *why they are not there yet?* It is certainly not a confidence booster. But the question is not meant to question your progress, it is meant to question your challenges.

When we track our progress, we only think about how far we are from the finish line. If we feel insecure that we are not close enough to our goal, we double down on our efforts and continue to drive ourselves into the ground, using the same methods. We don't look back and question the techniques that brought us to this place of dissatisfaction.

So let's evaluate: why are you *here* and not *there,* with your dream house and car, doing the work you want to do, with the great relationships you yearn to have? We must figure out what's holding you back to break through your wall of stagnation and get back to building progress.

The stagnation we experience is rarely because we run out of steam. Professionals are known for their relentless passion and dedication to a great idea. Our inability to move forward is far more subtle; it is the product of what I call, our limiting beliefs. Now, I only have a few thousand words with you, so I'll keep this brief! Our limiting beliefs are the unconscious anthems we stand by, and are dedicated to, unknowingly leading us to sabotage our own success. Our limiting beliefs also some of our earliest thoughts in life; a product of stories that our parents tell us about ourselves, early experiences we've had in life, and our coping mechanisms that we turn to in times of stress. These beliefs make us feel like we're not intelligent enough, good looking enough, brave enough, or just good enough period, to make something of ourselves.

The difficulty with limiting beliefs is that we often don't know we're controlled by them, unless we take the time to dig deeper. All we see is a lack of success, failed attempts, and a series of leads that got us nowhere. We think that our lack of progress is a consequence of factors outside of ourselves. But how liberating is it to know that a lot of this could be fixed by addressing internal factors that you do control?

You can read more about limiting beliefs, and the vicious cycles that cause us to remain stuck, in my book *Searching for Balance,* available on Amazon. The book outlines exercises to uncover your mental and emotional blocks that prevent you from aligning your life, and moving beyond your limiting beliefs, to achieve your goals.

To recap, your code is comprised of:

- Your upbringing

- Your successes and failures from childhood into adulthood
- The limiting beliefs you've developed over the course of your life
- Your alignment between your values and your goals
- Your vision for your business

To take the first step, you must move inwards. Admittedly, it's not exactly one of the key enduring business secrets of our time. But it can give you an edge on your competitors. Understanding yourself allows you to tap into both emotional intelligence and gut intelligence. Doing so improves your relationship management and ability to create your network, while garnering the skills to have people believe, and yes, *invest* in your vision. People are drawn to charisma and leadership. And surprise – you don't need to be an extrovert to possess these qualities. You just need to be able to understand people. And who better to start to understand, than yourself?

As you move inwards and start crumbling your wall of stagnation, you'll realize something else within you, your resilience and grit. If you think working 14-hour days to get your product to market is hard, try sitting across from a psychologist asking why you believe your self-worth is rooted in your need to amass wealth and emphasize ambition. Going inside is challenging, and a lot of people can't finish the job. Digging into your past, your insecurities, and your conditioning will make you question yourself and produce a lot of *"why?"*, about your past. However, if you can take the time to understand yourself, you'll also understand your "WHY", about what drives you to your future. Find out what makes you tick and what makes you stick, and you'll be unstoppable.

How you get there?

Let's look at a commonly understood model: Maslow's Hierarchy of Needs. Like scaling a mountain, you can't climb without key supplies and support factors. As we focus on reaching our desired personal and professional goals, we need to be equipped with foundational elements to help us reach our success.

We meet our physiological needs with food and sleep. And here's a special note to night owl professionals: according to Harvard Health

Publishing by Harvard Medical School, "structural and physiological changes that occur in the brain during sleep affect capacity for new learning…[and] promotes the consolidation of experiences and ideas" (O'Connor, 2019, para.2). A healthy regime including sleep hygiene, will set you up for success to develop mental, and physical endurance.

We scale up through the level of safety needs, on to social needs, which includes love and belonging. As we noted earlier, business professionals can make the mistake of over prioritizing their work. Ensuring you establish a support network is critical to the moments when you temporarily struggle with fulfilment in your work. As a business professional myself, I can wholeheartedly relate to the moments of second-guessing, and belief that there is no ROI on your work. Invest in your emotional network and connections, as it will build comfort, confidence, and self-esteem; the last step before self-actualization. What Maslow's model doesn't illustrate is that the way to scale this combination of factors, from physiological, safety, love, and esteem; is through self-reflection and self-awareness. These factors are key to understanding what does and does not work for you. Not unlike cracking your own code!

Self-reflection offers the first stage of connection, which is to figure yourself out. Understand your own emotions, to begin to understand the emotional drivers of others. Sounds like Marketing 101 right? It's not so easy though. There are multiple instances where companies have failed at emotional intelligence and connecting with their customers. One that comes to mind is the violent removal of a passenger (a doctor no less) from a United Express flight, after declining to offer up his seat for a United Airlines employee. The company's apology started with "This is an upsetting event to all of us here at United…" (Murphy, 2017, para. 5). They centered the company in the situation, not the customer.

Now contrast this with a letter written by Richard Branson of Virgin, to his younger self, on living and succeeding, with dyslexia. Such a simple act spoke volumes about representation, inclusion, and self-awareness, starting from the top of Virgin's structure. In fact, not offering simple acts of compassion can come with a high price tag.

Warnock (2019) of GetApp, estimates that companies lose $75 billion USD per year due to poor customer service.

The simple fact is, is that psychology sells. We can sell an ideal, we can sell gratification, or we can sell a memory. We are selling emotions! So why wouldn't you tap into your emotional intelligence to create a rapport and become an expert on your people, your customers, and your investors? Apple sells a lifestyle, Tony Robbins sells inspiration, and Disney sells wonder. All emotions, all successful, all enduring economic downturns, transcending through generations, and recognized across the globe.

So what does this all mean? *Business intelligence is motivated by emotional intelligence.*

In business and in personal lives, we work with people. People operate on emotions, and emotional intelligence is the key to understanding these variables. Emotional intelligence creates stability, certainty, and resilience. People will throw curveballs at you, and emotional intelligence allows you to maintain an agility to respond. Understand emotions, and you'll understand people. Ensure your goods and services reflect emotions and you'll create a constant supply of need. Your business choices will be astute, relevant, and targeted as you enhance your emotional intelligence, and those of your people.

How I can help

Balancing life and business is clearly a demanding task; the stereotype for example, of an entrepreneur, is clearly not a life of a balanced individual! We've reviewed how important self-reflection, self-awareness, and alignment are, in cracking our code to life and business.

Admittedly, this is always easier said than done. For a few years I was challenged to balance between focusing my energy on my relationships versus my goals. It seemed that I could not prioritize both together in the time that I had. In fact, there was a period of time where I not only grappled to balance these areas, but I struggled to draw a measure of success from my business at all. So what was my secret to endure and eventually succeed?

I created *my signature Rewire your Life and Business method* that has stayed with me for the past decades to succeed at my business venture and be present within my relationships:

1) **Be present:** Whether the process is painful, humbling, or frustrating, staying present in the pain or discomfort provides key knowledge and experience to help you build on past mistakes. It also helps you determine whether you're in a trajectory that you're meant to be on, or whether you need to backtrack or pivot direction altogether.

2) **Trust the process**: There's a reason behind what you're going through. You need the ebbs and flows to perfect your process. Most successful business professionals don't know the outcome of their end product, but they know what they want. There will be failures in the process, but the vision never waivers. If you are feeling frozen, it is because your fear is lying in the outcome, not the challenge. You may not have control on the former, but you can choose to work on your challenge every day.

3) **Defining your standards of integrity:** Your morals and ethics determine your lasting success as a business professional. People purchase products they trust from companies they trust. Don't compromise your human values over your business values. Rather align them, and you'll find fulfillment in your work. This is where leaders become legends, as they use their value system as a guidebook to navigate through crises – your integrity will shine light on your priorities and give way to your reputation.

4) **Using calculated judgements:** Risk without evaluation can be appealing but will set you up to fail. Trust your judgement, as your judgement is a combination of instinct and wisdom. Risk requires you to trust yourself and tap into your gut. You need acute gut intelligence, which is something you'll hone, in my program. Gut intelligence requires knowing yourself, to trust yourself. Without developing this gut intelligence, your business will plateau,

regardless of how brilliant your business idea is, as you will remain in fear and uncertainty. Just like working out, you create a mind muscle connection. Likewise, you need to create a brain/gut connection, trust it, and hone its capacity. Emotional intelligence is a prerequisite to know yourself. Know yourself, know your gut, and break through your personal and professional barriers.

5) **Evaluate priorities:** I often say that multitasking is *no-tasking.* In order to be present, you need to prioritize. Professionals who are aligned can more easily discern their priorities than those that have not undergone exercises in self-reflection. Clarity is necessary to maintain commitments, while confidence is required to discern priorities. Confidence is gained through presence, gut intelligence, and trusting in the process. Each component of this 7-step methodology reinforces the other.

6) **Manage expectations:** Much like priorities, business professionals feel obligated to appease a range of stakeholders in their personal and professional lives. At times, these groups will likely have conflicting directives and needs. Managing expectations is just as important for yourself, as it is for those around you. Emotional intelligence is key in this endeavor and will provide you with tools to negotiate while still maintaining long serving and collaborative relationships.

7) **Reflect on lessons learned:** Wisdom is knowledge that has been cultivated by time and experience. Evaluation in all things, whether it be our relationships, quarterly performance, or personal growth is necessary, even if it resurfaces past missteps. People don't just trust in leaders who have the technical knowledge, they trust in those with the wisdom accumulated from hindsight. Own your mistakes, and you'll give space to others to follow suit.

These skills gave me the grit and resilience I needed to endure when my businesses were failing, and when I struggled to feed myself. They also gave me the emotional intelligence to know what I was capable of, and to tap into those strengths to begin to take control of my reality and maintain alignment. When I started out, trying to get multiple business ventures off the ground, while supporting my family, I struggled to get a strong financial footing. People conflated my limited funds with limited credibility or aptitude. But I didn't resign myself to assuming that I would never make it. I focused on being present, focusing on the challenge ahead of me, maintaining my priorities and always emphasizing integrity. It's brought me here to a flourishing business, with several offshoots including coaching, books, consultations, and corporate training.

Success is not rocket science, but discovery is required. Regardless of how much you explore and address that which is outside of you, your lack of self-awareness will remain your most challenging factor. Understand yourself to understand your life and business, and ultimately your overall success. Your ambitious spirit is not an accident. It's a part of who you are, but it's embedded in a larger context of your character and your code.

Discover yourself, understand your code, and crack it.

So how can I help you *understand you*? I guide business professionals to rewire their minds to build emotional intelligence and perform in every area of their life. I help you better understand who you are and learn how to serve your life and business. Which is why each program is *uniquely personalized for the client's individual path, potential, passion and purpose.* I use my rewire framework of the 9P's as a signature performance model to optimize your personal power.

***

To contact Nadiya

Website: https://nadiyamanji.com/

You can also follow her on the following platforms

Instagram: @nadiyamanji

Facebook: https://www.facebook.com/rewireyourlifebynadiyamanji/

LinkedIn: https://www.linkedin.com/in/nadiyamanji/

"Change is inevitable, transformation is a choice." – NM

Sources:

Finklestein, J. (2006, October 27). Maslows Hierarchy of Needs. Retrieved September 13, 2020, from https://images.app.goo.gl/wXFTEPUEq6Dtgtz56

Margaret O'Connor, P. (2019, March 11). Aging and sleep: Making changes for brain health. Retrieved September 13, 2020, from https://www.health.harvard.edu/blog/aging-and-sleep-making-changes-for-brain-health-2019031116147

Murphy, M. (2017, April 21). CEO Fiascos Typically Start With A Lack Of Empathy. Retrieved September 13, 2020, from https://www.forbes.com/sites/markmurphy/2017/04/21/ceo-fiascos-typically-start-with-a-lack-of-empathy/

Darren Christopher Rowland D.H.F N.A.S.M

*Hi I'm DCR, and a Very **Warm** Welcome to you…*

I'm a Multi Award-Winning, International **VIP** Life Coach and Author.

Since 2012 I've had the *good fortune* to Coach Top VIPs from all over the World and I'm *Proud* to have received International Recognition for my Coaching (including Cracking The Rich Code) and this has been featured on International media including **ABC**, **NBC**, **CBS** and **FOX** news.

My Awards include: Best **London** Life Coach 2018, Best **UK** Life Coach 2019, Best **International** Life Coach 2020 **&** 2021. Leading **Specialist** 2021.

I'm the Author of **"Only for the Serious – Permanent Weight Loss"** and for 30 years I have helped over 100,000 people to experience a *"Better Quality"* of Life through my Books and Coaching.

In addition to being one of the World's Top **Experts** on Successful Weight Loss, I Coach Top Executives in the Business Environment and my Coaching extends into Finances, Health, Relationships and Emotional **Success**.

Due to my Success, I now Mentor other Life Coaches who want to progress from being *standard* to being Superior in the industry via my **Mentoring Program**.

I am the Chairman for a **UK Registered Charity** and I continue to Coach for *free for worthy causes* such as Cancer Research UK, Oxfam Headquarters UK, Police UK and others.

Secret Formula for Success

By Darren Christopher Rowland D.H.F N.A.S.M

My upbringing was a very humble one. Being the youngest of 5, I was last in line for most things and only ever received hand me downs. Growing up in a rented council flat was a massively limiting environment and so by the time I left school at age 16 I had nothing. No qualifications, no money, no prospects, no role-models and no confidence. **The year was 1989 and I was lost in life.**

So how was I fortunate enough to end up a Millionaire, a Top Awarder, receiving International Recognition and Coaching Top VIPs Worldwide?

This is the secret I would like to share with you. My story is not unique, far from it, but it is **my** story, and presenting it here to you I hope to instigate a reinforcement from within yourself that 'you' too can emulate this or even better, succeed in your area no matter what the perceived limitations are around you.

Allow me to share with you what I believe is the **Secret Formula for Success.** Before I do, please just remember 'one' thing. Never let this slip from your consciousness and always keep it close your heart…

*"Life is whatever you make of it (with the resources you have available to you + something **important**)."*

If you try to tell me life is what you make of it, then I would disagree. How could that possibly be a true statement! Try telling a man sitting on the ground, in a third world country, baking in the stifling sun, starving, exhausted and close to death with nothing but a cloth covering his back. There is not even a tree nearby for him to take shade, he is about to pass off into death from extreme dehydration, starvation and over exposure to heat.

If you walked up to this man and said, 'life is what you make of it,' I wager he would also disagree! Why? Because the resources he has, or in his case, he **does not have any.** Difficult to make some-thing from no-thing!

I know this is an extreme example and a pitiful sight, I want to highlight that this unfortunate man couldn't make his life better because he had NO options from which to choose.

Do you follow me?

In contrast, you and I and everyone else living in a wealthy country, with freewill, any portion of our health, time still on our side and opportunity all around us, almost beckoning us to take action, the bulk of the populous still end up in *'lack and survival mode'*.

How is that even possible?!

If life is whatever you make of it with the resources you have available to you, then by logic and measure, we should all be super successful people with everything we crave. Clearly not!

What's missing?

I believe it's the secret (something **important**) that I am going to share with you…

Internal World

Life is whatever you make of it with the resources you have available to you, however external resources as mentioned are great in and of themselves, but are of no use to you at all, if your internal world is not tuned into them.

So when I say "Life is whatever you make of it with the resources you have available to you" I am referring to the external world yes, but mostly your **internal world**.

Your internal World is EVERYTHING. This important something is without a shadow of a doubt the difference – that makes the difference!

Internal world is just my term, you may know it as mindset, or attitude or your Psychology. Whatever you want to call it, it's the same thing. '**What**' is going '**on**' inside your mind, your head.

When I coach VIP's I start by having them understand that there are 3 components to their internal world, and the same applies to you reading this right now:

1. **Dialogue**
2. **Pictures**
3. **Condition and use of Physiology**

I believe that early on in my youth, I succeeded (not perfectly, but enough) in learning how to manage, and eventually master my own internal world. In doing so, it gave me the base from which all my external success would be attained.

Trying to make more money in your life for example is clearly an external reality, but where do you think that reality will grow from? Your internal world first. Unless you are lucky enough to win the lottery or receive a hefty inheritance, then the only way you're going to make more money turn up in the external world is by **first tuning your internal world** into that.

Same applies and is no different if you want a better relationship, better health, more happiness etc…

B before A is illogical. A before B is logical.

Any and every external result – emanates from an internal action FIRST.

Remember we're talking here about success and human beings and how we function and how the 3-dimensional world, operating to the law of physics around us, all fits together like a jigsaw puzzle.

*Internal Actions = Dialogue + Pictures + Condition and use of Physiology = your Internal World and your 'Reality' = **what is reflected back out** to and on to and into – the external world.*

Let's briefly discuss each one:

Dialogue

This is the sounds you 'hear' inside your head when you think and when you talk to yourself. There are 2 major and separate parts to this:

1. *WHAT* you hear / say
2. *HOW* you hear it / say it

What refers to the content. Whether you say "I feel miserable" or you say "I feel great" they are 2 contrasting statements, but they are nothing but content at this point. Or if you think "I can't do that" or "I can do that", again these are the words used and nothing else.

How refers to the make up for the content. The tone of the voice you hear, the timbre or base or resonance, the volume, the location, does it come from all over or mostly the left side etc…

Together, *'what' you hear / say and the make-up of 'how' you hear it / say it, is your dialogue*.

Most people's internal dialogue is poor. This is not a judgment. It is from empirical data and observations over countless eons of time. Cultural conditioning, environmental triggers and accepted social beliefs all play their part in 'programming' you to 'be' a certain way.

There is nothing fixed about the dialogue that goes on in your own very private world. It is played out mostly due to our own compass, beliefs that tell us what is good or bad, right or wrong etc… However, **we can override this at any time we choose**.

That is what, in part, your conscious mind is there for. You have a tool that can lock on to anything you want to and can even provide the navigation required to get there. Your consciousness is powerful.

The tongue has no bones, but it is so strong it can break a heart and it can save a life. 26 letters arranged differently creates the entire encyclopaedia!

What

Begin to write down your thoughts. I know this may seem tedious to you, but it will save you decades of pain to come.

See in print what your thoughts 'actually are', once you see the negativity you may be shocked. You can then intervene and change it to more empowering words, thoughts, sentences, statements etc…

How

Just as powerful as the 'what', if not **more** important is the 'how' you hear what you hear.

Again, log the volume you currently have, is it low or medium? Log the location, is it from the front, top, back, left or right general area of your head? Move it to somewhere different and see if this makes you feel stronger, or weaker. Experiment. What is the tone you hear, is it motivating or drab?

There is a ton of information to share with you on dialogue but in the short time I have with you hear, I am trying to point you toward becoming more **conscious of what you currently, unconsciously do**, so that you can now step in and take over.

Pictures

The pictures in your mind are what's called your **imagination**, everyone makes pictures inside their mind. However, some people make pictures so fast, they don't see them. I assure you they are there. Also, most people's pictures are fuzzy and hazy and not crystal clear.

Regardless, you should know something rather extraordinary – your imagination is *Stronger* and more *Powerful* in terms of its *effect* on you, than your intellect / logic / reasoning / thoughts are.

Unused, untrained and unconditioned, this supreme tool can cause a disappointing life. It can also be the instigator of *wonders* beyond description so it's best, you learn how to use this device!

Same as with dialogue, it's both 'what' pictures you make, and 'how' you represent them.

What

Example, do you picture the worst case scenario in advance and feel anxious about something that actually hasn't even happened or, do you make pictures about the success coming your way tomorrow and feel the victory now as if it as already happened? 'What' is very powerful.

How

You've heard that a picture is worth a thousand words and that is true, also remember though a picture can be **interpreted** a thousand different ways!

Are your pictures panoramic or in a frame? What colour is the frame? Are the pictures close or far away? Lifesize or shrunken? Are they full of vibrant colour or black and white? Get the idea.

If you write down your discoveries, then you can experiment and see which of these 'sub-modalities' affects you the most. Then using this knowledge begin to modify your pictures accordingly *to your advantage*!

Condition and Use of Physiology

I saved this one for last because in my estimation it is the **MOST** powerful.

Physiology means your physical body. Condition means how it currently is, healthy and strong or weak and diseased. Use means how you use this physical body, in a good way or a poor way.

Let me explain.

Emotions

Every single feeling you have ever had, currently experience and will ever have in your future – is experienced through your body. Very powerful statement that if not properly utilised is a major self-created limitation.

You **cannot** feel something in your head. That is dialogue and sits in your mind. Yes it may lead to and evoke an emotional experience but that's the point, how do you experience that emotion? Answer is through your nervous system, through the physical vessel that contains muscles and bones and blood etc… Test this.

Try and 'feel' happy **without** a corresponding change somewhere in your physical body. Observe if your facial expressions change, if your posture shifts, if your muscular tension alters, do you breathe differently?

What about frustrated. Get frustrated for 10 seconds on purpose (it's okay to be a little eccentric – I am!) Did you breathe different? Did your face change? Did you sit, stand, or move different? Did you gesture with your hands? I bet you did.

An **emotion is one of the most powerful experiences** we can have. You want proof? Try calming yourself down when you're scared, and your heart is beating like the clappers by 'thinking' differently. As you well know it is quite futile. This is indicative of the fact that **emotions are King** (and Kings rule remember!)

The other point I want you to understand is that most people quantify an emotion as something extreme or significant. Whereas anytime you are **conscious**, it's highly likely you are experiencing an emotion of some sort. Society has conditioned you to believe an emotion is general thing, such as happy, and sad, with not much in-between but the truth is it could be mild like boredom, or confused, or curious or other.

Basically if you can begin to understand that an emotion is **10x more powerful** than a thought, that you are **always** experiencing an emotion (not just here and there) and that they can be **mild**, not just intense, then you can begin to understand where your power lies.

Thoughts and pictures are very important, they are an integral part of your second-by-second internal experience and without mastering them, you won't get very far.

When I say your emotions are the MOST powerful experience, then I hope it gives you some reference to just **how important** and powerful they are and need to be used, to your advantage not 'left to chance.'

Condition of Physiology

We have established that your emotional being is crucial to success. After all, if you feel depressed then you're not going to produce the behaviour called 'proactiveness.' If you feel fearful, then your behavioural response will **not** be confident and decisive.

Do you follow me?

As mentioned, these emotions that we feel (which are the **instigators** of the behaviours we produce) are 'experienced' from within our physical bodies.

How important would you guess it is that having a clean, strong, vital, healthy and energised physical body **IS** to any success in any area? Whether you want to make a million, or connect better with your spouse, or run a marathon, or pass an exam, or fast-track your career, you will need **optimum physical health** at the very minimum.

Would you agree with that?

Once you have that physical vibrancy, then the **potential** is there to be tapped into.

If your body is sluggish, tired, stiff, aching, carrying excess weight, diseased from tobacco, alcohol and a poor diet, do you think you can produce consistent effective behaviours, feel consistently on top of things and have the energy to get up early and stay up late consistently?

Hardly!

Just allow me to lovingly remind you here and nudge you – that your own physical body, is something that you will **never ever** escape from, and you are imprisoned inside this vessel for around 75 years! It's probably a great idea to ensure that this environment is wonderful (full of wonder) and *not a rubbish heap full of something you would put in a bin*.

Correct nutrition, correct hydration, correct movement – exercise, correct sunlight, correct breathing and other parts all play their part in this affectionate word we call health.

Health's literal meaning is to '*heal*.' Pretty important to understand. If you're not healing, that means you're busy dying from within.

So please today, take me up on a 30-day health challenge. Don't throw yourself off at the deep end of some extreme approach. NO. Just **eat better**, move better, **breathe better** etc…

If you are SERIOUS about success, then that will be measured by your actions, not by your words or claims. Top achievers understand that their health and emotions are precious, and require daily nurturing, pruning and attention just like an impressive garden.

Great gardens don't just appear by themselves!

Use of Physiology

Is it possible to produce great feelings, through a body that is diseased? Yes, but it probably won't last. Can you tap into energy and power necessary to succeed if none or little is available? No probably not. So, if you miss getting the 'condition' of your body into shape in the first place, then the ability to use it is massively **hindered**.

Remember the illogicalness of B before A?

With a strong and powerful internal world, including your physical body, it means that now you can actually use this to create the success you want. No success is guaranteed, but in reverse, without energy, health, emotion, control etc… It IS almost **guaranteed**, that you can only fail!

Using your physiology means to snap yourself out of limiting moods and emotions, move and gesture with purpose and confidence, stand tall with pride not stoop over, and remember that your emotions (the most powerful part of you) are experienced through that vessel called a body, so learn to **manipulate** your body in a way that gives you strength, energy and potential.

If I feel a limiting emotion creeping up on me, I move my body to change the circuitry so that the disappointment only lasts a few seconds and then disappears, or if I feel generally tired from travelling, I will purposefully move my body and perform what is called a **power move**, such as mimicking shooting an arrow! Or I will do the 'most muscular' pose from a bodybuilding contest, or I will clap my hands intensively for 3 seconds to break my state and become super focused.

Yes, I am a little mad, but you have to be in this world in order **to succeed**! Don't get me wrong, I am not perfect, I feel bad at times, but my point is I take action to minimise the duration spent there, few people go to a beautiful garden and look at the weeds, however that is what we sometimes to do with experiences!

Closing

I am going to assume you either have a great physiology or that you are inspired to go create it in the 30-day challenge. Great.

Now what?

You have (or will have) a powerful vibrant body. You have learned to modify your thoughts and internal dialogue to support you, you have tweaked the pictures to ensure the bad ones are diminished and don't affect you as much, and the good ones are enhanced. **The potential is now available to you**. For you to use your powerful body and mind in the best way you see fit.

This is exactly what I did early on as mentioned. I had to get the genesis of my future successes handled first, and that laid with the responsibility of **mastering** the mental and emotional part of me. Conditioning my mind and my body for the success that I craved. From that, would come the success in the external world around me.

May I encourage you to have a **dream** and make the necessary **changes** in your journey, to then reap the **rewards** in your own life.

Love Darren.

***

To contact Darren:

www.darrenchristopherrowland.com

www.darrenchristopherrowland.co.uk

dreamchangereward@gmail.com

www.linkedin.com/in/darrenrowland-lifecoach/

www.calendly.com/dreamchangereward

www.digitalmarketingmentors.com/Dannyo

Cindy May Grossmann, R.D.H.

Cindy is a licensed dental hygienist and graduate of the University of Pennsylvania college. She has been in practice over 25 years and licensed in multiple states. She is the owner of "Brilliant Smiles by Cindy," an in-home concierge, one-hour teeth whitening business. Cindy is a coach and a healer, and she is the award-winning author of the book, *Dentistry Shaken Not Stirred: Health and Controversy in Your Mouth.* She is host of the podcast, "Secrets Behind Your Smile." She has appeared on live forums and can be heard as a guest on several podcasts. Cindy is a model and 20 plus year SAG member in good standing. She is also trained in Reiki, Phlebotomy, Holistic Health, Therapeutic Nutritional Counseling, PEMF sessions and AO Body Scan. Her hobbies include Latin and Ballroom Dance and Hot Yoga. Cindy lives in NJ with her dog (and best friend) Buddy and has two grown sons who live in California. She would love to connect with you.

What if….

By Cindy May Grossmann, R.D.H.

What If…..?

What if I can do it and what if YOU can too………..?

"If you do what you love, you'll never work a day in your life."– Marc Anthony

"What if I fall? Oh, my darling, what if you fly?" – Erin Hanson

"When the student is ready, the teacher will appear." – Buddha

What if' are two dangerous words when used together. But, once we let ourselves get past them, magic can happen. Hopefully reading this chapter you'll allow me to be your teacher and guide you to where the magic is. Once we are really and truly in alignment with what we believe and what we know our purpose is, the words "What if" cease to exist.

What do you want to be when you grow up? This is a question asked by many, but an answer known by so few. How are you supposed to know what you want to do, or what you want to be at such a young age? And for the record, not everyone does 'grow up.'

Well, I knew what I wanted to be…. Miss America! I watched the pageant religiously every year, and then practice *the walk*. I would tear up just like the winner, tears of joy, and I could really feel what it would be like to win!

While awaiting my crown, I volunteered as a candy striper and volunteered on a crisis phone hotline. I did that throughout my high school years. I also would help at the local animal shelter and was on the lookout for every stray animal in hopes of reuniting them with their owners. I grew up watching "Lassie" and would get emotional at the thought of poor Lassie running so much to help others. The reward for me of helping people and animals was priceless. I was very aligned with what I was doing and knew I would want a career where I could be of service to others. I did not want to go to Medical

School, so being a psychiatrist was out. I could not be a vet because I would be too emotional and attached to the animals. I was told that working as a Dental Hygienist was a great profession, one that came with flexibility and a great salary. I then decided the answer to "what do you want to be when you grow up" and went to the University of Pennsylvania to become a dental hygienist.

Although I didn't grow up with much, I consistently had a dental checkup twice a year. I can remember being young and not wanting to get X-rays and to not have a fluoride treatment. The X-rays gagged me and even at that very young age, I remember thinking why do I need these? I just had X-rays 6 months ago and I never had a cavity. I can still see the metal fluoride trays that gagged me as well. They were larger than life and the fluoride in them oozed out the side dripping down my throat. To make it worse, a timer was placed in front of me. The timer was set for four minutes and if I tried to move it, it got reset to the full four again. The only thing to make the visit tolerable was the costume jewel ring I'd always pick. The round one with lots of colors and facets. Again, a very vivid memory. I did at some point in my late childhood begin to like dental checkups. My experiences were a great value in being compassionate to my own dental patients and I wanted to work in a pediatric dental practice.

After taking the board exams, I chose to get licensed in several states. The scariest part of the job for me was calling patients out of the waiting room. I was worried I may call the wrong name or that the patient I did call may not there. So, just as I had done in Dental Hygiene School, I would have someone else get my patient for me. I did and still do enjoy my Dental Hygiene profession but knew I was meant for more than just cleaning teeth. I knew I needed to teach and share something with the world.

Although I did not pursue being Miss America, I did do some modeling work, and then some acting in TV, movies and commercials. Even with my success in obtaining various roles and my true desire to be there, the fear of failure and fear of success ran through my mind simultaneously. I would tell myself *"there is no fear here, and if it is so easy for others, why is it so scary for me?"*

The answer is, we create our own fear. We create our own lives, and we manifest what we believe we can achieve.

I can still feel how real the fear was, but now I understand that 'what if' is a self-created fear. We will never know the answer to 'what if' unless we try. And we will never move forward if we hold ourselves back. No matter how many people believe in us, if we do not believe in ourselves, it really doesn't matter.

So, why don't we go for the stars? Why don't we live out our dreams? Why don't we like to exit our comfort zones? What if 'what if' didn't matter? And what if we do it now so we never have to worry about 'what if we tried?'

> *"Twenty years from now, you will be more disappointed by the things you didn't do than by the ones you did. So, throw off the bowlines. Sail away from the safe harbor. Catch the trade winds in your sails. Explore. Dream. Discover."—Mark Twain*

Thoughts are a powerful precursor to what becomes reality. We manifest what we believe we should have, what we are good enough for, and what we deserve. What if we realize we deserve only the best? What if we put our intentions out there and make them happen? What if we succeed? What if we can make an impact and what if we can do what we love and share the gifts we all have? What if we acknowledge our fear but not lot it overtake us? Just once…and what if just once leads to just twice…and so on.

For those who think you cannot create your own reality or manifest your future, let me share this brief story. While at dinner for my son's birthday at Benihana, at the last minute a girl we did not know came and sat with us. My dad struck up a conversation with her and learned she was a dental hygienist. She happened to be in town for work—not cleaning teeth but inspecting dental offices for the state. She mentioned she lived some distance from the area and was going to look for someone else to take over the position. My dad mentioned that I was also a dental hygienist, and I soon started inspecting dental offices. I was able to set my own hours and still had the freedom to clean teeth, model, and best of all, be present for my kid's activities! All because of a random, almost impossible scenario.

My dental inspection job ended some years later, as they ended that position. I knew I wanted to have my own schedule and do something I loved, something I knew. I still loved being a dental hygienist, but I knew I didn't want to work full-time cleaning teeth. There was more I needed to share with people, more help I could give them. I did a lot of research and came up with the idea of mobile teeth whitening and named my business "Brilliant Smiles by Cindy." I planned to charge less than the dental office, be able to see people in their home or mine (where they could be comfortable, not waiting in a waiting room) and receive true one-on-one service. I was very excited, and it all seemed perfect. My LLC was formed, my website was up, all needed supplies were purchased and then...

'What if'...What if teeth whitening didn't work? So, because of my fear, my business sat in my garage and I went back to my safe zone of cleaning teeth. What if all the 'what ifs' were just an excuse?

Then one day, I got a call to do teeth whitening for a large group. Everybody got a great result. This turned into word-of-mouth referrals, and later led to corporate days, bridal parties, and one-on-one bookings. To this day, I am still happy and grateful to be making people smile, whether it is one person or a group of people. And to think, I held myself back by thinking 'what if.'

I learned a lot of alternative medicine modalities over the years. Some of these were incorporated into my business. This way, I could offer more services to people; if someone was not a good teeth whitening candidate, I was still able to offer something. I trained in various modalities including Reiki, Phlebotomy, PEMF sessions and body scans. I began studying to get a Holistic Health Certification as well as Therapeutic Nutritional Counseling. The mouth and the body are connected in so many ways.

I started taking business and self-development courses. I realized I wasn't the only one with 'what if' fear. It seemed to be a common thing. It sounded so easy to "just believe in yourself." When negative feelings and thoughts lie deep down, it doesn't matter what you say on the outside, because what is deep inside is way stronger. In the same way that you can think about someone you haven't talked to in a while only to have them call you, you can also think about where you want to be in your career and your life. You really can make it happen.

I am the author of a book that got released December 2020. The title is "Dentistry Shaken and Stirred: Health and Controversy in Your Mouth" and it took almost two years to complete. There were nights of falling asleep while I wrote because I just was not feeling it. I was concerned that if the information was not stimulating to me, how could it be stimulating to the reader? I knew something was lacking, but what? Then one day, I heard a startling, and somewhat controversial, dental fact on the radio. I went home and researched it, deciding THIS was the type of information I needed to share, not the same old, boring, outdated dental facts. I never fell asleep again while writing. It was at this point I realized what my true purpose was. When you are aligned with what you love it just flows. Everyone has a gift to share and once you figure it out, you shine, and a snowball effect happens. My book became #1 bestseller in new released books after only one day on Amazon! This was total verification that I really need to spread the truth in Dentistry. I am so passionate on the topic and I feel like Dentistry was something I resisted. I remember that my first patient in Dental Hygiene school was a thirteen-year-old. I forgot to give her a fluoride treatment. But did I forget or did I know something more back then. I really do believe there is never any mistakes in the universe. And everything and every person you meet happen for a reason.

I got asked to write about holistic dentistry in a magazine and asked to write a dental blog. I was also invited to be a guest on several podcasts! I finally was not blocking myself from launching my own podcast "Secrets Behind your Smile." I answered dental and health questions on social media and love connecting and helping people. A lot of people are interested in learning something new. And I am grateful to be the one to explain it all. And after all who would be excited to speak on brushing and flossing only?!

'Believe' is my favorite word in the English language. What if we all chose to believe? To believe that we can. To believe in magic. To believe in ourselves and believe we are magic.

Figuratively speaking I did become "Miss America". I held my head higher, I smiled more, and I waved hello to people I didn't know.

"Money comes and money goes, but time only goes,"—Cindy May Grossmann

"We are all given the same time, but we are all choosing different priorities"- Cindy May Grossmann

***

What if I did it…and what if you did it too?

To Contact Cindy:

Facebook Cindy May Grossmann

Instagram. Cindy.m.grossmann

Linkedin   Cindy Grossmann

Email   cindy@brilliantsmilesbycindy.com

Phone.   856-500-2375

Belinda Ellsworth

Belinda Ellsworth has been a professional speaker, mover, and shaker for more than 25 years. Having built multiple successful companies, she has helped thousands of entrepreneurs make better decisions, create successful systems, and build business strategies using her "Four Pillars of Success" system. More than 200 companies have hired her as a consultant and conference speaker.

As a speaker, her engaging style and immense knowledge has made her a highly sought-after presenter. Sales organizations have reported a 35-139% increase in sales within 90 days of her presentations, which is why she is often invited back by companies year after year.

As a consultant, she has a track record of increasing sales and profits on average by 200%.

Known as the "Left-Brain Entrepreneur," Belinda has been called "a trailblazer in the industry of coaching and speaking."

Her iconic messages of good solid business practices will stay with you forever and positively impact your bottom line.

Belinda is an International Best-Selling Author. Her podcast, Work From Your Happy Place, where she interviews other successful entrepreneurs, has been consistently in the top 10% of podcasts.

Falling in Love with Your Numbers

By Belinda Ellsworth

I hear this from business leaders every day - "I'm not a numbers person."

In reality, there is not any part of your life where you don't work with, and understand, numbers. From the moment numbers wake us up in the morning via our alarm clocks, we look at numbers in the weather forecast, our calendars, and bank accounts. We get in the car and drive to work looking at numbers on our speedometers. We get to the office, we log in to our computer using passwords, which have obligatory numbers in them to make sure we're safe. We pick up the phone, dial phone numbers, and begin our, hopefully productive, day.

We get home after work, check the thermostat, and set numbers on the oven to preheat it for dinner. After dinner, we sit down in front of the television to chill for a little, using the numbers on the remote to choose what we want to watch. We make sure the correct numbers are set on our alarm clock in order to wake us up the next morning and do it all again.

It's not that people are not "numbers people;" it's that some people are afraid of their numbers. How do we behave when we're afraid? When you are afraid you do things like avoid the scale because if you don't see it, it's not real. You don't keep track of spending habits because you don't want to know that you spent $150 on coffee, $400 on clothes you barely wear, or $1,000 eating out this month.

Out of sight, out of mind is not a strategy!

If you don't know it, your brain doesn't think you need to change it. Knowing your numbers changes your feelings, your motivation, and your behaviors. When you wear your fitness tracker, it makes you move more. When you become aware of how much unproductive screen time you've used, it causes you to use your time more wisely.

Knowing your numbers puts you in control. Without them, we would be late, hungry, and broke.

Realize that numbers are not only your constant companions but are also your trusted advisors and friends. They should be celebrated as the game changers they are. That is why it's time to fall in love with your numbers.

Falling in love with your numbers means you think about them all of the time. Thinking about them excites you. You appreciate them, you want to do things FOR them, you make smarter, more deliberate, and thoughtful decisions that benefit them.

So what does falling in love with your numbers look like when it comes to your business? When you fall in love with your numbers, you can quote them at the drop of a hat. You're ready, happy, and excited to share when someone asks you about them.

If you develop a great working relationship with your numbers, you not only make better decisions, but you can take your business to a whole new level.

Your Numbers as Motivation

As both a business owner and a consultant, I felt compelled to choose this topic because while knowing your numbers may not seem glamorous or exciting, it could mean the difference between a successful company and a struggling one. Over the years, when I've been focused on my own numbers, I've seen growth. When I've not focused on the numbers, there's been no growth, or worse, we've flatlined or even gone backward. More crucial, we've lost precious time and money.

At 12 years old, I had my very first business. It was a paper route that I had to petition to get because there were only paper boys at the time! I was awarded a route of existing subscribers. The list was decent, and I immediately decided how I was going to grow my route and make more money.

I focused on getting to know each customer personally and providing excellent customer service. The results of doing those two things well were that it caused customers to keep their subscription and it gained me higher tips. A third benefit these practices brought was it allowed me to ask for, and get, referrals.

I kept a notebook with customer information. It included how many new customers I was adding monthly, and how much money in tips I was making weekly. I began logging that information for one reason...so that I could see if I was improving. I ended up building one of the most successful routes in my area and made a good amount of money doing it.

That was the first time I fell in love with my numbers. I was 12 years old.

My next business was where I learned to take numbers to an even greater capacity. With my direct selling business, I tracked everything; how many calls I made, my ratio of yeses vs nos. I set goals of how many nights I wanted to work and then worked toward that. I counted how many opportunity packets I took with me, and how many I gave out at each event. I made servicing calls and calculated how many reorders I would get per week. I set goals and then set out to crush them. I was now in my twenties.

As my team started to grow, I kept records of everything: what my team sales were, how many leaders I had, what was my activity rate and what was my average monthly sales per consultant. I tracked what percentage of each of my leaders made up my overall downline sales. I tracked how many of my new team members recruited one person in their first 30 days and worked to increase this percentage. At the beginning, it was 20%, but quickly rose to 30%, then 50%, and on average was regularly over 75%.

Because I knew the numbers and watched them, I took action and tried new things to increase these numbers. This resulted in my reaching the top of the career plan at age 29 and earning a six-figure income. The year was 1990.

When I ask leaders or companies today what these numbers look like for their team or company, most have no idea. That boggles my mind. When I was serious about this and tracked it, I would coach better, I would strategize better, and my sales and team grew.

When I would become complacent or lazy, I'd see my sales, as well as the retention of my sales reps, start to drop.

After 16 successful years, I started my speaking and training business. I became obsessed with my numbers once again; how many calls I made in a day, how many new connections I made, asking for referrals, how many speaking gigs would I get in a month and how much I would make selling my products in the back of the room after an event. I attended NSA meetings and talked to other successful speakers to learn what 'averages' in the industry were. I watched the growth of my email list, and how many new customers we were adding per week. I knew what percentage of an audience would make a purchase, and what steps I could take to increase that.

By year four, I had a million-dollar business. In the past 25 years of running that company, I am proud to say that we have maintained or exceeded that revenue every year.

However, as I added more employees and the business grew, I became more complacent. I had other people running reports. I didn't always see them or study them like I did back when I was totally in love with my business.

With each changeover in new employees came new opinions about my numbers. Some didn't see the importance of some of these numbers and just quit tracking them altogether. I can honestly say that I was just so busy doing other things, working with clients, and growing my consulting side of the business, that I just wasn't paying attention.

In light of Covid-19, and all of the changes that happened in 2020, I had to make drastic changes to my business. The first thing I had to do was to get in the mindset of thinking like a new company. I made a new list of everything I wanted to track.

Realizing that the 12 year-old girl with a notebook was now coaching me, I got refocused.

Some of those numbers looked familiar, while others were new to the list, such as social media engagement and online marketing KPIs. We had no idea of how we were really doing because we weren't tracking anything! I once again started tracking all of the numbers. We began our staff meeting each week with them. Back on track, and having fallen in love again with my numbers, we see an increase every week, and the team is feeling excited again. It's an exciting time here at my business, and we are starting to see revenue increase again - as it always had whenever we consulted our most trusted advisor, the numbers.

During the past 25 years as a sales consultant, the number one thing that has shocked me the most is that most companies DON'T know their numbers. They're not at their fingertips. When I ask the question, "What are your sales so far this year? How do they compare to this time last year?" business owners have to look at their latest spreadsheet to give me a ballpark answer. Even worse, they say, "We'll have to have someone run that, and get back to you."

If you were in love with your numbers, you would be able to say, "We're 25% ahead of where we were at this same time last year." You would be able to share quickly and enthusiastically. We would be able to set goals based on where you want to go. If you don't know your numbers, it's difficult to set realistic expectations. How can you strategize? How can you forecast? How can you adjust? How can you change your behavior?

You can't.

When I consult with a company, I spend the first month in discovery. I see what programs they have in place, but I ask for the various numbers to see how many of those programs are effective. I can tell you that most companies have no idea about the numbers I'm asking for, and it takes them several days or even a week to compile that information. In some cases, they aren't sure what they are looking at.

They certainly aren't tracking this information on a regular basis. But as we begin to create reports and start following the numbers, we start to see increases quickly.

Why?

Because we are adjusting marketing ideas, incentives, and training to support the behavior we want that will move the numbers. The companies who do this typically see anywhere from a 150% to 300% increase in sales revenue. The ones who don't see the importance of tracking or refuse to send me a daily report, only sending two times a month or even monthly, don't see these types of increases.

That's because, if you wait till the end of the month to see where you landed, you cannot do anything to change the outcome. You are just hoping for the best.

Hoping is not a business strategy.

In one example of this, I was able to work with a company whose annual sales were $800,000. In just two and a half years, we were rounding the corner at $20 million in sales. In another case, in just six months, we were able to increase productivity by 250%. All because we had the right reporting in place to watch all of the necessary behaviors, and then adjust accordingly. We were able to see if what we were doing was working. When we see that it is, it creates excitement and energy amongst the whole team. If we see a decrease, we take a look at what they did this same week last year. It might cause us to implement a campaign that was super successful that we have overlooked.

If we weren't watching that closely, we would have missed that altogether.

What Numbers Are We Talking About?

Let's start at the beginning. All numbers are not created equal when it comes to your daily motivation. There is a set of numbers that will ultimately determine whether you thrive or struggle; numbers that change your behavior and make decisions for you.

The numbers to have at your fingertips on a daily or weekly basis are your current monthly sales (percentage increase) as compared to this same time last year, your goals (are you hitting them?), and your customer/rep growth (quantity or quality), social media engagement and your customer list. Those are the numbers that will affect your actions, behaviors, choices and decisions.

There are numbers that can be tracked in QuickBooks or other software and looked at on a monthly or quarterly basis. These can include payroll, expenses, your profit and loss ratio, receivables, payables, taxes, budgets and bank accounts, just to name a few. But those daily numbers are the lifeblood of your business. They save you precious time, because they help you to catch things quickly when they are off track and adjust.

If you have ever spent any amount of time in a Kohl's department store, you've probably noticed that a voice comes over the intercom two or three times an hour and says something like, "Associates, way to go! We are at a seven. Let's go to nine. Thank you." What are they doing? They're tracking their numbers in real time and letting their team members know where they are in respect of their goals, and what's left to do. This is an example of a company keeping their foot on the gas pedal. When you have goals, and you have momentum, you want to keep it going. When you give it more gas, you are more likely to reach, or even surpass, your goals.

Many leaders I have coached have had a goal to do $1 million in sales. Each year they would fall short, but they would never really do anything differently. They would just wait for the end of the year, hoping for a better result. The first thing I suggest is we break down the goal into ten months instead of twelve. That gives them a grace period of two months. To reach their goal, they would need to generate revenue of $100,000 per month. Next, I ask for the activity rate per sales rep. How much each rep would need to do in sales? How many new reps would you need to add? I ask them to share this goal with their team so that everyone feels as if they are a part of or a contributor to the overall success. I encourage them to keep this alive by giving regular updates and sharing the numbers.

Every single leader I do this with hits the million-dollar mark. I had one leader who had fallen short for seven consecutive years. The year we implemented these strategies, she had $1.2 million in sales. When she set her sights on $1.5 million the next year, she knew exactly how to do that.

When you have numbers in place, share those numbers with everyone, it will make them feel important and involved. When you keep your focus on your numbers, you will almost always get the result you desire. Just like any good relationship, you need to make time for it. The entrepreneurs I work with are often driven and motivated and energetic; they wake up every morning doing, doing, doing. It's sometimes difficult to slow down enough to have a date with your most important business partner...your numbers. You have to set intentional time to spend with your numbers as if they are a trusted advisor (because they are!). When you see the growth and excitement in your numbers, your competitive nature shows up, your creative juices flow, your brainstorming is at an all-time high and you can't wait to get to work!

If you don't set aside time to nurture that relationship, going to work is a daily grind, you begin to doubt yourself, and wonder if what you're doing even matters. Even in times when I don't FEEL like things are going well, my numbers tap me on the shoulder and let me know we're doing just fine. Sometimes you need to trust them more than you trust yourself. That is how important they are to your business.

Sales vs Profitability

Quick, answer these questions about your own business:

Are you making money? Losing money? Maintaining money? Where are you today? Where were you last week? Last month? Last year at this same time? Might you be able to do less work and make more money?

I read a statistic that 80% of small businesses do not keep month to month profit and loss statements, and if they do, they never take the time to look at them. I've seen companies get nervous that their sales are down and get in the habit of running 'flash sales' more often than they should. By the time they look at the commissions they paid, plus all of the other costs associated with it, like the cost of goods and shipping, they sometimes realize they barely broke even or actually lost money.

Some companies never take the time to figure this out, and that's how they find themselves in a reorganization, or worse, a bankruptcy situation.

Over the years, when I have kept up with my monthly profit and loss statements, I have been able to see exactly where my revenue is and what my expenses are. I can make adjustments accordingly. Sometimes you might have more sales and are working harder, but your number of employees has gone up, as well as the cost of goods or additional expenses, and you are actually making less money than you were before...all while working harder.

When you can see exactly where you are, you will know what adjustments are needed and where it's important to put your energy.

After the loss of an employee, I decided to outsource my bookkeeping. I was rarely receiving monthly profit and loss statements. At best, I was getting them every six months, or worse, just at year end.

In the past two years, we've moved more toward an online platform of sales and courses. On the surface, it appeared that our sales were doing great, but we were barely paying all the bills month to month. I was very frustrated and started running the report myself. I discovered that, even though the sales were up, my expenses were now exceeding revenue. There was the expense for the ad team, the cost of the ads themselves, the copywriter and all the tools that were needed to run an online operation. I discovered that we would buy one program for $299 a month and were paying $199 a month for a similar product because no one had canceled the first when we went to a new platform.

It was a rude awakening as to where the money was going and explained why profit was down. My decision, once I had that statement in hand was obvious...I needed to bring this back in-house.

I needed to fall in love with my numbers again.

When you know your budget, where your money is going out and coming from, you can adjust your behavior. You can eliminate products or services that you don't need. You can put more effort into the three things that are working instead of working on ten different things, seven of which are draining your finances. Falling in love with my numbers helped me fall in love with my business again. It rekindled the spirit that was there at the beginning.

Your numbers are talking, are you listening?

Communication is key in any relationship. I encourage you to fall in love with your own numbers. When you do this, you will not only get clarity on where to put your effort, but you will see the growth that follows. This will help you find joy in working, and help you fall in love with your business again.

***

belinda@stepintosuccess.com

734-426-1075

www.stepintosuccess.com

www.workfromyourhappyplace.com

https://Linkedin.com/in/BelindaEllsworth

https://facebook.com/StepIntoSuccess

Mike Weiss

Mike started his career in 1987 in the financial markets. He's spent the last 15 years as a digital marketer. During the last five years he's become a global leader in online education.

He's made every mistake while creating and running five successful multi-million-dollar companies. He knows what'll work for you and what won't. Which is why he offers "done-for-you" programs to ensure your success.

After many years of frustration and wasted money on Facebook ads, Mike ran into Gary Vaynerchuck. He said, "if you are not crushing it, right now, on LinkedIn you're a fool.

Now, LinkedIn and referrals generate 100% of Mike's company sales. His Done-for-you "LinkedIn Leadership Lead Generation Program" gets you leads and sales.

You can use Mike's company to write your online course curriculum and create your content. To build your personalized e-learning website. His technology will scale your coaching, consulting, and mastermind programs.

Some of his clients include: Digital Marketer — Ryan Deiss, Agora Financial, GKIC — Dan Kennedy, Matt Bacak, AdvantageForbes Media, Profit First, and many others.

A natural-born entrepreneur, Mike Weiss, enjoys the challenges that come with genuinely promoting change. He's a technologist and problem solver. Yet, his true passion is helping you achieve your dreams.

When he's not working, Mike spends time with his soulmate, Carolyne, their son Joshua and dog Lottie. They have a powerful spiritual practice which focuses on treating all relationships with human dignity.

How to Monetize LinkedIn

—Without Losing Your Shirt...

By Mike Weiss

Founder, Client Engagement Academy

Hi, my name is Mike Weiss and in the next few minutes I am going to show you "How to Monetize LinkedIn Without Losing Your Shirt!'

First, I need you to stop posting on LinkedIn - stop immediately! You're wasting your time and degrading the platform.

In the next few minutes, I'll share three secrets that less than 1% of the 660,000,000 LinkedIn users are utilizing. These secrets are being used by people just like you, right now, to create consistent sales on LinkedIn.

Ever tried monetizing social media? Dream come true? Or disaster...

If you're in business you've likely heard that LinkedIn is the place to grow your network and get sales. Yet most people don't know where to start.

If you're like others, you may have already spent untold numbers of hours and large sums of money to create a presence on LinkedIn. Like others, you got no real return. You wasted time and money and that's a disaster.

It means that you're not taking advantage of the business-to-business (B2B) gold mine. It means that your product or service never gets out to the 675 million monthly users on LinkedIn. It means that your unique selling proposition stays unique — to you!

Your lack of visibility and inability to create consistent, qualified leads will put pressure on your profits. It could cause you to cut back on spending, marketing and advertising because the consistent sales you dreamed of aren't happening.

Struggling to create consistent sales and riding the revenue roller coaster is miserable. Even worse, it can lead to watching your dreams dry up.

I've been there and I know first-hand how it feels watching the expenses rise faster than your revenues...or listening to your sales force constantly complain how hard it is to get quality leads.

Or to manage the so-called "guru's" who always promise to start the next profitable Facebook ad campaign or build a sophisticated funnel that makes money while you sleep.

Or buy expensive software like HubSpot which forces you to spend more money on experts to run it with very little in return.

It's hard facing the fact that the mounds of wasted money and time spent haven't generated the sales you need or expected.

You feel yourself between a rock and a hard place and that tiny space gets tighter...until it squeezes the life right out of you.

At this stage, you might have to decide to skip the family vacation, and work weekends. You push yourself to work harder to make sure you keep everything moving in the right direction.

As you work harder, miss family time, skip workouts and start eating crappy food, doubt sets in. You ask, "Why am I struggling to get consistent leads, sales and grow profits? What now?"

Well…

Massive Sales Lead To A Better Life…

Imagine waking up in the morning… rubbing your eyes… getting your coffee… patting the pup… and then checking in with your business to find your sales appointments in your calendar have shot through the roof—while you were sleeping.

Every day, you're now getting consistent, highly qualified inbound leads like you've never seen before. All on LinkedIn. People you've never met are messaging you to book sales calls. They're requesting product brochures, watching your videos and asking to be part of your network.

And so it goes for the next 6 months.

Your spouse or partner finally begins to support the time you've been devoting to this effort. Business colleagues start wondering what your secret is.

Soon you're thinking about taking a nice little vacation—and bringing some work with you so you can sit back and watch the astonishing results roll in. Or maybe just taking the afternoon off.

Because you can. Because sales are skyrocketing. Because your private, personal mission—your passion—your brand... is spreading around the world.

And you're reaping the results. The dollars. Your peace of mind. The rewards of controlling your own destiny. You'll never be embarrassed again by failure to finally "figure out" the online lead generation and sales game. You're the success you knew you could be.

Hey, my name's Mike Weiss...

And not too long ago—I was just like you...

By the time you finish this chapter, you're going to know exactly how to get consistent, qualified leads on LinkedIn—and radically increase your sales.

Trust me. I've been there. I turned it around. And I want to show you how to do the very same thing.

If you want...

To get more qualified leads...

To make more sales...

To get branded as a global leader and authority...

Then this chapter's for you.

But first the question... why hasn't it happened for you yet?

Come on... admit it.

This isn't the first time you've tried to find solutions to use the internet, social media or advertising to create consistent lead flow.

Let me tell you a quick story.

There I was, a business owner running a startup, struggling to get consistent high-quality leads to scale my business. I was trying to get more traffic, build funnels, write blog articles and advertise on Facebook.

The thing is, at the time, I was laying out so MUCH cash with no return on investment. I struggled with the complicated funnels and systems. I also struggled with the number of vendors and technology needed to try to get qualified leads.

The big problem was that I couldn't figure out how to make all of it work. I spent over $25,000 and made back $8,000 and none of the vendors would take responsibility for the loss of time and money.

I was so disappointed, and I couldn't take it anymore. I'd had enough and I did the unimaginable. I shut everything down!

That meant I gave up on my aggressive growth dreams and the hope of quickly scaling my company. It meant I had to share the bad news with my investors and employees.

What's worse… I was so disappointed in myself. It meant that it would take a lot longer to hit my target of helping 100,000,000 learners achieve their goals and get the outcome they desired, deserved and paid for.

Then, as if by chance, something amazing happened…

I heard Gary Vaynerchuck speak live in New York City. He spoke about taking advantage of LinkedIn's current business cycle. He shared why the clock was ticking and said it was time to start!

Instantly, it became crystal clear to me how to give LinkedIn what they were looking for to achieve their goals. I understood how their algorithm would hunt for consistency and great content. I understood that if I gave them what they needed they would propel my business through to their 675,000,000 users.

I knew I could use my extensive content creation knowledge to produce posts and videos on LinkedIn.

I saw that I could rapidly expand my viewership, engagement, leadership position and get high quality leads…without spending a bunch of money on ads.

My plan was to start becoming an expert at "everything" *LinkedIn* and learn how their algorithm worked to propel my business.

So, I started posting on LinkedIn every business day. Twenty days a month. Ten video posts and ten written posts. But I didn't stop there.

I started devoting a massive amount of time to researching profile optimization, hashtags and LinkedIn engagement through comments and messaging.

After that, I hired some leaders in the LinkedIn space to flatten the learning curve and started developing my own data points and analytics.

Bottom line: In the end I was able to exceed 1,000,000 views of my videos and posts on LinkedIn in 2020 with only 9,000 connections.

These views have generated all the qualified leads I could wish for and all of my clients now come from LinkedIn.

When I realized I could use my own LinkedIn profile to focus on teaching and delivering great content, I started to understand how to get qualified leads on LinkedIn really FAST!

LinkedIn Is the Place For You If...

LinkedIn is THE PLACE if you sell to the affluent, professional or business community or if you're a consulting or service-based business. LinkedIn is perfect for you if you're an agency or sell enterprise solutions to the corporate world. It's also perfect for you if you sell products from $1,000 to eight figure solutions.

It's important for you to know that as you read this, you're at a pivotal moment. The same pivotal moment I experienced when I gave up on traditional online marketing.

Gary Vaynerchuck provided me with the opening—the top-level strategy—and it took me four months to get results.

I'm going to do you one better, I'm about to share the three LinkedIn hacks that you can put in place right away to get moving in the right direction.

You need to know that once you get LinkedIn working for you, expanding your reach, branding you as an expert and providing you with engagement opportunities... your life will change dramatically for the better.

The consistent growth of your sales, income, or company will give you the flexibility to create the life you want, the marriage you want, the family you want and the free time to enjoy them all.

This Opportunity Won't Be Here Forever!

First, I need you to understand the *why*, and then we'll get to the *how*.

Every social media platform goes through a business maturity cycle. When they are aggressively trying to expand their network, content and engagement, they open the algorithm for us to step in and provide them quality content and engagement.

When you give them what they need, they propel you forward and grow your business for you. Every platform gives us this opportunity and when the platforms mature, they close the door. It happened with YouTube, Facebook, Pinterest and Instagram. I missed all those opportunities which is why I'm so excited about LinkedIn.

You only get one shot at events like this.

You also must know that you absolutely have to move now and follow the steps I'm about to share with you.

In addition to the LinkedIn window closing, every day you wait is another day your competitors scoop up your leadership position on LinkedIn. It's a lot easier to own that leadership position first, than it is to take it from a competitor.

And here's one of the most exciting facts to get you to take action today...over 700,000,000 people use LinkedIn every day and only 1% of them know how to be effective. Act now for this will change!

Now let's get into the three secrets that you can put in place right away.

Quick Tip—go to my LinkedIn profile page: https://www.linkedin.com/in/mikeweiss/ to examine each section and end the guesswork.

The first secret is you have to completely revamp your personal profile. Yes, I said personal profile. I get it, you own a company, are an executive at a company or work at a company so why are you optimizing your personal LinkedIn page and not your company page?

Because your personal page is the only page that matters.

In today's lighting fast, transparent world, people are buying from people who happen to work at a company. In order for you to get an abundance of qualified leads from LinkedIn, YOU need to be the brand alongside your company brand. Which means, you must optimize your personal LinkedIn page.

Here are the most important areas to optimize...

The first is the "look" of your personal page. The look covers your LinkedIn profile cover photo and your LinkedIn profile picture.

Here is your job, hire someone to make your two images look great. If you're not a graphics expert—don't do it yourself. The big mistake I see so many people make is that they attempt to save money or time doing things like this themselves. Don't do it because in the end you'll waste both and repel people instead of attracting them.

Next focus on your "About" section and your "Experience" section. Both of these are crucial if you want to generate quality inbound leads or want to have success doing cold outreach.

Think of it this way, if someone said something smart and you wanted to determine if they should be in your network, what would you want to know?

You would want to know "about' them and what they "do."

Carefully craft these sections and put yourself in someone else's shoes. Determine how YOU are impressive and clearly state who you are, what you do, what you offer and who you can help.

I invite you to go to my LinkedIn profile to see how it's done.

The next secret to focus on is your messaging. Have you ever been to a sales seminar? Read a sales book, been to any sales meetings, worked on a sales script or role played how to handle objections? Of course you have. So why wouldn't you develop your messaging capabilities on LinkedIn with the same vigor?

Almost 100% of all the people who enter our LinkedIn Leadership Done-For-You Program need work on their messaging! So, you're not alone.

The dirty little secret is that you should never use canned messaging. You should only use genuine messaging modeled from scripts that you put into your voice.

If you meet someone in a restaurant, do you use canned messaging or are you listening, thinking and responding so you can be engaging?

LinkedIn is the same conversation happening online, on your phone, desktop or computer. Be real and find out something about your potential connection and incorporate it into the conversation.

When you are real, you'll stand out because automated canned messages are becoming an issue on LinkedIn which creates an opportunity for your authenticity!

The final secret is the biggest of all three and that is...

Immediately stop posting on your LinkedIn profile. Stop, cold stop.

Now that I have your attention, you must radically change what you are posting. Don't post cartoons, promotions, your podcasts (promotion), webinars, sales events, or any other type of self-serving promotion.

What should you post?

You should post videos and text-based posts of you teaching. Teaching? Yes, teaching.

There are four ways to establish yourself as a thought leader—write a book, speak on stage, sell your company for $100,000,000 or teach using videos online.

Your goal is to give value with each of your posts. To establish yourself as a thought leader. To connect with people and show them that you are knowledgeable, trustworthy and perhaps funny.

Here's the rule of thumb that I teach in my done-for-you program and that is...anytime someone visits your LinkedIn feed and looks at your post, they should say to themselves, "He or she knows their STUFF!" That's it. So simple. Yet almost no one does this.

This is what aligns you to LinkedIn's mission: to provide great content, increase their engagement and the number of people on the platform.

When you shift your mindset from "What can I get from LinkedIn" to "What can I GIVE," you will be greatly rewarded by the platform.

The three secrets I shared lead to conversations with new and amazing leads. These new leads understand how you think, your belief system, and methodologies. They believe that you are trustworthy and know your "stuff."

They ask to meet with you and during the first few minutes, they repeat back what they've learned from you and frequently ask how they can get more.

This is the big secret to LinkedIn.

When you put in place what I just shared you'll be able to turn your experience and knowledge into a lead generation machine. You indoctrinate your connections with your process which creates inbound leads who want to learn and buy more — from YOU. You'll crush your competition by owning the leadership position in your field.

What I've shared with you is exactly what you need to get started down the path to success.

Yet, as an educator, a thought leader and someone who genuinely cares about you and your results...I don't want to leave you here, without a speedy path forward, when I know there's more that you need to know.

I heard someone mention this quote from Tony Robbins:

He said, "If you want to achieve success, all you need to do is find a way to model those who have already succeeded."

Which is why I created the LinkedIn Leadership Lead Generation Program.

This took months of focused effort and data analysis to create and cost me tens-of-thousands of dollars in experimental and optimization cost. But it was totally worth it…

And I can make it worth it for you too. A hefty increase in in-bound leads. Massive sales—while you sleep. Or while you slip away to go fly-fishing. Whatever you wish.

What used to take me years of torture, I can now get done daily and the longer I'm at it, the bigger the pipeline gets.

It'll be like this for you too.

In fact, here's just a sample of what you'll get…

Done-for-you program that directs you and does most of the work so you can start getting consistent and qualified inbound leads within the first 30-days.

Brand yourself as a global thought leader—an authority—and out-compete your competition so you can scale your business when others are struggling to make sales.

Create shorter sales cycles because your inbound leads are better qualified so you can build or grow your sales team.

Learn 5 messaging openers that instantly grab attention so you can kill off your non-profitable marketing efforts and start LinkedIn outbound lead generation.

Discover how to engage new prospects on LinkedIn in a non-sales-y way to get a TON of new appointments so you can fill up your schedule with all the buyers you need.

But don't just take my word for it. Take a look at this—I've generated over 1,000,000 views of my LinkedIn posts and videos with only 9,000 contacts. All my sales now come from LinkedIn or referrals.

Is that what you're gunning for? I hope so… because I can deliver it to you.

But before you get started let me ask you this question…

Would you like to get access to LinkedIn Leadership Lead Generation Program?

Now, while it would be impossible to show you all the benefits of the LinkedIn Leadership Lead Generation Program, I want to show you some things that you'll experience as soon as you're on the inside.

* Done-For-You Daily Posting of Your Morning and Afternoon Content

* Done-For-You Daily LinkedIn Accountability

* Weekly LinkedIn Data Results Reporting

* Access to Your Daily LinkedIn Reporting

* Monthly LinkedIn Sales Training

* Monthly LinkedIn Challenge

* Monthly Live Group Q&A and Hot seat

* Re-design Your Messaging

* Re-design Your Content

* Re-design Your Profile Page

* Re-design Your Bio

* Develop Your Content Marketing Strategy

* Develop Your Content Posting Schedule

* Develop Your Call to Action

* Develop Your Irresistible Offer

* Develop Your Comment Messaging

* Develop Your Private Messaging

* Develop Your Cold Connection Messaging

BONUS #1

* Weekly 1-Hour Live Mastermind Calls

BONUS #2

* Done-For-You Rewrite of Your Call To Action

BONUS #3

* 30 Minute Consultation with Mike Weiss

Why all this for you?

Because just one new client pays for the investment ten-fold.

Would it be worth it if…

— The *only* plus was to show you how to generate inbound leads?

— You could stop wasting money on advertising?

Of course, it would!

Want some even better news?

I'm going to take on all the risk and give you my "Mike Loves LinkedIn Guarantee"!

Get in touch with me at MikeLovesLinkedIn.com to get involved… to get the scoop on exactly how to do this… to outrageously boost your sales… to finally get what you've been wanting… authority, financial stability… and the time to enjoy your rewards…

If the LinkedIn Leadership Lead Generation program doesn't show you exactly how to get more qualified leads… if it doesn't take you by the hand and walk you step-by-step into more sales… or if it fails to help you get branded as a leader and authority, then you'll receive a full refund.

That's my guarantee… No Questions Asked!

But you must act now because…

* A LinkedIn content strategy locks you in as THE expert.

* There's no faster, less complicated and affordable way to make money than from LinkedIn.

* LinkedIn is giving us this opportunity and like all the other social media platforms…it will go away— NOW is the time to act—just visit MikeLovesLinkedIn.com to get started.

Imagine what life will be like when you know how to get qualified leads on LinkedIn…

WARNING:

Are you succeeding with lead generation on LinkedIn now?

Probably not!

And if you want to keep struggling and never figure out how to get qualified leads on LinkedIn… keep doing what you're doing.

But if you want instruction and encouragement from someone who has successfully "been there and done that!" with lead generation, check out MikeLovesLinkedIn.com.

This Done-for-you program will get the lead generation success you've been chasing… and deserve!

Never before have you had such a unique opportunity for me to take you by the hand and help you get qualified leads on LinkedIn…

Act now so you can get more qualified leads, make more sales, and get branded as a leader and authority just like I did…

If it worked for me, I can make it work for you…

So, if you want to get out of your rut… and into massive sales through successful lead generation on LinkedIn… check out MikeLovesLinkedIn.com.

After all, what have you got to lose?

And remember, whether you take what you learned and do it yourself or you join my program you must act now!

Your LinkedIn content strategy locks you in as THE expert and boxes out your competition. LinkedIn is providing us this opportunity and like all the other social media platforms…it will go away.

***

To Contact Mike:

linkedin@clientengagementacademy.com

Phone: 917-938-7900

https://www.linkedin.com/in/mikeweiss/

https://www.clientengagementacademy.com/

MikeLovesLinkedIn.com

J.D. WildFlower

J.D. WildFlower has been a celebrity branding and global business growth specialist, as well as a holistic success coach helping professionals create lives and businesses they love since 1997.

Her client list includes Academy & Grammy winners, New York Times best-selling authors, high-profile professionals and globally recognized companies like Samsung, US Bank and Dish Network. J.D. has been featured on NBC and PBS, as well as in publications like Woman's World Magazine, Star Tribune, and numerous other global media outlets.

J.D. is a professor of marketing who graduated with honors with a degree in Advertising and Multimedia Development from Minnesota School of Business with an emphasis in advertising psychology.

As a Marketing Executive, J.D. created VIP Global Media in 1997, the world's first "Organic Branding Agency," where she has inspired millions to achieve success in business and life. She loves sci-fi movies, bonfires and a good cup of tea and is based in Minneapolis and Las Vegas.

Learn more about J.D.'s "VIP Global Client Formula"—her signature program that helps experts brand, build and launch a high-end signature training platform while elevating celebrity-expert-authority status and creating an online group inner-circle style program—plus the Ultra-High-End VIP Private Program Suite in 8 Weeks. Her platform also includes the Celebrity Branding Formula Program, VIP Global Entrepreneurs Inner-Circle Club, VIP Mentorship Programs or "Done-for-You" Business Solutions, which can be explored in depth at http://www.VIPglobalclientformula.com

Photography by Shane Van Boxtel

VIP Global Client Formula

By J.D. WildFlower

If you are an expert, coach, author, consultant or service business owner, you know that getting clients and scaling your business without burning out can be challenging to achieve. After being in business for over two decades as a celebrity branding and global business growth specialist, holistic success coach and recording artist, and going through a burnout of my own in 2012, I knew there had to be a better way to manage and scale my business to financially thrive while leveraging my time so that I didn't burn out again.

So, I set out to find a way to do just that. I tried so many different things to build my business and leverage my time. I created low-end $27 online products. I also tried to become a social media superstar but ended up with a ton of vanity followers who didn't pay me. Many of the strategies I used became so time-consuming that I was left exhausted by the end of each week. I realized I needed to take a step back to get what I called the "Hubble telescope view" of my business model. By viewing it in a new perspective, I was able to deconstruct my broken business model and instead develop an easy-to-follow system that I could share with my clients to help them scale their expert businesses while having a life too.

I combined this comprehensive business development system into a framework that I call the VIP Global Client Formula. The VIP Global Client Formula is a framework you can follow to create a client generation machine within your expert business, while leveraging your time so you can have a financially thriving business without burning out.

Let's face it, it can be confusing to know what to do to get clients and best leverage your time when it comes to your expert-based business. There are so many options out there; it can be mind-boggling to determine which strategies you should try or not. You might find yourself asking the following questions:

- How do I brand and market my business so that I stand out as a coach, expert, author or consultant in a sea of noise?

- Should I charge low-end rates under $3,000.00 or high-end rates $3,000.00-$10,000.00+?

- Should I offer one-on-one private programs or one-to-many programs, like online group-coaching programs, continuity mastermind programs, inner circle programs, VIP days and keynote speaking services?

It can be confusing to know what to do with all of the options available.

Instead telling you what to do, I'm going to start by inviting you on a journey—a journey to discovering a smarter way to build your expert business. Upon this journey, what you remove from your business is just as important as what you add to it, so you can scale your business and leverage your time without burning out.

The number one thing that most experts, coaches, authors, consultants and service-based business owners do wrong is SELL SERVICES. Why? Because people are far more interested in the solutions you are helping them create for their lives or businesses than they are in simply hiring someone for a service, like coaching or consulting.

SELL SOLUTIONS, NOT SERVICES.

Solutions are compelling because people are looking to solve problems in their lives or in their businesses. When you sell your services by marketing them as solutions, you are addressing the main reason people want to hire you in the first place; they have some kind of problem that you can solve or make better.

When you sell solutions, you can charge high-end rates, or ultra-high-end rates, because you are focusing on helping people create the end result they want to see in their lives or businesses.

Having Your Own Signature Coaching or Training System

You may have a myriad of certifications, doctorates or experience, but in order for you to charge high-end rates, you must have a signature coaching or training system that is based on your own solution-based system— one you have distilled into a user-friendly system based on many years of either education, experience or a combination of the two.

Now, you might already have your own signature coaching or training system. If you don't, now is the time to take your methods and turn them into a process. Chart a path to the common client's journey that will create results and translate into a user-friendly, step-by-step process. Design a program that teaches your clients in a one-to-many fashion.

Your clients aren't only interested in learning the exact methods and strategies you've learned; they also want to learn your take as well. Creating your own signature system allows you to communicate the value of what you bring to the table as an expert.

Creating Celebrity-Expert-Authority Status

I started working as a branding, marketing and business coach to Academy and Grammy winners, New York Times best-selling authors and globally recognized companies in the '90s. The one thing that always stuck out to me about the celebrities I worked with was that some of them had worked for years to cultivate their celebrity status, while others took strategic shortcuts to skyrocket their careers quickly.

The thing that most people don't know is, celebrity status only means that a lot of people know about your business. As long as you're making money and enjoying what you're doing, that can be a great thing.

What does celebrity-expert-authority status mean for the expert, coach, consultant, author or service provider? It can mean having articles published in prestigious magazines or newspapers, being interviewed on TV or podcasts or being asked to be a featured speaker at industry conferences. Why should that matter to you? Look, I'm not talking about fame or celebrity just for the sake of it; it's a strategic business move. If you need to up your self-esteem, do so in other ways.

The game of celebrity-expert-authority status is an art of strategically aligning with reputable industry media sources, events and companies to help your ideal clients get to know, like and trust you. As a really cool bonus, it helps amp up your professional credibility by association. Are you going to be famous enough to be on the cover of a magazine? It's possible. It just depends on how you craft your approach to the media.

Now, I could write an entire book just on amping up your celebrity-expert-authority status alone, but one quick tip that you can use to get started is to write three articles that showcase your expertise. In each one of these articles, weave in something that connects your topic to either a current event or an upcoming holiday and send it to industry publications as a pitch. Journalists are always looking for fresh new material that is time relevant because of the ever-present need to produce time sensitive journalism.

High-End VIP Rates ($3-$10K+) vs. Low-End (under $3k)

Now, you might think that just because your aunt Sally couldn't afford high-end rates, no one can. It's just not true. There are many people out there willing to pay high-end rates for high-end services because they want it done right the first time.

High-end rates work best when you are solving a major life or business problem your clients are experiencing, as opposed to just providing trivial services.

So only charge high-end rates if you can truly help people solve major life or business problems, then help them create their "hero's journey"—the path taken to achieve their goals. People pay high-end rates to have an experience, not just receive a service. So, make sure that every step of your client's journey is met with strategic experience-building tactics.

The Scaling Principal

How do you stop trading all your time for dollars and still make high-end rates without burning out? Scaling your business without getting burnt out requires a certain kind of strategy that allows you to provide high-end, VIP services for clients in ways that leverage your time.

One-to-One or One-to-Many?

For many experts, this involves having one or more one-to-many business offerings. Some prefer to provide both one-to-many services and one-on-one services, in addition to offering keynote speaking as a service as well. Others like to stick with only the time leveraging approach of one-to-many programs. It really just depends on the business model that's right for you.

I have found that in order to have a scalable expert-business, providing online group-coaching mastermind programs, with a hybrid of online video trainings and live Q&As with you as the expert, is the best way to start scaling your business. Why? Because creating an online group-coaching mastermind program is a way for you to help bring your clients through the hero's journey of reaching their goals. It allows you to provide fundamental training online to everyone enrolled in your program, while still providing personalized support by way of live Q&A calls hosted by you on a weekly basis.

I recommend having an entry program that is between 4 and 12 weeks long and brings your clients through the hero's journey to realizing some kind of tangible goal in their lives. Having a hybrid continuity program that involves you providing live masterclass trainings each month, as well as live Q&A calls and/or private sessions, can also be very beneficial. Because this includes your personal time on the live Q&A calls, you can charge high-end rates. I recommend between $3,000 to $40,000 and up for these 4 to 12-week entry programs.

Why not focus on creating $97 online courses and selling them to many thousands of people?

Because, while that may sound appealing, attracting the thousands of customers it would take to have a financially thriving business is a lot harder than it looks, especially in a crowded marketplace. Many experts waste a lot of time creating low-end online products that fail to bring adequate revenue, instead of strategically creating a live, interactive program that generates high-end rates. Plus, because there is no external accountability, many people end up not finishing online training courses without an interactive component. It is estimated that up to 95% of customers fail to complete the program in the first place; so they simply will not receive the kind of results they could if they were able to interact with you as the expert.

After your clients finish their entry-level program, I recommend having a continuity program, club or association that has either a monthly or yearly recurring fee. This is where you continue to provide master classes pertinent to their continued success with your topic, as well as in-person or online retreats to help them with any ongoing issues they may be having in their lives, encouraging them to be proactive about creating their future, rather than letting their future be created by default.

Having both an entry-level program and an ongoing continuity program can help you solve one of the biggest problems in an expert-based business—inconsistent income. Having both an entry-level and continuity program can create more consistency in your income, while you help support clients in staying goal oriented and proactive in their lives.

You can also provide VIP days or VIP retreats for individuals (a select group of people or private company retreats) or ultra-high-end, private program suites where you can charge an ultra-premium price for your one-on-one time. Also consider the tried and true path of keynote speaking at conferences and organizations. It really just depends on what works best for you.

Why Ultra-Niching is the Secret to Cracking the Rich Code for Experts.

In this day and age, there is a sea of noise out in the world of experts, coaches, consultants, authors and service-based businesses. How do you stand out from all the noise?

One simple answer: ultra-niche.

What is ultra-niching? It is a term I coined to define creating a deep level niche of services for a specific audience who have a problem that you specialize in solving and the money to pay high-end rates. Focus on a narrow audience that either has a common problem or common network, rather than generalizing and pitching your program to everyone.

An example of this is a men's weight loss coach who focuses on helping executive men lose weight. This person is going to have a much easier time communicating to his target audience than he would broadly teaching and coaching men in general.

Look, just as it is with a medical practice, the specialists are the ones that make more money. Why? Because often, by the time the patient gets to the specialist, they've already seen other doctors and are in the market for the final solution to their problem. And that is what you should strive to do in your programs—help your clients achieve definitive success with a specific goal and progress using your own signature coaching or training system.

Spending Your Time Wisely to Attract High-End VIP Clients

Let's get real here, as a celebrity branding and global business growth specialist since the '90s, one of the most important things I've learned about marketing is that "your vibe attracts your tribe." If you're putting out a low-end vibe and under charge for the important services you provide, you will attract people that can only afford the low-end rates.

Frankly put, you can spend time in your business working to get low-end clients or you can put that exact same amount of time towards getting high-end clients. So why not put your energy towards attracting high-end clients which can yield more income for the same amount of time spent building your business?

That is what you must be willing to do in order to go forward and scale your business. You must invest time and energy to deliberately build your success.

Is it going to take work? Yes.

Is it going to happen overnight? No.

Success in business does not happen overnight, even though it may appear that way sometimes. Success in business happens when you follow a set of proven principles and strategies in a comprehensive framework. How long will it take? Well, that depends on you and your willingness to shift your paradigms, upgrade your mindset and step up to be the leader you always knew you were meant to be, helping your tribe achieve their goals while creating a financially thriving business.

I have seen experts dramatically shift their business within a month or two (at times even in a matter of a few weeks) by using VIP Global Client Formula strategies.

What's Confidence Got to do with It?

Do you have the confidence to amp up your celebrity-expert-authority status and charge high-end rates?

Confidence can be a tricky thing. One minute you have it and the next, you might feel like a fraud and have imposter syndrome. You may even ask yourself, "Who am I to step into this ball game of being an expert authority in my industry?" Look, you don't need to have superhero levels of confidence all the time in order to be a highly paid expert in your field. You just need to be good at what you do—at your particular field of expertise.

No, you don't need to be perfect all the time or feel confident 100% of the time. The secret is showing up for yourself and your business and standing up for your life by charging forward, even if you feel less than confident. Just show up. Minute by minute, hour by hour, day by day, week by week, month by month and year by year. Just show up and take the strategic steps to make it happen.

The Next Steps

The first thing that I ask all of my clients and students to do when they start working with me is to define their 'why.' Because when you know why you want to create your dream business, you are willing to do what it takes to make it happen.

So right now, write down your 'why.'

Why do you want to be successful in business?

Is it because it would help you purchase the home of your dreams?

Or perhaps help you buy a new car, buy a car for your kid, put money into college for your children, take your family on all-expense paid vacations?

Do you have a favorite charity or cause that you would love to donate money to when you are financially thriving in your business?

Knowing your 'why' is the first step.

The next question to answer is, "What would it mean to you to have a financially thriving expert-business?"

Would it mean not having to worry about how you're going to pay your bills anymore and help you have less stress and anxiety?

Would it help you feel more confident?

Would it help you quit a day job that you have been at for years?

Would it help you to have more time and freedom in your life?

Look, as an entrepreneur there are 10,000 things you can focus on every single day in your business, but 9,999 of them are the wrong focus.

The right thing to focus on is, "What's next?" That way you don't waste your time busying yourself with a minutiae of details that do not contribute to moving the needle toward success in your business.

Now, these tips got you started, but there is a journey ahead of you. Building or upgrading a business doesn't happen overnight, but with deliberate action and implementing a strategic framework formula, you can scale your business and leverage your time in a matter of months, creating a financially thriving expert-business without burning out. Cheers to creating a financially thriving expert-business while having a life too!

If you would like my help every step of the way to build the business of your dreams, you can learn more about my VIP Global Client Formula 8-week Business Accelerator, Celebrity Branding Formula Business Accelerator, VIP Global Entrepreneurs Inner-Circle Club, The Quest For Holistic Success, my VIP Mentorship Programs or "Done-for-You" Business Solutions at www.VIPGlobalClientFormula.com.

Moe Falah

Moe Falah is fortunate to be living his dream: establishing wealth by mentoring others in the skills and mindset needed to better their own circumstances while connecting customers to products that make the world a better place. He discovered his gift for sales - which he says is related to his being voted "Most Talkative" in his high school yearbook - at the age of 21.

Now 25, Moe is the CEO and founder of Simple Solar - a solar panel sales startup which grossed over $25 million in sales in its inaugural year of 2020. Moe's biggest joy is helping his salespeople exceed industry standards while watching them succeed personally, professionally, and financially. Everything he does revolves around the pride he feels in watching his team grow and excel.

As soon as Moe heard about the benefits of solar panels for his customers, their communities, and the environment, he knew that this product was what he wanted to do with the rest of his life. He's since used his gift for sales to train wildly successful sales professionals and help thousands of California families switch to solar energy.

Head First

By Moe Falah

I'm the last guy you would expect to find heading a multi-million-dollar startup at the age of 25. I don't have an MBA, rich parents, or even a college degree. That's why I want to share exactly how I did it.

To me, wealth means freedom. I watched my parents struggle and saw how my dad had absolute power in our house because he was the one with a paycheck.

From childhood, I was obsessed with making money. But none of the schools I attended taught me how to do that. So where could this knowledge be found?

In this chapter, I'll share how I found the answers that allowed me to succeed, and my top three lessons about how *anyone* can attain their goals using a simple formula.

I know that the advantages of my early life — some of which don't *look* like advantages, such as being the target of racism, or getting robbed at gunpoint — helped me get to where I am today.

Being forced to be self-reliant taught me to plow through obstacles. And every time I realized how fragile my comfortable life was, I found a way to do better.

I developed a penchant for putting myself in high-stakes situations where I had no choice *but* to learn what I needed to know to succeed. My willingness to go all-in, and the knowledge that I could not afford to fail, has allowed me to pull off miracles.

So let me tell you how I became the CEO of a $25 million company at the age of 25— and how you can do it, too.

My Palestinian family moved to small town America when I was six years old. We arrived in the U.S. just months before 9/11/2001.

Oops.

Suffice to say, I developed a thick skin growing up. People didn't usually hurl racial slurs at a six-year-old, but seeing racial attacks leveled at my dad and older brothers left little doubt about how people in our town felt about me.

I was not a popular kid in my elementary school. In fact, I was a total outcast. I had to learn not to care if people rejected me. I had to learn to plow through uncomfortable conversations and win people's trust despite being someone they viewed as inherently untrustworthy. I also got the idea pretty quickly that I'd have to fend for myself in the world.

By late elementary school, I was fascinated with making money. I'd heard my parents say too many times that we couldn't do something because we didn't have the money. I'd noticed that my dad had final say over all decisions in the house. Anything my mom, my brothers, or I wanted, he could approve or veto with absolute power.

And why was that? It was because he made all the money. He allowed us to have a house and food, so he got the final say on everything. I learned one thing very early on: money is power. If you don't have money, you don't have autonomy.

So how did I get money?

My classes in school didn't answer this question. Fortunately, I was born in the Information Age. I took my question to the Internet, and soon I was up to my eyeballs in personal development and entrepreneurship videos.

By fourth grade, I'd started my first business. I'd buy things on sale at WalMart and put them up on eBay at a markup. In that way I could make $50 in an hour, and that was huge to me.

I invested all my profits back into my "company," keeping wads of cash on-hand in case I saw something I could buy and resell at a profit. In high school, I'd even buy and sell used cars.

Back then, college was seen as the only reliable road to success. Kids were "irresponsible" if they didn't go, and we were told it would be easy to pay off our student loans. I assumed college must teach things about making money, then, but to my disappointment it didn't. My college classes were no more useful to someone trying to get rich than my high school classes had been.

Then, disaster struck.

I'd invited a stranger into my apartment to talk about my business. He was recommended by a friend, so I trusted him. I showed him the merchandise I'd bought to resell and the cash I kept on hand for making purchases.

I trusted him until he pulled out a gun and pointed it at my forehead.

"Put everything in the bag," he commanded, his voice deadly quiet. Terrified, I did what he said.

I escaped with my life, but I lost over $12,000. For 19-year-old me, that represented years of constant struggle to achieve independence. All gone.

I was shaken. In just one day, years of hard work could be wiped out. If I wanted true freedom, then, I had to be able to turn profits so massive that nothing could hold me down.

So, I turned to real estate.

I knew nothing about real estate, except that the analysts said it was a good bet. Property values almost always rose, sometimes drastically if you were able to fix up a broken-down house.

So, at 19, I bought a dilapidated house in my college town for $47,000. Then I called up my brother, who was a home improvement contractor.

I put in drywall and flooring, laid tile and painted. For a teenager still in college full-time, it was a tremendous amount of work. I woke up many days hating what I was doing, and wanting more than anything to give up.

But I couldn't give up. I'd invested too much. If I backed down now, I'd lose everything. And that fear kept me going.

I ran out of money because I hadn't realized how much renovations would cost. I couldn't give up, so I went online and searched "how to find real estate investors."

I ended up at a local meetup. As I walked in, everyone turned to stare at me. I was by far the youngest person in the room. They thought I had no idea what I was doing.

They were right. But it didn't matter. I had to finish this project.

When my turn came to speak, I announced that I was renovating a property and I needed an investor. Everybody laughed. Nobody volunteered to invest their money in the harebrained scheme of a woefully underqualified college kid.

But the next day, I got a phone call from one of the investors. When he came to look at the house, I think he was surprised to see that any work had been done at all. Looking over the pristine new floors and the half-finished drywall, he made me an offer: he'd give me the funds I needed — at a 15% interest rate.

What could I do? I'd sunk nearly $80,000 into this project, and I'd lose it all if I didn't finish it. I said "yes."

A year later, I sold the house for $165,000. I was able to pay back my investor, pay my brother, and still pocket almost five times more money than I'd lost in the robbery that drove me to take the leap.

Now I had a taste of making real money. But I'd also learned that I hated renovating houses. Fortunately, in the course of the project, I'd met Alex.

Alex was the wealthiest person I'd ever met. Only a few years older than me, he drove a new Audi R8 and a matching G-Wagon. He lived in a penthouse in Toronto, where he entertained guests with expensive parties any time he wanted. He seemed to have full control over his life. And he gave me some of the best advice I'd ever gotten.

"The only way to get rich in this world is sales," he told me, "You sell people what they want and you can make any amount of money."

I'd learned a version of that truth through my childhood exploits. But I'd never had guidance. Fortunately, this guy saw something in me: the potential to sell.

I was voted "Most Talkative" in my high school yearbook. I thought it was a bad thing, that people were annoyed with me constantly blathering about whatever was on my mind.

But Alex saw something different. He saw that I could fearlessly connect with anybody. He saw that my earnestness made me trustworthy, and my ability to plow through rejections made me an ideal salesperson. So, he made me an offer.

"Come to Toronto, Moe," he said, "and I'll take you under my wing. I'll teach you everything I know."

At 21, I threw myself into learning sales. I knew I had to learn to overcome any objection — internal or external — because if I didn't, I had no backup plan. There was no career that I wanted other than the one that could make me rich.

I'll tell you another truth: sales skills can be learned by anyone. Since starting my own business, I've been able to teach a whole team of salespeople how to drastically exceed industry quotas.

Alex was in the energy and water space. Soon I was going door-to-door, offering people products that could make their lives better. Within months of moving to Toronto, I was making more money than I'd ever seen.

Still, I might never have become a CEO if not for a series of calamities that, had I been less determined, might have made me give up.

First, Ontario banned door-to-door sales. But Alex knew how to turn a disaster into an opportunity. "Let's go to Miami," he told me. "The people there use more electricity than anywhere else."

We moved to Miami and began selling AC units. The money was great. I began to diversify, working for different companies in the disaster preparedness space.

But then, I ran into a bizarre problem. I could sell so much that I bankrupted the companies I sold for. This had never been a problem when I worked with Alex, but these other company's pipelines weren't designed for large volume. When they sold a product, they had to pay the cost of installation before the buyer paid them in full. That meant that when sales increased, costs rose before profit rose.

At the age of 23, I watched the company I worked for collapse because I'd sold too much of their product.

With that company gone, I needed somewhere to go. Fortunately, that somewhere found me. I arrived at a home to make my sales pitch at the same time a solar sales rep was finishing up.

"Don't mind me," the solar rep, Scott, said as he checked boxes on the clipboard in his lap. "I'm just finishing my paperwork. Go ahead and make your presentation."

As I spoke about the benefits of hurricane windows, graphically demonstrating the damage done to homes by hurricane-force winds, something funny happened. I looked up to see that Scott was entranced. He stayed until I was finished, then followed me out to my car.

"Your presentation was amazing," he said. "I'd like you to come work for me."

I didn't make this sale easy for Scott. I had preconceptions about solar panels and thought no one would want to buy them. But as I listened to Scott talk, my jaw dropped.

Here was a product that would permanently eliminate a homeowner's electric bill at no up-front cost. Having solar panels would leave them independent, unaffected by calamities that may strike the electric grid. And they'd be fighting climate change.

I knew that this was what I wanted to do with my life.

But there was a problem. In Florida, the permits to install solar panels took 4-6 months to obtain. So, Scott's company was way behind on serving my customers, and I wasn't satisfied with that.

I turned the calamity into an opportunity. Where could solar panels be installed fast? The answer turned out to be California.

California was leading the U.S. in solar power purchases, by a lot. This meant there was a ton of business there — but it also meant the market was saturated. Would moving to California be the right move? For now, the numbers said 'yes.'

So, knowing no one in the state and little about my new industry, I moved to California.

When I knocked on my first door in California, my worst fears were confirmed. The man who answered rudely told me: "What are you, another solar rep? This is your tenth visit this week!" before slamming the door in my face.

My stomach dropped out. I'd left everything behind — my lease, my contacts, the industry I knew.

I've made a huge mistake, I thought.

But I'd never let rejection stop me before. I drew myself up, put on my most confident smile, and knocked on the next door.

I made sales. A lot of them. Then I ran into familiar problems. The installer my company worked with was not up to my standards, and I wasn't happy with the service they were offering my customers.

In frustration, I decided to do something radical: if no existing company could meet my standards, I'd start my own company.

I was about to turn 25, and I'd been in California selling solar for less than a year. But I knew one thing: as long as I didn't give up, I couldn't fail.

In January 2020, I started Simple Solar with a team of myself and four other people. I addressed the supply chain problems that were causing slowdowns and insufficient funds for companies that weren't expecting to sell a massive volume.

We expected volume. We created a culture of expecting constant growth and spectacular performance. We became like a family: supporting and expecting each member to realize their fullest potential.

As I write this on Thanksgiving 2020, eleven months after starting Simple Solar, we have 41 members. We've surpassed $25 million in sales in 2020.

These truths are the keys to my success:

1. Wealth comes from connecting people to things they want in a convenient way. People will pay a premium for ease of access.

2. You can learn to do anything if you ask the right questions. I've always made decisions — at least the major ones — based on good, solid data.

3. I went into real estate because I knew it was a safe bet for growing wealth. I went into sales because a rich person told me it was the best way to become rich. I moved to Miami because it had a unique need for my products, and I moved to California because it was the best place for the industry I loved.

4. This was all publicly available data. And I didn't learn any of it in school. Instead, I used the Internet to research.

5. If you have a goal — any goal — you can learn exactly how to attain it by asking the right questions.

6. If you don't give up, you will win. I put myself in positions where failure was not an option. To some, these leaps may seem scary.

7. Imagine if I had given up on renovating my first house. Imagine if I had given up on sales when Toronto banned door-to-door solicitation, or when the Miami company collapsed under my sales volume, or when I got my first resounding "no" in California.

8. But I *couldn't* give up, because failure was not an option.

9. If I hadn't bought that house in a state of semi-panic, I might never have had the confidence to move to Toronto to become a salesperson, or to start my own company in California. Each experience taught me that I could do more.

10. All I had to do was go all-in and refuse to give up. The same is true for you.

These truths can be made into a formula that will allow you to accomplish *any* goal. It's so simple that you may have heard similar formulas elsewhere, but I bring you this one directly from personal experience:

Step 1: Identify your goal. What do you want? For me, it was wealth and the freedom that comes with it.

Step 2: Conduct research to identify your strategy. For me, the best way to obtain wealth was to sell high-ticket items that people would benefit from.

Step 3: Research where to start. What is the hottest industry near you? Or, what's the best place to move for what you most want to do?

Moving may be a deal-breaker for some, but it may also be the difference between success and struggle.

Step 4: Follow through. Pour your whole self into excelling. This is both simple, and deceptively difficult. There's no magic formula to reduce your effort. There is only research, strategy, and effort, through which you can learn any skill and conquer any obstacle if — and only if — you commit yourself.

Step 5: Don't take "no" for an answer. From yourself, or from anyone. When you want to give up, remember how much you want your goal. If you hate your first strategy — like I hated real estate — find another strategy and commit yourself to *that*.

I started a business that relied on door-to-door sales just before the COVID-19 pandemic hit. Disaster, right?

But I learned to re-cast calamities as opportunities. 'More people will be home when we knock now,' I reasoned. So, we suited up and kept a respectful distance as we stood on porches, explaining the benefits of solar panels for times of crisis.

I had no advantages except my hardships. You, too, can strike it rich if you research and follow through.

Many people find the demands of the entrepreneurial life to be too much. But to me, it's easier to get rich once than to stay broke forever.

***

To contact Moe:

Instagram.com/Falahtheleader

Linkedin.com/in/moe-falah/

Facebook.com/moefalah6

Simplesolarllc.com

moe@simplesolarllc.com

Phone: 305-807-9572

Brenda Jones

Brenda Jones, MA is an international speaker and board-certified Master Trainer of Neuro-Energetics (a unique blend of Neuro-Linguistic Programming, Hypnosis, Reiki, and other modalities) who supports business coaches, mastermind owners, and entrepreneurs to turn their hidden mindset roadblocks into their path using her signature BELIEF COaching™ Method + Certification Program.

She combines her unique expertise in behavioral psychology and her love of the subconscious mind to help her clients and students end self-sabotage, eliminate overwhelm, and finally put a stop to inconsistent results to maximize their impact and influence – with their clients, loved ones, and themselves – so they can manifest their kickass vision board lives.

After impacting thousands of lives as an autism specialist, she now continues to impact lives around the world as the co-founder of Belief Company, training and certifying others to continue the ripple of impact, and as a senior columnist for The Los Angeles Tribune.

Brenda lives in Southern California with her husband where she homeschools their two daughters around their competitive dance and theater schedules… all while putting the "ME" back in mommy.

Success Can Be Found Wherever You Look – Even in a Restroom

By: Brenda Jones, MA, MNLP

"What are you going to do?"

I remember pulling up to my daughters' dance studio, just a few days after it reopened following the first "shut down" of 2020. Before I could even turn off the engine, my friend ran over to my car and asked, "What are you going to do?"

Bewildered, I simply stared at her, wondering what I'd missed. The girls had been at the dance studio for only a few hours. Having spent way too much money the day before by going shopping to keep myself busy while they danced, I had attempted to set up a mini-office – laptop, phone, charger, etc. – at a local "patio-only-dining" restaurant in the Southern California summer heat hoping to get some work done.

After months of working from home, one child taking 30+ hours of dance upstairs in the loft and the other taking her 30+ hours per week of class downstairs in the same room I was working in, we were FINALLY back at the studio. Due to the new regulations on crowd size, parents could no longer enter the building; my new challenge was finding somewhere I could continue to work – seeing clients virtually, creating online content, and building my company – while they danced 5-7 hours per day… five days per week… at a studio an hour away from home.

I'd come up with the perfect plan. While things eased back to "normal," I would go back to working at the local outdoor food court. It had food… coffee… power… Wi-Fi… and restrooms, a necessary part of the plan. A little hot in the summer sun, but it would work. And it was better than 4 hours of commuting back and forth to drop off and pick up the girls each day.

Scratch that. Restrooms status: closed.

Plan B: find a local restaurant with outdoor dining, tip the servers well, and bring a portable charger. Restroom crisis averted. Phew!

Until... "What are you going to do?"

As she explained that the newly reopened restaurants were closing again, her voice faded into the distance as my mind raced, that little voice in my head repeating between "What am I going to do?" and "Wait... no restrooms?" Ok... and probably several more colorful phrases.

Have you ever thought you had figured out the perfect plan only to have life laugh as it knocked you down?

How did you respond?

Did you let it knock you down? Or did you smile in gratitude as you took that as an opportunity to course-correct?

Me?? I said a few choice words... and rented a restroom. Yes, a restroom.

Are you done laughing yet?

How about now??

I didn't realize it at the time, but as soon as I recovered from the initial shock, my years of training in mindset had already kicked in.

As I sat in traffic driving the hour home, that little voice in my head whispered, "Offices have restrooms. What about an office?"

For years, I had prided myself on not needing an office... building a coaching and training company that allowed me to work from anywhere, including sitting in a dance studio; using daily office spaces as needed and renting various hotel and other spaces for in-person certification and personal development events; and teaching my students to successfully do the same.

I didn't want an office.

I didn't NEED an office.

But I did need access to a restroom while my children danced 30+ hours per week as I had zero intentions on getting to know all of the local gas station attendants as my friend had done.

So, I went home and scoured the internet for any offices that were available and sent messages to each. The next morning, I was touring (and signing a lease agreement) at the only office that had responded, not knowing if business was going to pick up or if everything was shutting down again.

What I did know is that my kids needed to keep dancing in-person and with friends as long as their studio remained open; and I needed to find somewhere to go so they could do that.

When friends ask me if I'd rented an office, my reply was and still is, "Nope! I rented a restroom, and it came with an office!"

Years of training had all come together in that moment. I had done what my mentors had taught me to do and what I teach my clients and students to do.

Now, while many people believe you simply need to do what others do to get the results they get, it doesn't really work that way. It's about adopting the deeper mindsets – beliefs, values, and identities – the things that really drive our actions and determine our success.

Looking forward, I never could have guessed that something as simple as renting a restroom with a bonus office could massively and profoundly shift the trajectory and success of my business… and my life.

Looking backward, I see how that "simple" action wasn't simple after all; it was actually a culmination of years of self-development work.

So, while you can go out and rent yourself a restroom and hope for the same, let's dive into what really happened.

10 LESSONS LEARNED FROM RENTING A RESTROOM:

#1: KNOW WHAT YOU WANT

Have you ever noticed that when you ask someone what they want, they often respond with something they don't want? And after they empty out all the things they don't want, they still don't know what they want?

You have a conscious mind and a subconscious mind. Your conscious mind is aware of <1% of all the information your subconscious is taking in at every moment. We call it our "reality" and it's simply the information your subconscious thinks you should know based on your personal filters – things like your values, beliefs, memories, identities, words we use, mood, etc.

When you are clear with what you want, it's like telling your subconscious what information to bring into your awareness and what to store for later use.

Imagine you're at a buffet with over 2 million menu items. To prevent you from feeling overwhelmed, a server is available to bring you a plate of 126 items. You can either tell the server nothing and hope for the best, or you can tell the server exactly what you want and have the best meal ever.

The best way to "know" something? See it. Hear it. Feel it.

I didn't set out to rent an office. I definitely didn't predict the impact it would have. What I wanted was a restroom. And if that restroom could be somewhere with power, Wi-Fi, and where I could record content and see clients virtually, that would be icing on the cake.

#2: KNOW WHAT'S IMPORTANT

One of the easiest ways to make life feel easy and effortless – to move out of hustle and grind and into flow – is to be aligned at your core. Eliminate conflicts between what you say you want (your conscious mind) and what you actually do (your subconscious mind). When these conflicts arise, your subconscious always wins; and when it does, people often label it "self-sabotage."

When you know what's important to you about work, success, health, relationships, impact, self-care, or any other large or small area of your life and you release the deeper mindset roadblocks that hold you back, making decisions becomes simple. And when making decisions becomes simple, so does taking action. And when your actions align with your core values, you no longer have to effort at making them happen.

When I rented that restroom, this is what was most important to me: ensuring my girls could continue to dance and continuing to serve and support my clients and students as I had been doing while I was stuck at home for those first few months of the shutdown.

#3: GET OUT OF YOUR COMFORT ZONE

It doesn't matter if it's a tiny step or a massive leap, do something every day that stretches you. Challenge yourself. Each step moves you into becoming a new version of you. And once that becomes comfortable, take another step. Every time you stretch your comfort zone, you achieve something and/or you learn something. And that something may change your life.

I had avoided renting an office because I wanted flexibility. I thought I'd be "stuck" in a single location. I worried I'd become a "workaholic" again and miss family time. When I did the scary thing and signed that lease so I could have a restroom, I discovered that having an office was the best way to have the flexibility and freedom I desired. It created boundaries that allowed for harmony between work time, family time, and me time.

#4: MAKE DECISIONS… QUICKLY

I had heard from my mentors, including Mark Yuzuik (another author in this book), over and over that successful people make lots of decisions and they make them quickly. I'd heard it and I'd taught it, but I didn't always live it. I liked to weigh pros and cons. I liked to comparison shop. And I'd often get stuck deciding and never actually decide. I used to play the "what if" game so often, typically focused on what if something went wrong, that I created the "What If" Technique to complete my studies and earn the title of Master Trainer of Neuro-Linguistic Programming (NLP).

But this time, I didn't have that luxury. Only one office had returned my email overnight and I needed somewhere to go ASAP.

Not having the luxury of time, I made a decision on the spot. And that decision changed everything.

#5: BE FLEXIBLE

In NLP, we have several beliefs that we choose to accept as true because it makes it easier to move through this Earth-dance. One of them is the Law of Requisite Variety. In everyday language, it states that the most flexible person in the system wins.

It was my ability to be flexible that allowed me to remain calm and focused as my plans were falling apart around me. I didn't know what the next step was going to be, but I trusted in my ability to bend with the constant changes vs. having them knock me over.

#6: TAKE BIG ACTION

Newton's Third Law of Motion states "For every action, there is an equal and opposite reaction." If you take small action, you'll get small results. If you take big action, you'll get big results. Want massive results? Take massive action.

It's not necessarily what you believe is "massive" action.

I thought I was renting a restroom. Universe saw it differently. Universe saw me rent an office on the spot. Almost as quickly as I'd signed the lease, opportunities began flooding in; opportunities that were likely always there, but, without a consistent office space, I wasn't able to see them.

#7: GO ALL IN

Make the decision, then own it. Tell the Universe that you are ready.

Before the ink of my signature on the lease dried, I was on the phone with my business partner and we were making plans to meet up and shop for fun décor for the office. Within a couple of weeks, we jumped on an opportunity to grab a second office we didn't "need" at the time, trusting that the need would arise as soon as we took the step, and it did. Within a couple of months, Universe rewarded us again as we upgraded to larger offices. And now, only 6 months from the initial decision to rent that restroom, Universe has continued to reward us with opportunities that have us expanding yet again.

#8: RELEASE THE FORM

So often, we get stuck on how we think things are supposed to go. We make plans, and when something throws us off course, we get lost. Sometimes, we get stuck.

But what if getting lost is the path to dreams far bigger than ever imagined?

When restaurants closed back down, I instantly felt the fears and worries begin to build. And because I've changed how I respond to those feelings, they instantly jumped into me feeling focused and in control (thank you NLP).

I had my plan… until I didn't. And I discovered a path that had always been there waiting for me, a path that I had never seen before.

#9: LISTEN TO THE WHISPER

If you learn nothing else but this, listen to that voice. Trust that gut feeling that is guiding you. Teach it that you're listening so that it continues to talk to you more frequently.

This was one of my hardest lessons learned and one that I didn't understand for years until that first weekend I fell into learning how the mind works and how to program it for success.

That voice – that whisper – is you. It's the "you" that's aware of all of that information that the "conscious you" is not aware of. It knows more than you or I can ever know. And it's working for your best interest.

#10: HAVE FUN

At the end of the day, the question to ask is this: Am I having fun?

Your subconscious mind is the part of you that likes imagination and play. The more you find the fun in everything you do, the more you move into activating the most powerful parts of you… and that is where you unlock all of the amazingness that awaits you.

So maybe you do what I did… and you run out and rent a restroom.

Or maybe not.

Whatever your next step is on your journey to success, let these lessons guide you.

***

To contact Brenda:

Website: www.beliefco.com

Start your NLP journey: www.learnNLPfree.com

Hang out with me on social (FB, IG, and more): www.beliefco.com/letsplay

Robin Bela

Robin Bela is an International Bestselling Author, Speaker, Success Mindset and Manifestation Coach & Transformational Teacher for over 15 years. Robin is from India and lives in the UK since 2003. She is the author of 'Break the Pattern: Connecting to The Power Within To Create The Life You Want' & Co-Author of the book 'The Successful Mind: Tools To Living A Purposeful & Productive Life.'

Robin is an MBA graduate with a corporate background. She has helped thousands personally and professionally come out of challenging situations where they seemed stuck, especially in their minds for their personal and professional success. She shows you how to tap into the flow of the Divine for moving into the flow of higher positive vibrations to bring your success.

Robin shows how to improve the way one thinks and feels about themselves, their business vision and achieve their success. She helps Leaders & Entrepreneurs to manifest their greatest potential by cultivating a Success Mindset.

A regular international guest speaker in media and events, Robin also offers various online programs, seminars, offline and online retreats.

If you would like to learn more about Robin and access free resources to help you manifest your success, please visit her website.

Manifesting Success Through the Power of Mind

By Robin Bela

➤ **The Power of A Relaxed Mind Creates Success**

Everything we create first begins in our minds. It starts with our imagination, often a wild imagination like that of Thomas Alva Edison when he invented the light bulb. He imagined light in the dark was possible through an electric bulb! And he was able to make it a reality after a thousand trials! But Edison never thought of those trials as a failure. Once a reporter asked him how it felt to fail a thousand times, and he replied, "I didn't fail 1000 times. The light bulb was an invention with 1000 steps."

Our success always begins in our perception. The hard work put into our work can seem frustrating to some, but exciting to others who are focused on the result and never for a moment doubt that they will get there. How our mindset is while we perform our work determines our achievement. So, it is imperative to study and know about the power of the mind in our lives, especially at work and through testing times where we need to create results to come out of challenging situations.

It may be said that our mind's power lies in being resilient and versatile rather than being rigid in approach and execution. This is possible only in a relaxed mind, which is focused on the present moment and its potential, rather than being energetically drained by past regrets or guilt or undue worries or stress about the future. We can so train our minds that while we give our best to the work put in daily, it is not only productive but also joyful and fulfilling. Often, some people get so worked up for the result that they cannot relax and be joyful in the moment, and instead, live in anxiety, frustration and fatigue. From that energy of the mind, one cannot manifest any success.

We have to train the mind to be comfortable with our physical reality and be able to maintain a higher vision in our mind about where we are heading. We are always in charge of creating our reality as long as we are comfortable with the nature of duality between reality and vision.

➢ Asking & Setting Intentions

When we are curious to find solutions, we also enjoy the process of treading on the unknown route, excited to see how we can make things work. When we focus on the thought 'I wonder how I will get there', ideas show up, because you asked and God / Higher Consciousness whatever you like to believe in, gives your mind the power to see and know more, sometimes intuitively. The asking puts you in a receptive mode instantly. Sometimes a formal asking like a prayer to God / Higher Consciousness is powerful, especially if you are struggling to surface above some turbulent waters. The asking process is like setting an intent and helps to put our minds to think powerfully and to keep the faith. I recommend doing this daily, first thing in the morning, so you are manifesting your success and getting the best support for your exponential growth.

A mind has the power to imagine a positive outcome, even under difficult circumstances and then manifest what it envisions. I have always been fascinated with power of the mind right from my school days. A month before my dreaded exams, I would tap into my mind's power through mindset techniques and pass those same previously terrifying exams with ease and good grades!

Our society is programmed to think logically, to see the world through the rational mind. Like with the Law of Universal Gravitation, when an apple falls, it does so because of gravity. If I say you can make massive amounts of money and achieve great success even when you don't have any opportunity in the present, it may sound unreasonable to anyone with a rational mind. So, we continue on our path of hardships, limited vision and limited growth, while we could be manifesting miraculous success and opportunities and growing exponentially, if we could just give the logical, rational, mind a little rest.

➤ The Art of Thinking BIG

We need to learn to train our minds to think big for a start. Are you ready to think big? I can talk about it, but if you don't decide and allow your fears to drop and surrender to the unknown confidently, it's going to remain a theory and mystery as to how others achieve massive success. I will now attempt to help you to move in that direction. When people work with me in my coaching practice, I handhold them through the process, but I hope this will be a good start for all as well.

I am sure the big idea of the company Amazon first came to its Founder Jeff Bezoz's conscious mind as an idea from his imagination, and he then went ahead with his big vision. Perhaps some may have considered it a wild risk in the nineties. But he went on to create one of the most prominent companies that the whole world uses to sell and buy products for personal and business use via the Internet.

You can ask yourself, are there any big ideas that you have and are afraid to think deeply about? What is the vision that you carry now, and would ideally like it to be? You can activate your mind to produce success for it when you allow yourself to dream big and not let your fears stop you.

Our mind can carry many unconscious thoughts. All these thoughts are meaningless. We create our thoughts randomly, and when our minds are not trained to differentiate between what is real and what are just fears, we tend to believe in thinking that these fears will become real. When we mindfully create our thoughts, we decide what to give importance to and make our reality. We could weigh the pros and cons, allay our unfounded fears and choose to side with our big vision and go for it. Are there thoughts in your mind about what you would like to really do, but have buried beneath a thousand fears?

You do have the power; you are a co-creator with the Universe. Everything progresses naturally, like the nature around us. No one stops a river from flowing in a direction, nor an embryo from growing. We may need to take a thousand steps to get somewhere, but that's all! And when you work with faith and work along with the Higher Consciousness, you can create instant manifestations and miracles. But the mind has to start believing that it is possible and expect it to take place.

I have a personal anecdote I would like to share of a time when my mind started to think bigger in an instant and how I started spontaneously manifesting opportunities that I had not previously imagined. All out of the blue I had received an offer for work with a monthly payment that equaled my then annual income. I wasn't actively looking for an offer at all. But I was surprised that someone thought that, that was the value of my work. This experience was a turning point in my life, when I began permitting myself to think big and receive more. It wasn't also about putting more hard work. It was just about thinking big and more for myself and have greater self-worth. And more opportunities like that started coming.

Let me also add to the above story that a month before receiving that offer, I had allowed my mind to think that I would love to have a certain amount of savings in a month. At that time, I had not realized that I would manifest an offer with that very amount per month. I realised what's possible and what more I can create from there. Where the mind goes, the reality follows!

I am sharing this here because sometimes we think life is all about limitations and block our minds from thinking of what all is possible. The steps may be new but trust the Universe to show you opportunities to manifest your wildest of ideas. Your past doesn't have to be your present, and you require no proof of what will happen in the future to begin on the path to accomplishing your big vision. So, start dreaming big!

➤ Progression Happens When You Ask and Let Go!

You begin your vision with what you like, as opposed to what would work. You have to not worry about all the steps needed beforehand, as you would know by now that it doesn't matter as long as it's moving you forward toward the goal you desire and makes your life more meaningful. You will eventually figure out all the steps along the way. It is possible you may learn how to get to step 10 only after you reach step 9.

With your vision, you can also ask in prayer or intend in your conscious mind that you will have all the financial support or any other support that you require. And just let go of worrying about the process of how. 'Ask and let go' is the motto. Everything progresses naturally, like in nature. If we only stop worrying, which pushes our minds to think the exact opposite of success.

Sometimes the human mind is addicted to controlling what will happen and think of the worst. I have clients who ask me how they can be peaceful and joyful at a given moment, when they are so worried about the future. For them, the act of staying in the moment unconditionally in joy is also a controlled process, and it becomes futile to manifest anything positive from this constricted, anxious place.

Letting go is surrendering of the control of results. Learning to be happy for no reason is like being how you were as a child. You would never think of the worst then. You lived for the day happily and expected to do the same the next day. We need to deprogramme our minds of the need to control outcomes. We cannot manifest and experience success or witness incredible synchronicities and receive unique opportunities by having a controlling and fearful mind. Sometimes people are so used to that way of being that the other way of life seems abnormal or a fantasy, or even scary as one lets go of control.

➤ Heal the Mind To Tap Into Its Power

Life offers the best when we expect and look for the best in situations, especially from people. When we look for goodness, we see more goodness. When we train our minds to look for the best and see the best in everyone, we see more of that and have good experiences with these people. Most importantly, we are at peace instead of suffering with turmoil and confusion in our heads.

We cannot be a vessel to receive good if we are unconsciously defensive towards the world around us. It is like building a wall. It may just be with one person, but the toxic emotions from the situation could have taken over your life.

What we need to do is to make our minds a haven. Be protective of our minds to which thoughts it carries. The more we are focused on positive thinking and look for the good with patience, we start seeing that people around us notice our open, forgiving and peaceful mind, and change their behavior too.

Best of the best people in stressful situations can show their human nature that is not appropriate, and at that moment it is crucial to know how to handle our emotions. Learn not to judge, learn to forgive, and allow the mind to be clear of any baggage. One cannot manifest anything positive with toxic emotions in the background. Healing the mind is essential to tap into the power of the mind to manifest any success.

Our thoughts are powerful. When it is hard to control thoughts because of external influences or emotional pain, emptying and healing of the mind is essential. Prayer and meditation are beneficial. Bringing God into our mind makes our mind a sacred space as it is a pure and divinely peaceful experience, which reverts us to our usual calm and peaceful selves.

You may say that all these emotions, fears and doubts are just illusions and not real when we go back to our usual self and recognize our divine power to feel whole, healed and complete, again by connecting to God / Higher Consciousness. We are powerful divine beings capable of erasing our painful pasts and manifesting success just by planting the seed of that thought in our mind. Let us now talk more about manifesting power!

➤ Manifesting Success Powerfully!

When you know what your vision is, have eliminated all worries, anxieties, painful memories, learnt to tap into your inner joy and practiced seeing the best with the support of God / Higher Consciousness, you are in the perfect fertile energy to visualise that the seeds you sowed are manifesting!

Move into the flow of the Divine by connecting your mind to seeing the best. This, dear reader, is what having a winning mindset is all about. Life is here for us, and we now embrace it, rather than fearfully inch towards it in small steps or fight it altogether. I ask you to relax your grip, give away control, and shift from driving yourself to sitting and relaxing. It is time to allow yourself to receive the success you deserve.

We want to become a magnet for success by connecting to the unconditional joy within. This absolute joy is within us naturally when we learn the power of having a relaxed mind.

The world around us usually suggests doing more - push, fight, be an opportunist and so on. While in the place of no control or push, we allow the Universe to co-create miracles by bringing opportunities, sometimes for which you may not have to even lift a finger! They occur just because you thought, stayed joyful, relaxed and expectant. It will feel like a natural and organic process that leads to fantastic results. A person only needs to fight for success when he doesn't believe that it's really possible. Instead, relax and feel confident that all is well.

We can grow at an incredible speed when we can perceive this can happen, and we begin to think big. I came from a corporate background and had Masters in Business Administration and Marketing degrees under my belt way before I embarked on my coaching practice in 2005. But what brought me my success was first thinking big, then tapping into this divine success mindset and manifestation flow, and not so much by my marketing strategies at all!

Business strategies work the best when we know how to be in good energies – with a healed mind, a winning mindset, the right vision and in the Flow of Divine Manifestation, of asking and receiving. It is a healthy mind that is not swayed by emotions and circumstances, and as a result is powered with a strong vision. It is not masculine energy as you might think. It's feminine as receptivity is of ease and relaxed self, and not pushing through. So yes, a sale does not have to be pushy! In fact, it never works that way, does it? How about you attracting clients and work like bees to a flower?! Just as the way nature is designed and progresses without any resistance, we move forward naturally with our thoughts aligned to our actions.

➤ A Mind of Faith Can Move Mountains

It's a delicate dance between 'reality' and 'vision', as we live in the reality and design the image of our future joyously, with no doubts in our minds of course. Such consistent faith can move mountains!

Finding faith is the second step after letting go of controlling outcomes. We may have had no successful result for a long time, but it is then we need to ensure we are enjoying our task and staying in the moment. Faith is something we will repeatedly get tested on in our lives. Once we realise there is nothing we can do about results, other than to let them unfold, we need to believe that life wants the best for us because we all can have the best opportunities and support from God / Higher Consciousness. The question is, do we keep the faith in tough times or do we go back to feelings of our doom and gloom and stay small? It requires great training of the mind to stay on course. In my profession, I am always helping my clients to keep their faith and shine their brightest by learning to always stay in the fertile energy of manifesting success.

Here are some quick questions to assess if you are in the flow of manifesting success. You can answer the following as 'yes' or 'no':

1. Do you usually find it difficult to be relaxed as you go about the essential things that you are focusing on at the moment?
2. Do you like to control outcomes and results?
3. Do your fears block you from dreaming big and bold?
4. Are you constantly feeling the world is against you and having resentments from the past?
5. Do you find creating results is all about pushing, pulling and being an opportunist?
6. Do you run out of patience when desired outcomes don't show up?
7. Are you afraid of failure?
8. Do you struggle with enjoying the present moment as you focus on the work?

9. Do you have a big vision but struggle to keep the faith when difficult situations arise?

10. Do you feel the best strategies don't work because of bad luck, or mistakes?

If you answered all or most of the answers as a 'Yes', then you need to focus on learning to manifest your success through the power of your mind. Only when you can get a 'No' for all the above, you are in the Divine Manifestation Flow, where everything flows to you effortlessly. And you can then indeed live the life of ease, charm, joy, and success that you truly deserve.

***

Email - mail@robinbela.co.uk

Website - www.robinbela.co.uk

Michelle Guinn

Michelle Guinn is a Personal Productivity Strategist, Success Mentor, International Speaker, and Coach who has found her passion helping others become even more successful.

After over 25 years as a self-motivated and accomplished corporate professional, Michelle began her entrepreneurial journey and has never looked back. Today, she is empowering business owners, individuals, and entrepreneurs to transform their lives, achieve their goals and turn their dreams into reality.

Through her speaking, training and coaching programs Michelle incorporates key learnings and life lessons from personal experience and successes to help others in their own personal journey of self-discovery, personal growth, and goal achievement.

Michelle's approach is simple and profoundly impactful. She will empower and inspire her audience to take daily action in their personal and professional lives.

She proves that by incorporating the right systems and daily success habits, anyone from serial entrepreneur to the newest online solopreneur can generate exciting momentum as they move closer to building a life and business they love.

You Wake up in a Panic Again. It's 4am

By Michelle Guinn

You wake up in a panic again. It's 4am. Your heart is racing, and you are trying to get your bearings. Then you remember. Your mind starts spinning thinking about all the things you didn't get done yesterday and the things you must get done today. You begin feeling guilty. Could you have done more? You begin to berate yourself for not doing enough, for not being smart enough, for not being good enough. You start feeling fear and doubting yourself. The dread that no matter what you do, you will never make this business work.

Sound familiar?

Unfortunately, for many entrepreneurs, this is a common occurrence.

Our minds are powerful. You can either allow your mind to continue to disrupt your dreams and visions of prosperity, or you can take control of your thoughts and use them to attract the success you want and deserve.

Having the right mindset and learning to address your habitual thinking is the foundation to a system to change the course of your life and ultimately accelerate your success and increase your revenue.

Every accomplished entrepreneur and businessperson will tell you they succeed because they have the right systems in place to ensure their success. They have instilled time-proven habits and daily routines.

It is not difficult to learn about these habits. Many books have been written on the subject. But if you lack one piece of the success system, and the accountability to keep you focused on that system, then your chances of succeeding drop significantly.

So, I'm going to make it easy for you and lay it out right here.

Step 1: Master Your Thinking to Crush Your Goals

As I stated, developing the right mindset is the foundation to all success. So, if you are spending your days mentally beating yourself up, putting yourself down and being generally negative you will struggle to achieve anything you set out to do.

Here are some tips on maintaining consistent momentum, productive and positive thoughts throughout the day:

First, when you focus on what you want, you tend to attract that into your day, right? Also, when you focus on what you don't want, what happens? You attract that as well. You have a choice. This may sound like common sense but ask yourself how often do you find your thoughts lingering on the what ifs and everything that could go wrong. Instead, imagine your life and how it will change once you achieve your goals. Focus on the feelings of being successful. Spend time each day envisioning your definition of success and daydreaming about what your new life would look like and how it would feel. These daily thoughts will help to rewire your brain and give you the new habit of focusing on the positive outcomes.

Next, transform negative self-talk into positive self-talk. Identify the habitual thinking patterns that have likely been there for many years. You probably have stopped noticing how often you put yourself down. Stop being so mean to yourself! Make a note every time you speak down to yourself so you can start to identify how your inner critic is blocking your success. Is your negative self-talk sabotaging your good intentions? Once you have learned to identify it, then you can start to fix it. Find positive statements you can use to replace those negative thoughts that run through your head. And whenever you catch your inner voice saying something unwanted, acknowledge it and immediately replace it with something positive.

Finally, do not believe everything you think. Our reality is all a matter of perspective. We have a natural tendency to make up stories and dwell on things that are not true. I love this example: You walk into meeting room with a few people and say good morning. Everyone says good morning back except one person. You immediately start to wonder why they ignored you. Did you say something to offend them in a previous encounter? Maybe they do not like you? They are just being rude! And more excuses will run through your mind. But here is the reality: This person had her headphones in listening to a phone call and never even heard you say good morning. Now ask yourself, how many times does something like this happened in your life?

Step 2: Find Clarity and Know Your WHY

The most successful people succeed because they are clear on their "why." Your "why" is going to give you the fuel to keep going when your motivation and inspiration fail you.

A business coach once asked me about my "why" and I can tell you my children have always been the driving force behind everything I do. So, he suggested I print a picture of my daughter and tape it somewhere that I will see it every night before I go to bed. So, on the days where I chose to get distracted or procrastinate on the income producing activities I committed to, I can look at her face and confess I didn't care enough today to honor my commitments. I understand this may sound a bit harsh, but for me, it is what I needed to hear. It is the emotional attachment to what may seem like meaningless daily activities that, in the long run, will lead to increased income and the success I have envisioned for myself. To this day, I keep her picture on my bathroom mirror.

You must understand what drives you. What are you passionate about? What is your "why"?

Your "why" is the driving force behind what you do. It could be your family, your children, travel, helping your community, freedom to do what you want when you want to do it. Your "why" is very personal.

It is not a difficult concept, but if you have never put thought into it, it is sometimes hard to voice or put on paper.

The question we usually do not ask ourselves is "What is the purpose behind my actions?" Which is really a question you should ask yourself daily.

Here are critical "why" questions you should answer:
- Why do you want to take your income from where it is to a "next level"?
- Why do you want to start your own business?

- Why do you want your company to evolve, or to quit your job, or to rise up through the ranks of your current job?
- Why do you want your parents or spouse to retire?
- Why do you want to lose weight, have more passion in your actions, have more joy on a daily basis, and live a life with more smiles than frowns?

When you can uncover your true "why," your driving purpose in life, and translate that into actions, you obtain the momentum you need to push forward, faster than ever.

Step 3: Craft A Powerful Vision

It is easy for all of us to get lost in the mundane activities of daily life. Crafting a vision provides hope for a better future. It also gives meaning to certain activities we indulge in.

I have always been a dreamer. I would lay in bed dreaming about all the things I would do when I won the lottery. What I would buy, where I would live, who I would help. But then my inner voice would squash that telling me it would never happen, and I would go back to my day-to-day routine and not give those dreams another thought. Do you sometimes find yourself doing the same?

Over the last few years, I have learned a lot about the power of visualization. There are far too many stories of people who have manifested their dreams by visualizing the things they want. Of course, you must put the work in as well. Crafting a powerful vision is an integral piece to the foundation required for achieving all your goals and dreams.

A vision board is one of the most valuable visualization tools available. It is an inspirational collage that serves as your image of the future. A tangible example or idea of where you are going, it should represent your dreams, your goals, and your ideal life. It is meant to be a visualization tool.

How does a vision board work? Think about a time when you got a new car. Let's imagine for a moment it is bright red and you think, "Wow, I have never seen this car in this color red before. It must be the only one like it! It'll really stand out on the road." Then, the next thing you know, you see that make and model in the exact same bright red color everywhere. The reason is that you have put your attention on something specific and are unconsciously scanning the world for items that match it. It is not that those cars were never there before; it is simply you never noticed them.

So it makes sense if you put your attention and focus your feelings on the images on your vision board (e.g., pictures of your dream trip to Hawaii) that the energy will more likely be in your awareness (e.g., commercials for Hawaiian Airlines might keep popping up on your TV, or your job might unexpectedly send you there for a work project).

This is what a vision board can do for you. When you continue to give your attention to the things you want and have a picture of them, you attract those things into your life, and what once seemed like an "ideal life" can become your reality.

Step 4: Become A Master Goal Setter

Once you have the foundations of your mindset, your why and your vision in place, you need to take action and begin the work. This is where your goals come in. Without goals, you have no real focus, no real purpose to make things happen.

Goals help you focus on the possibility for success. As we have already established, what you focus on expands. Creating and focusing on concrete goals will open more opportunities and give you a sense of direction.

In this busy world, you can be overwhelmed by opportunities and choices and end up doing nothing but standing still. People with goals succeed because they know exactly where they are going.

In my corporate career, I spent a long time rejecting the idea of goal setting. At the end of every year, I was required to write down and submit my goals for next year. I came to hate that exercise. On the surface, I believed goal setting was a waste of my time. Do you know anyone with that same belief?

I've come to realize it was not the goal setting I had a problem with. It was the fact I had no passion or ambition to succeed in my job and I had a fear of disappointment. A fear that if I wrote my goals and did not achieve them, I would be a failure.

Today, I write my goals, review them daily, and revise and adjust as I go along. Quite honestly, I have adopted the believe that I never want to achieve my biggest goals. Why, you ask? Because then I will stop pushing forward, I will stop growing my success. So, I set very lofty and sometimes scary goals and keep revising them as I go along in order to reach even more success. Then I break them down into smaller steps, take action every day, and celebrate my small achievements.

This is how you too can become a master goal setter. Remember to keep your goals SMART: Specific, Measurable, Achievable, Realistic, and Timely.

Step 5: Implement the Right Time Management Habits

Highly successful people hold tight to the belief that time is your most precious commodity. You can sell it, but you cannot buy more, and everyone is given the same amount every day.

When it comes to time management, there are success habits that should be built into your daily routine to face the challenge of staying on task.

The first-time management trap you should recognize and work to eliminate is multi-tasking.

There has been a ton of research which proves multi-tasking does not work.

Did you know it can take up to five minutes for your brain to properly refocus on a given thought process or task? So, when you continually jump from task to task you cannot truly focus your proper attention on the work to be done. As much as you can, you need to avoid trying to work on multiple things at once. You will be much more productive and get so much more done in less time when you do.

The next time management habit to establish is to time block your most important tasks for the day. Make a list of what needs to be done (preferably at the end of the previous day), then set up your calendar in time blocks based on the amount of time it should take to complete the task. This may be difficult given interruptions, but when you block your calendar, you can actively avoid interruptions and distractions. This includes email time. Be proactive with your email by allotting times throughout the day when you will check and respond. Your goal should be to stay in proactive mode and not spend all day reacting and allowing email to run your day.

Be sure to leave a little wiggle room between your time blocks also. No one should have a fully stacked calendar with no time for a break. Block out buffer-time on your calendar in between meetings and tasks. Your future self will thank you when your days are more productive, and the hours are less exhausting.

My next time management tip is to do your most difficult tasks first. Block the first hour of your day to complete your most difficult tasks or those that take you out of your comfort zone. The morning is when most people will have the most energy, so use it to your advantage and stop putting off those difficult or important matters. Don't allow the quick, menial tasks to get in the way. Set a deadline for important tasks as well. Many of us work best under pressure, so when you set a deadline, a given day and time to complete a project, you are more likely to complete it within a timely manner.

Finally, make sure you take regular breaks. The body runs on 90-minute energy cycles, so when you work longer than 90 minutes on a given task, your energy will drain, and you will lose focus. It is not only good for you physically to get up and take a short walk or to bend and stretch, but you also need that mental break to allow your brain to recharge and get ready for the next cycle.

Step 6: Make Every Day Count with the Right Success Habits

The most powerful life you can live is one in which you control your own habits. To succeed in anything you do in life, you will need: strategy, accountability, commitment, grit, and patience. You will face obstacles such as: laziness, procrastination, and feeling overwhelmed. This is where your habits will either propel you forward or hold you back.

Imagine waking up each day knowing what tasks you need to accomplish, having an action plan to complete them, and knowing exactly when you will complete them. Instilling habits such as goal setting, time blocking, taking action, rewarding yourself and getting out of your comfort zone will put you in a position of power and control over your own life.

Use these proven steps to develop new success habits:
- Decide specifically what your new habit will be and set your environment up for success by writing it down, telling everyone who will listen, posting it online and putting sticky notes everywhere.
- Build an emotional attachment to the outcome. How will your life be different when you implement this new habit?
- Have a morning mirror discussion with yourself by spending 30 to 60 seconds giving praise in advance and affirming you are the master of your new habit.
- Celebrate and reward yourself daily, weekly and after 90 days of maintaining the new habit.
- Find an accountability partner. Not friends! Someone who will hold your feet to the fire when you need support and be firm and direct with you.

Now, imagine this…

You wake up, it's 7:00 a.m. You have slept through the night again and you feel at peace. Last night, you celebrated yet another achievement that took you one step closer to your goals. You have a full day ahead, but you are not stressed because you are excited by everything you accomplished yesterday and are eager to see how much you complete today. Your focus has changed. You no longer wake up in a panic. Your thoughts are productive and positive.

This will be your reality when you implement a proven success system.

I love seeing my clients get amazing results from this system. I recently received the following note:

"Michelle, I thoroughly enjoyed your program. It was a very simple and brilliantly structured which made it easy to comprehend resulting in huge breakthroughs and takeaways. I was able to see things from a new perspective, allowing me to step outside of what I've known to be true. It has helped me to get clear on my business and how to move forward fiercely."

I look forward to hearing from you and how we may work together to get you the results you desire and deserve.

***

To contact Michelle:

Email: info@themichelleguinn.com

Phone: 443-550-1822

Schedule a Breakthrough Discovery Session:
https://calendly.com/michelleguinn/discovery-session

Social Media:

Facebook: https://www.facebook.com/MichelleGInspired

LinkedIn: https://www.linkedin.com/in/michelleguinn/

Kevin T. Robertson

Kevin T. Robertson is a top consummate professional speaker, CEO and Co-founder of Speakerfocus.com. Internationally recognized as America's Leading Focus Expert, Kevin has delivered over 2000 customized leadership programs since 1988.

KTR teaches Fortune 500 clients, across the US, toured overseas in

30+ countries like North Africa and Italy. Successful companies like; The International Association of Venue Managers, McDonalds, Burger King, Verizon, and over 100 companies each year invest in his teachings, booking him again and again.

In 2012, the 6X Super Bowl Champion Pittsburgh Steelers hired Kevin TO DELIVER THE FIRST EVER ONSITE TRAINING OF IT'S KIND at Heinz Field celebrating the historical; "Year of the FAN", 80th season of the franchise, and the 40th year of "The Immaculate Reception".

KTR has earned a reputation where high profile celebrities and top brands trust in his leadership, experience and unmatched proven track record to deliver powerful results on the mark every time.

He is a regular contributor to the Pro View Magazine and The Business of Wisdom on CBS Radio, has written for numerous trade publications and is a frequent media guest on national Radio, TV & Podcasts.

KTR's strong skill as a facilitator has educated over 1 million conference goers with "How To Techniques", "Common Sense Approaches" and "Simplistic Practical Application Strategies".

Leadership Strategies That Magnify Success

by Kevin T. Robertson

A leader is born

From the beginning my Mom say's I was screaming coming through the birth canal. She could feel her youngest child's vibration as I made my way to the world. I came into the delivery room with a loud cry so you could say I was destined to be heard. On my birthday, my oratorical prowess was unleashed upon this earth.

I thank my dear Mother for staying on my ass about spelling, articulating my words properly and making sure me and my brother became gentlemen of the first order. The focal point of my life has been centered around communication and it always came natural. I can never recall having the fear of stage fright or was ever nervous about speaking in public.

I knew I had the gift of gab but that is not enough to cut the mustard and earn a great income as a high fee speaker (and deep down I knew it). My blind ambitions of wanting to chase dreams of being a "motivational bloviator" would later prove to be detrimental but just the shot in the arm I needed to clean up some sloppy habits that were holding me back. The wakeup call came when I had to get serious about learning the speaking business.

The unknowns of the industry changed a young man at 18 years old who knew nothing about transferring knowledge and raised me up so I could stop operating out of broke, begging and desperation mode. 7 years into my journey a shift started to happen, and I could finally call myself a consummate professional speaker.

If you want to crack the code and experience success like never before, then be prepared to give up quarts of blood from all the battles you will encounter. You will cry gallons of tears that will fill the deepest sea, sweat bullets of frustration and live with constant disappointments. Fight through the pain without complaining. Code crackers… mount up and let's ride!

Young leadership should be nurtured

My English teacher Mrs. Pronk helped build my confidence, supporting my dreams and nurturing my talent as a writer. It gave me such a jump start on my career and enough belief in myself to attract anything I wanted to accomplish. I felt powerful, fulfilled, and special. Public speaking made it possible for me to do all the after school and extracurricular activities I could handle.

I was a curly headed little kid from Capital Heights in Prince George's County. We lived in Seat Pleasant and then moved to Maryland Park. I grew up eating fried bologna and cheese sandwiches, playing in the hood with my friends and seeing rats rummage through the neighbor's garbage cans on the regular.

Some things about growing up in an underprivileged environment exposed me to the harsh realities of a cold world. I learned how to survive really quick and street smarts is something you could simply not afford to live without.

I used to love watching "The Adventures of Letterman". It was a series of animated skits that was a regular feature on the 1970s PBS educational television series The Electric Company.

I could literally see word sequences flying through the air 24hrs a day. My creativity was jumping and jolting with action like a pinball machine. The gift would never leave me alone not even in my sleep.

I responded to the calling of becoming a professional communicator a long time ago. I accepted the gift and responsibility that comes with walking in your purpose. The moment you fully acknowledge your destiny and establish a mind-set that's free from censorship, you seize opportunities of exponential growth.

My testimony is a kaleidoscope of talents that have been recognized for as long as I can remember. Writing & the gift of communication have been paramount in my life always. I had no idea these skills would be the primary reason for the longevity of my success.

Adversity & Failure

The failures in my life both personally and professionally have been brutal. The devastating financial losses have been nothing short of torturous. Navigating stormy seas in the smallest boat can be a rough passage and flat out tumultuous.

There are no perfect scenarios in business. The painful setbacks have been like a bike with no kickstand causing me to be in a tailspin of perpetual motion with no support system, or safety net to break the fall.

Before you take off the training wheels you must first learn to master unimaginable practice repetitions to gain the confidence to fly solo into the wild blue yonder. In order to "crack the code" of success, you must endure incomprehensible pain, learn the patience to overcome and develop self-discipline plus emotional control.

Falling down is all part of process improvement and failure is imminent for us all; however, failure does not necessarily have to become a permanent fixture in your life. These stepping-stones of FOCUS will equip you with the wisdom to push through the toughest days even when you feel like all hope is gone.

Learning how to grow a successful business is a rough road to travel and a tough pill to swallow for sure. No matter how hard the game may be, you must stay true to your vision.

Entrepreneurship is like being on a secret mission full of pending danger no matter where you go. It's landmines everywhere, so you must not deviate from the road map and get off course.

Organize your Focus

A big part of achieving focus is having the ability to see things other people don't see. I have spent years studying the keen eyesight of birds.

For example, the Peregrine Falcon is a bird that has binocular vision and can see eight times better than humans. Studies show they can see their prey from a distance of more than three kilometers, that's a little over 1.8 miles.

Develop eyes in the back of your head with laser-like focus! Lock into your (foresight) to see deep into the future and execute your daily, weekly, monthly and yearly goals. Most entrepreneurs don't prepare with a plan of contingency.

Always remember setbacks, challenges, difficulties and the unknown is not a point of "if", it's just "when" it will happen again so govern yourself accordingly. You must be tenaciously aggressive to survive in a vicious cycle of negative opposition. Predator or prey… the choice is yours.

Peregrine Falcons also have a third eyelid to protect their eyes as they stoop to dive. This spreads tears and clears debris without obstructing vision when hunting prey.

Most people in business try to focus on 20 things at a time. They are delusional at best, not delegating tasks effectively, being under the influence of their own ego, with a break-neck management style of multi-tasking in a world full of chaos.

Going nowhere fast with a crash & burn kind of mindset is one of the most common traps among busy people. Busy people squander the most time; meanwhile productive people are action oriented from sun up to sun down.

Belief based leadership

Lacking belief in their plan, success evades them because they suffer from "possibility blindness". These distractions can prove to be lethal, extinguishing the flames of your passions as you watch your dreams evaporate into thin air. Where is your focus? What are you focusing on? Are you focused at all?

Studies also show that a Peregrine Falcon sees more clearly when its head is turned at a 40-degree angle.

Do you have your head on a swivel? Does your vision allow clear and pristine panoramic views with techno colors so bright like a Pixar Animation Studio, CGI film production? If you can't see it clearly you will never manifest the clarity of true success and that's why focusing on your dreams with telescopic accuracy is why the most effective leaders bust the code wide open.

The steps I've taken to build a global brand started from a simple idea and a massive amount of belief. Belief is a strange thing to most. Belief in your dream is not a physical thing, it's mostly mental.

You're asking your brain to believe in something you can't, see, hear, or taste. A dream is all visual in your head and is driven by the powers of your subconscious mind.

That's why most people find it difficult to dream, because they look at the dream like it's an inanimate object. In case you are confused, let's define INANIMATE OBJECT: a thing that is not alive, such as a rock, a chair, a book, etc.

So, if you are not looking at your dreams like it's a real living and breathing thing, how the hell are you going to visualize the key components that are the building blocks of certainty that will connect you with your destiny?

Marathon based leadership

When you are living your dream, walking in your purpose and connected to your mission with every fiber of your soul, that's when the universe starts to conspire moving mountainous obstacles out of your way so you can live without limits and have other deserving people partake in the riches of your success as well.

Business is a marathon, yet most people are not prepared to put in the training miles equivalent for cross country and long-term success.

In 1984, I made the cross-country team at Eleanor Roosevelt High School, going to the state championship my first year. Thanks to one man that I will forever remember... Dan Rincon was an outstanding distance runner for Dover Air Force Base High School.

While in high school, he won two state cross country titles (1969 and 1970) and (2) two-mile championships (1970 and 1971) with a personal best of 9:33.0. He also won Henlopen Conference championships in cross country (1969 and 1971) and in track & field (1970 and 1971).

While at the University of Maryland, he was the ACC six-mile champion and a cross country All-American. He qualified in the marathon for the 1976 Olympic Trials with a 2:20:07, running for the Delaware Sports Club.

Cross country is a grueling mental sport and it's not for the weak minded individual. It's a team sport that relies on you doing your part, training together and acting as a 7 man/woman unit to win the cross-country meet. Your body must be in shape, but I learned the hard way that your mind must be in better shape.

I can remember one of our regular practice sessions was at Maryland University College Park golf course. The first time we went there, I was like "WTF is this?" Why are we here? Curiosity quickly turned into the most grueling workout of my life.

Mentorship based leadership

Coach Rincon believed in pushing us to the limit. The workout was tough to get through because we would literally sprint from one hole, jog to the next hole and keep repeating the process until we completed all 18 holes on the golf course.

The first time I did the workout I thought I was going to die. I remember thinking to myself, "Is he crazy or something?" I asked one of the seniors on the team, "Why does he have us doing this kind of workout"? Coach Rincon would run beside you not breathing hard while talking in conversational mode with his brand of brutal motivation (meanwhile you needed to be resuscitated gasping for air).

He would blow past you at a fast pace and meet you at the other end of the next hole. He would wait for you, so he could see the look of depletion on your face and say, "Do not walk, keep jogging to the next hole and then take off running fast again!!! Do not put your hands on your hips and control your breathing".

His stamina was amazing. I had never seen anything like it. It's like he never got tired and gave no mercy. He knew exactly what he was doing. His leadership, strong character and mentorship made us all better as a unit and those workouts at the golf course were always hard but got easier each time.

Running cross country is deeply embedded in my entrepreneurial DNA. I have outworked most people in business because they are consumed by mediocrity. I was taught since the age of (15) to manage physical pain, push through your adversities and never accept being average.

I will forever be indebted to my cross-country coach for pushing me mentally and physically. He was able to get the most out of me because he was tough and did not allow us to make excuses about anything. It's impossible to give up when you are under the tutelage of the right guidance and leadership.

Maverick based leadership

Trailblazers and pioneers see the world differently. They see a problem and they don't complain about it. They go out and create a product that will service that need.

Over the years I have taken countless seminars, workshops and trainings of all kinds working on my skill set, always getting better at my craft. I must admit marketing and branding gave me the most trouble. The specific set of skills required to excel in these areas are simply not mastered overnight.

Every business suffers from the same dilemma. Where are you going to get new customers from? How am I going to generate leads? What is my marketing budget? How am I going to generate sufficient dollar revenue to survive, thrive and reach profitability before I lose everything?

When my dear friend, colleague and mentor Les Brown asked me to come speak at one of his events called "Motivational Monday", over 25 years ago, It was without a doubt a turning point in my career. I secured a TV deal with the Dream Network and picked up pharmaceutical giant Bristol Myers Squibb as my first fortune 500 client.

It only takes one magic moment in your career to turn things around if you know how to leverage these opportunities and spin them into paid public speaking profits. After that performance, I started to develop an insatiable appetite for micro-specific marketing knowledge that would take my brand to all 4 corners of the globe.

I started contracting with the biggest public seminar companies in the world. It was like going to Speaker College for a crash course in the art and science of facilitation. Most motivational speakers are good at the feel-good part of the presentation but offer very little value. Professional speakers actually know how to transfer knowledge at a high level and hold your attention for elongated periods of time.

As a result of this, I can remember doing a keynote in NYC for a ballroom full of corporate meeting planners. Right after my presentation a woman with a heavy Italian accent walks over to me and asks if I would be interested in speaking overseas. Once again opportunity was knocking so I kicked in the door and hopped on a plane.

I had to fly to North Miami to the Johnsons & Wales University campus for a meeting of the minds to discuss a special management and leadership training they were putting together. I was on a short list of the top facilitators in the US. I was offered a professorship to teach their curriculum and delivered onsite training to over 30 different countries, serviced over 78 different nationalities and my works books have been translated in over 30 different languages. I've also worked with sign language, multicultural and hearing-impaired interpreters.

It's time for the teacher to give back

All this experience as a celebrity insider, trusted advisor, specialist, subject matter expert, leading authority and service provider to top brands has afforded me the ability to experience work-travel to exotic destinations and love every minute of it. I have taken the time to do research and study the top 3% of the most successful people in the history of the modern business era.

Technology based leadership

These time-tested strategies from the early part of the "Industrial Revolution" to the "Technological Revolution" are designed to increase productivity and efficiency. Technology has influenced every aspect of daily life in some way or the other.

The World Wide Web is an extraordinary exhibit of new ideas getting to the market faster and business professionals control the narrative building brands that are powerful and influential.

This unprecedented shift in wealth is supported by sustainable growth as underpriced attention becomes more and more affordable. Opt in pages are exploding with email addresses, sales funnels are attracting new target prospects, converting those leads into consistent and predictable revenue.

Companies that can quench the thirst of an insatiable appetite for e-learning will rule their space with absolute domination. Prepare to set sail on the high seas and never look back. The barrier to entry is low for innovative companies who have the foresight to see a "blue ocean".

Blue ocean strategy is the simultaneous pursuit of differentiation and low cost to open up a new market space and create new demand. It is about creating and capturing uncontested market space, thereby making the competition irrelevant.

Fear and creativity cannot reside in the same space so in 2017, I became CEO/Co-founder of SpeakerFocus.com along with CTO/Co-founder Auston Troyer. We create innovative products to help subject-matter experts grow their speaking revenue.

Life puts you on a path that sometimes you least expect, so I have always learned that you should be open to new ideas that push the envelope of conservatism and take risks.

This is exactly why you should believe in being disruptive and study what pioneers, mavericks and trailblazers do when proposed with a problem they feel others should have solved. Go out and build some new shit and take over.

***

To contact Kevin:
www.speakerfocus.com
ktr@kevintrobertson.com

Joe Leone

Joe started his career in entertainment at the age of eight when his 3rd grade teacher suggested he should try out for the Phoenix Boy Choir. He endured the ups and downs of the entertainment world and was even forced to live out of his car. Never one to quit and guided by his voracious appetite to succeed, he ascended to music management.

In 1993, he moved his family to Las Vegas, starting over again. Working as a part time stagehand at the world-famous Golden Nugget he diligently worked his way up to Director and ultimately Vice President of Entertainment. After the sale of the Golden Nugget and joining Wynn Las Vegas he quickly ascended from Executive Director of Entertainment Production Services to Senior Vice-President of Entertainment Production; eventually making his way to corporate as the Senior Vice-President of Design & Development for Wynn Resorts.

Joe has experienced incredible success leading and retaining diverse talent. Joe shares his vision, specialized expertise, and exceptional facilitating skills from walking the walk in all facets of entertainment and corporate leadership. His bold desire to drive meaningful conversations on even the most difficult workplace topics separate him as a true visionary.

Described as creative, focused, and deadline driven, Joe has effectively navigated and led on the world's largest stage over three decades of live production. The opportunity to be part of a creative team that nurtures a client's vision into reality has fueled his passion for execution and creating a memorable moment for audiences throughout his life.

Where's Noah?

By Joe Leone

When pulling out of the driveaway from my family's home in Mesa, Arizona, I only saw my little brother waving goodbye. I knew the destination was going to be Los Angeles, where I didn't have a job, nowhere to live and $400.00 in my pocket. The next morning, I woke up in the back seat of my car looking out towards the ocean in Venice Beach thinking I was the luckiest man on the planet.

Seven plus years later after working my way into producing and managing Reggae artists on major tours and being a part of albums and songs that made the Top-10, I found myself mopping the stage in a 400 seat Theatre in downtown Las Vegas, Nevada as a Steady/Extra stagehand. I asked myself "is this the right career move?"

Over a decade later after retiring as Corporate SVP of Entertainment/Design & Development for one of the premier brands in the gaming industry the question is, "were they the right/wrong moves?" For every decision I made that I can lookback on and maybe do better I can find one that had I not done it would have changed the trajectory of my career. In most cases I believe the things I would have NOT done would be more of a reason for me to be less effective than the so-called mistakes (lessons).

Understanding leadership is critical in today's world regardless of your goal. Whether it's to be the leader or to follow and/or support a person or a group's vision. Understanding the motivation and source of the leader or leaders you choose to be, or follow will allow you to be successful.

What I do know is throughout my journey there may have been divergences that others could not understand but the vision was always clear to me along with my standards on how to achieve them; and the price it would cost.

I used to call it the Santa Claus Syndrome. Everybody loves Santa but all he gets for his hard work is cookies and milk! Who's his Santa? Of course, he has Mrs. Claus who has been by his side in support of him and the incredible dedication and loyalty from the Elves; but who is thinking or asking him what he WANTS for Christmas? The basic premise of this is that strong *true* leadership is constant work that really is never complete even when finished; but in the end a lonely one. Because of that it is imperative that a Leader have as one of her/his traits

COMPASSION.

I don't mean empathy or sympathy; although needed unfortunately, our own biases and judgments can come through as we try to feel as others feel. Empathy can make us feel good about ourselves but a lot of times it does not provide what the individual or group we may have been trying to help needs: relief from suffering

Leadership is about helping, teaching and giving your team all the tools and support they need to accomplish your vision. It is difficult to guide your team down a path if you have not made an effort to take a *"walk in their shoes"*.

If you ignore someone's journey, how they got there, and how they became the person in front of you; inevitably you will not understand why you are not communicating, or your message is not being received.

If you are the one people are looking to for the vision whatever the responsibilities of the one you are trying to reach, the accountability to fix it lies with **you**. That is one of the things I believe made me pivot this year from the Santa theory to NOAH.

Do you have a clear understanding of not only the storm you are currently in but the one you are heading into? How are you going to accumulate and acquire the tools, materials and skills to accomplish the goal? And once you have, do you have a message that can clearly communicate to a wide audience from different backgrounds, needs, and desires? In the end, do you have a barometer and/or systems in place to know you are on course? You must be bold in your thinking, almost every challenge should start with throwing everything out that you used to use to fix it.

To be clear, I did not say tear everything **down**! The process of change and vision always begins and ends with yourself. There may be inherent obstacles or barriers that must be addressed within an institution or entity, but if you start with what is wrong with them are you trying to lead or control?

I used to say about brick wall challenges that I would go *"around it, over it, under it or through it!";* but one of my mentors said if you go through that brick wall you are left to clean up the mess and/or rebuild it. Plus, when you broke through what were the consequences you imposed on those that were behind it?

Whatever obstacles that lie ahead of you, make them build the wall longer if you're going around them, build it higher if you are going over or have them build a deeper foundation to keep you from going under.

If you find yourself "banging your head" against that wall maybe it's time to look in the mirror again and re-evaluate either the goal or how you are getting there. That doesn't make it your fault or the goal wrong. Remember, my definition of successful Leadership is RESULTS! There is always a reason an idea or product cannot be done. The question is are you the one who decides we can fly?

If the person in front of the room can tell you every reason why it was not successful and list the people and things that prevented it from succeeding but does not go over the list of what the organization could have done better; that leader will eventually come up against a challenge they are not prepared for or willing to confront. I know sitting in a meeting with the Boss telling everyone all the reasons the goals were not met and how none of them were in your control may make you feel better but how secure are you really? Hence it is important today to find or be Noah.

What is Vision and why do we need to understand the need for it to be an effective Leader?

First let me define what I believe vision to be: I use it in the context of Webster's definition- *the ability to think about or plan the future with imagination, inspiration, intuition.* Keep those three words in the back of your mind in having a vision to lead in today's lightning speed environment:

Imagination-Inspiration-Intuition.

The foundation for that path starts with valuing the people we want to lead. To value someone you must know them. You must know them not as the "group" you are leading but understand what as an individual they are adding and bringing to the group with their own unique perspective and vision. It will also allow you to be more effective when a mob mentality arises in being able to communicate to the group as a whole but also give you tools to address specific needs and attitudes within the team. You may be successful in getting them to follow you two by two, but you better be prepared to continue to bridge the gap of their individual needs and concerns.

When I say, "get to know your people", I mean actively find something with each person that allows you to relate to that person's passion whether professional or personal. If you really want to unleash the talents of your people find out what they are hungry for! Hunger will out work Passion every time!

Remember, even if you are trying to engage on a personal level you are the *"Leader"*. Most of the time you will be perceived as talking from a position of authority. In contrast if you ask a question that feeds their personal or professional passion it allows them to take the lead. Doing this consistently not only makes them feel they can share their personal thoughts with you they will be more apt to share with you their professional opinions.

It is also important to value TIME. By understanding your team, you will be more effective in communicating the particular goals at hand. Often the inability or difficulty in communicating the enterprise's goal may be perceived as incompetence. Which in many cases is just two parties "not connecting."

If you have prioritized your time to focus on getting to know and understand your team you will be armed with what all true strong leaders have, INTUTION (insight).

Now on the surface insight may seem obvious but if that were the case there would not be so many examples of very smart people and institutions who did not have the insight in the markets or industry they had totally dominated for a long period of time. Sears and JC Penny are two perfect examples. Had either of those enterprises foreseen how to use and even more importunately how their market was going to use technology I do not believe Amazon would be the behemoth it has become.

The reason I say this is not that someone might not have entered the same space as them and not been able to compete, but they would have been at a significant disadvantage. They certainly had insight early on, you could make the argument that they pre-saw the internet buying habits of the public with their home catalog. They possibly could have been more successful than Amazon because the older generation that currently may only use technology in a limited way because it intimidates them would be more likely to get past it or learn how to use it because they would have the comfort and familiarity with using the on-line "Sears Roebuck Catalog".

An example of a successful eye to the future is todays modern "Block and Tackle" store. In many cases the services they were providing for the "cowboy/rancher" a 100 years ago: field tools, pickax, shovel etc., are still being provided today, but now you can also drive your truck up and put gas in.

So why is it that some have this *vision* and others do not? I do not believe it is that they do not see the vision, but they do not understand the climate we are in. Noah started building the ark long before the storm arrived. The more complicated an issue, the more difficult it is to break it down into a simple problem to solve.

I would like to reference a story I used when I interviewed new stagehands; I would ask them to tell me what they thought the problem was and how they would solve it?

"We have a headliner on stage in the middle of the set and their wireless microphone goes dead; what do you do?"

Some would begin by telling me that they would start by calling the mixing board to see if they knew the problem, whereas others who had more audio experience may tell me they would start at the antenna station, or check the power etc.

Remember I was interviewing for a stagehand, the person I would hire is the one who said, "I'd walk a different microphone out on stage."

My point being is that you could be correct in stating that the reason the microphone wasn't working was because of an RF issue or power but the true issue at that time was "THEY NEED A MICROPHONE!"

I believe we find ourselves today in a similar situation. There are a lot of smart people trying to solve a lot of very complicated issues in a diverse, challenging world. The anxiety a lot of those folks are feeling is because their solutions or proposals do not work or provide the projected results. I believe that is because they do not see the fundamental change in our world. The fundamental need for the microphone has not changed, you can get one at Sears or Amazon. The way we acquire our needs is changing.

Every generation is left to enjoy and deal with the decisions and consequences of the one prior. The ocean we have been navigating in my lifetime is the BOULDER that dropped in the water during WWI and WWII. Now I know I can go further back in history with the same analogy but bear with me for this point.

The waves we have had to navigate, and some have been large, '70's gas shortage, Savings & Loan scandal in the 80's, 9/11, multiple wars, and of course recently 2008 financial crises. Are all just ripple effects of that boulder, what is significant is we are dealing for the first time in our lifetime with our own boulder, 2020!

We must therefore rethink everything we do. It does not mean that the lessons learned from the past must not be heeded and used but the underlying foundation of the world we live in has changed, period. And it will NOT go back to a NEW NORMAL.

Today's leaders are now tasked with building the future from this perspective and moment in time. We must find a message that resonates with a wide spectrum of people. We need to help build and sustain strong institutions to weather the storm, provide security, safety, timely information to our teams so we all can bring our talents to the table.

Every individual has a responsibility now more than ever, you cannot just BE an employee anymore or have an "it's not my problem" attitude. We truly are in a global flood and if you think your bank account, zip code or anything else is going to insulate you from this flood I believe you will be disappointed. Those may only delay the issue of "getting you another microphone!".

So, with that in mind it stands to reason that we will come up against challenges that we have seen before or look familiar, but we do not understand why this time it is NOT working. Understand we live in a time that you may just have to send out a dove for some hope and if so, communicate that clearly and why to your team.

A leader does not need to know every answer but should know the right questions!

***

To contact Joe:

vision@joeleonespeaks.com

www.joeleonespeaks.com

linkedin.com/in/joeleonespeaks

Instagram: @joeleonespeaks

Twitter: @joeleonespeaks

Ron Jahner, ND, LAc(MT), DACACD

Founder Clarity & Creativity Coaching & Training Systems

Ronald Jahner has been recognized as a National Board-Certified Naturopathic Physician (ANMA) with a Diplomate in Acupuncture and a Diplomate in Addiction Medicine. He is a Licensed Acupuncturist (MT) and on the faculty Of the American College of Addictions and Compulsive Behavior Disorders.

Ron has over 40 years of personal and professional experience in applying the universal principles of health and spirituality for mastering life challenges. He has participated in over 5000 hours of postgraduate training and education in health and vitality enhancement and now holds numerous certifications in a variety of medical disciplines including functional neuro-kinesiology, clinical nutrition, orthomolecular therapies, mental health, oriental medicine, pharmacology, homeopathy and botanical medicine. He has extensive experience in hospitals and medical clinics collaborating in the development of integrative medical protocols for metabolic management of chronic health issues.

Dr Jahner currently focuses on teaching & mentoring executive mastery.

He is a Certified Addiction Recovery Coach (CAd) specializing in Emotional Trauma Resolution and neuroscience-based Personal Development Coaching.

He is also a Certified Health Coach working with international colleagues to combat the epidemic of obesity, eating disorders and the co-occurring health issues associated with them.

Grizzly Bears & Two Year Olds

*The Hidden Secrets of Neuroscience that Dissolve,
Relationship Conflicts, Business Stress, Over-eating,
Habitual Discouragement and Worry, Fear of Failure,
PTSD and Addictions*

By Dr Ron Jahner

6 Weeks to Live

My father was diagnosed with extensive metastasized bone cancer in the mid-1970's. It had invaded all the major bones of his body. His doctors gave him 3-6 weeks to live and a prescription for all the morphine he wanted. Then they sent him home to die. He was just 40 years old.

My father stubbornly insisted he wasn't going to die a "drug addict" and so we began a search for alternatives, certainly not a cure, which we had been told was impossible. We simply were looking for anything which might help control the terrible pain he was suffering without being drugged all the time.

At about the same time my father became ill, I had begun to experience severe symptoms of what we now know to be severe case of Immune Deficiency Syndrome (CFIDS) along with severe neurological disorders and cardiac dysfunction. Perplexed doctors told me repeatedly that, although they did not know why I was so sick, I probably had only a few years to live. I was just 20 years old.

Actually, my father did die, just recently, some 46 years after that terminal prognosis. Dad passed peacefully in his sleep cancer free for over 40 years! And I live a full life lecturing and teaching with a busy consulting practice.

My father and I had worked for many years as industrial painters with high exposure to multiple toxic solvents and chemicals. At the time, none of the doctors we saw recognized the connection between the hazardous toxins (most of which have since been outlawed) and our life-threatening health issues.

I am often asked how we did it. Ultimately there is no one secret to amazing life transformations. No single technique or healing ingredient can account for my father's recovery or mine.

Yet, we know so much more now than we did then!

New research in neuroscience, biophysics and psychoneuroimmunology, is changing our knowledge of what really work every day. These discoveries, combined with practical experience from over 40 years of clinical work, has led me to teaching and coaching these amazing practical tools for life success.

Would you like to get the benefits of these discoveries for yourself, your family and your business?

My name is Dr.Ron Jahner, for over 40 years now I have studied, researched and been certified in multiple systems of healing and life transformation. I began my career dedicated to creating healthy recovery for patients with life-threatening degenerative diseases such as cancer and chronic viral disorders. Along the way, I learned that chronic health and life challenges have many things in common.

One of the really interesting things we have discovered is that there are really only four primary causes. And one of them is the key to unlocking long-term issues such as chronic diseases, dysfunctional relationships, destructive compulsive behaviors, reversing obesity, and even addictions!

What are they?

    TOXICITY

    DEFICIENCY

    PHYSICAL TRAUMA

and...

most would say "STRESS" but that's not really it!

Now, before I share the fourth cause of dysfunction, let me give you a little background.

Interestingly, modern medicine, yes, even the formal training in so-called natural, or complementary medical schools, leans heavily on what we call an "Acute Care Model". This is exactly the four-step protocol model you would expect to receive if you suffer an accident & go to an ER Doctor.

> Symptom
>
> Cause
>
> Diagnosis
>
> Protocol

For the most part, all doctors are trained in this model. We tend to differ significantly only on step 4. Surgeons do surgery, acupuncturists use needles, chiropractors do spinal manipulation, etc. But the thought model is the same. What's the presenting "symptom" and here's our pat solution.

And it's a great model, for ACUTE issues.

However, today we are experiencing an epidemic of CHRONIC health challenges: heart disease, cancer, diabetes, pain and addictions. Even viral infections are most serious for those with other long term or chronic, co-occurring issues.

And, long-term social issues, from prejudice to domestic violence to finances and child abuse are just as serious and creating havoc in our world. ALL follow common patterns that regulate "chronic" or, long-term, human behaviors & metabolic activity.

Unfortunately, this acute care model is flawed when it comes to these CHRONIC life issues. Why?

For one thing, the first two steps of the model, which are usually obvious with an acute accident or infection, are seldom so evident with chronic issues. There are often few or mostly vague symptoms for months or even years (often decades!) when you are developing things like heart disease, cancer or even an eating disorder or alcoholism. Or, perhaps, hanging on in a dysfunctional relationship or failing business strategy.

And so, by the time you can identify the symptoms or issue as an acute crisis, it's often too late. We go to the doctor or social worker or bankruptcy lawyer with a serious issue that requires crisis management! By then, the original causes are obscured or there are so many of them that simple protocols based on presenting symptoms are inadequate.

By the way, in neurophysiology there are good reasons to believe that any social situation, behavior or metabolic process that persists more than 3-6 months, or, in some cases, even 3-6 weeks crosses the line from acute to chronic. And remember, these issues often fester unawares for decades before a crisis, or series of crises, make the issues unavoidable.

So, what is that fourth causative factor that regulates long-term healing and emotional resilience? Surprisingly, it is NOT how much STRESS you are experiencing in your life!

The key fourth factor that unlocks the key to creating amazing health and life success is how YOU, automatically and even unconsciously, REACT, to stressful people, events and personal memories. The fourth vital cause of chronic life dysfunctions is:

4. Our personal SURVIVAL COPING BEHAVIORS

These are automatic, mostly non-cognitive behaviors and reactions to what we, or our subconscious, mid-brain perceives to be life-threatening or intolerable stresses.

These SURVIVAL COPING BEHAVIORS come in two flavors, those that are genetically encoded, we are born with them, and those we learn and memorize instinctively from our families & cultural environment, mostly as small children in the first five or six years of life. They are also deeply imprinted with any significant trauma or institutional routines at any time.

So, what do we do about it? If these SURVIVAL COPING BEHAVIORS regulate our bodies ability to heal and deal with stress, then how can we ever be successful in life?

How do we change them if they're not working for us?

What can you do when your health, relationships, business, or mental-emotional stability is compromised? How do you identify & change patterns that have been running in the background of your mind for decades? Especially, when they are running automatically in a non-cognitive, auto reactive, part of our subconscious neurology?

Enter…

Grizzly Bears & Two-year Olds!

Some 40 years ago now, I did my residency and associate practice in rural Montana with a brilliant naturopathic physician, acupuncturist and pastoral counselor, Dr. Brazos Minshew. We saw patients with chronic health challenges, often 250-300 patient visits per week, from all over the world in our small clinic near Glacier Rocky Mountain Park. As we began to get a better understanding of how individual temperaments and non-cognitive stress responses were affecting our client's ability to heal from serious illness, we made up "Grizzly Bear" stories to explain what was happening in their bodies.

In fact, everything we know about how your body, brain and nervous system reacts to serious stress and physical trauma can be easily explained with a metaphor of an attack by a wild animal like a grizzly bear or lion.

In addition, since the vast majority of these unconscious reactions are either genetic or learned in early childhood, everything we have learned about how to heal and repair these aberrant behaviors and dysfunctional reactions can be explained with a metaphor about a two to four year old child!

Hence, "Grizzly Bears & Two-year Olds".

Fight - Flight - Freeze

We are all familiar with the genetic automatic reactions to physical stress and trauma. It's commonly called, Fight - Flight - Freeze.

Or, in doctor-speak, Sympathetic Adrenal Dominance or Arousal. This genetic reflex is why a newborn baby is spanked after birth. It gasps & has an autonomic reaction in Flight/Fright to start breathing. Not a very kind way to start life if you ask me!

Whether you are a doctor or not, we all have a pretty good idea of what happens in our body if we were chased by a real grizzly bear! If you were really running from an aggressive, vicious bear, would your body & nervous system:

Continue digesting a big breakfast?

Continue activating immunity to fix a cold or hay fever?

Stop and rest to heal a sprained ankle or scratched knee?

Be focused on life-threatening heart disease or cancer that might kill you in the next few years?

Stop to contemplate & enjoy the beautiful flowers & bunnies you see?

or

Run like crazy focusing on nothing but being killed & eaten by a vicious bear!!!

Well, duh! Lol.

OK, so we all get it. In sympathetic adrenal dominance/arousal, commonly referred to as Fight/Flight syndrome, your body is concerned with nothing other than physical survival. Everyone knows this. Even doctors know this!

However, there are three exciting new discoveries in neuroscience and neuro-physiology that most doctors are not aware of yet.

These three factors are the difference between how your body and your nervous system responds to an acute trauma or condition, and how it reacts in an entirely different way when something has been running in your nervous system for more than a few weeks, especially a few months.

Don't blame your doctor. Remember most of his training was in an acute care model. He is highly skilled at recognizing a presenting symptom and giving you the value of his expertise and training with what to do about that symptom.

Chronic conditions are chronic, unfortunately, because we don't know how to fix them with that model! Otherwise, they wouldn't be chronic, would they? They would be cured!

What are these three potent game-changers from neuroscience that have revolutionized our understanding of long-term human behaviors and coping strategies?

When I teach doctors in the postgraduate American College of Addiction and Compulsive Disorders (ACACD) classes, at this point in my "Grizzly Bear" story I always ask the same question.

How long does it last?

How long does the stress response, the fight or flight down-regulation of digestion, immunity, tissue repair and long-term healing systems, last? The bear is gone. The park ranger shot him with a tranquilizer gun, and you are home safe.

How long does it take for your body to reset neurologically to where it was before you saw the bear?

The answers from most medical healthcare professionals are startling! Most commonly they will say a few minutes, a few hours, a few days. Occasionally a week or two.

Conversely, when I give the exact same lecture to a group of laypeople, the answers are very different. Most say it would take quite a while to recover from that sort of a traumatic experience. Some will even say, "I would never get over it! I would have nightmares about bears forever!"

Why the difference?

It took a while (I can be a little slow) but eventually I understood why doctors answer the way they do. Most of modern medical science and research is based on autopsies and animal studies. If a gazelle is chased by a lion and gets away, what is it doing 15 minutes later? It's eating! It's completely forgotten the lion attack and is getting on with her life.

Are people gazelles? Not exactly. Actually, humans have something called a neo-cortex coupled with creative imagination and long-term memory. We have this amazing capacity to re-run personally created "movies" of our memorized experiences over and over, all the while reacting emotionally as if the event was real, even though it's just running in our mind!

The best answer we have now from neuroscience is that one traumatic event can continue to run in our nervous system, suppressing digestion, immunity and tissue repair for two to ten years! Two to ten years!!

So, my next question for you (and the doctors) is,

"How many two-year periods have you lived in your life with only one stressful event?"

(Ok, you can stop laughing now!)

Hmmmm… What happens when you pile one stressful event on top of another or have ongoing stressors like relationships or financial issues that go on & on?

And that brings us to the second thing we have learned from the neuroscience of trauma neurology, healing mechanisms and social behaviors.

Once a stressful event or metabolic reaction runs in our nervous system for 3 to 6 months, sometimes just 3-6 weeks, it is memorized as a non-cognitive (subconscious) automatic reaction program!

I have my clients internally visualize miniature grizzly bears running continually on hamster wheels in our subconscious. How many do you think you have now? And every one of them is controlling your automatic reactions in life, including the efficiency of your immunity and healing systems, even your success in relationships and business, without you even knowing they are there!

I'm sorry, it gets worse.

There is still that third neuroscience factor about how we react to trauma and long-term stress that even most doctors are not aware of…

If our bodies or, subconscious neurology, perceives any of these stressors to be life-threatening, even if it just FEELS life-threatening, the nervous system doesn't just memorize it as a subconscious habit or behavior.

Your body and nervous system will record this trauma memory in the exact same part of the mid-brain that regulates survival coping mechanisms!

In effect, your body will come to believe that holding onto this trauma and continuing to react to it is helping you to stay alive! This is the exact same part of the midbrain where addiction and dysfunctional compulsive behaviors exist and destroy your ability to cope and respond rationally to stressful situations for the rest of your life. The body effectively believes that suppressing immunity, digestion and tissue repair may be hazardous to your long-term health! Oh my!!

Unless you learn how to change it.

So, what do we do about it? That's where two other exciting discoveries in neuroscience can radically change everything about this scenario.

The first discovery, unfortunately, is that we made a big mistake in modern medical theory over the last couple hundred years or so. (Ok, so maybe more than just one, but let's keep this manageable!)

What we did was split medicine into two broad areas and put all health issues in one box or the other. The two "boxes" were, Mental-Emotional versus Physical. Most doctors, trained in that acute care model, focus on the physical side. Interestingly, some version of addressing the first three physical causes of illness, Toxicity, Deficiency, and Physical damage, will usually allow a patient to heal from acute symptoms.

You break your leg, get it set properly, put on a cast and then in six to eight weeks it heals stronger than it was before. Ditto most common acute symptoms. However, if the symptoms persist for more than six to eight weeks (90 days is a common rule of thumb), it often can become chronic, a life-long issue.

And that's where we made our mistake. First of all, the body is a holistic unit and separating parts out instead of seeing it as an integrated system is problematic. However, if you're going to split it up, current research in neuroscience indicates that the correct "boxes" are, Mental/Thinking and Physical/Emotional. That's right, the part of your brain, the neocortex, that regulates mental processes and thinking is very different from the part of the brain that reacts only to emotions and controls all your autonomic physical responses and behaviors.

In fact, we now know that about 95% of your emotional processing occurs from the neck down! In fact about 60% of it in what is called the "enteric brain", your digestive system! Another huge neurological "brain" is in the heart tissue and actually sends more information to the brain than it receives in return.

And, most importantly, this emotional-physical-metabolic neurology that controls unconscious processes and behaviors does not understand words! So, using some form of talk therapy to change compulsive body behavior is doomed from the start. Your body isn't listening! If you don't believe me, what happened the last time somebody, (even you) told yourself not to eat that second hot-fudge sundae or drink that third scotch? Nobody was listening!

The body reacts automatically to a completely different communication system especially in response to what it perceives as chronic life-threatening stress and trauma! And the biggest part of that is running non-cognitively in our subconscious neurology, 24/7. We're not even aware of it.

It requires a completely different, systemic approach if you choose to change long term compulsive behaviors and survival coping responses. And that's whether they are creating over-eating, a chronic disease, dysfunctional relationship, a compulsive disorder or addiction, or even, continual failure in business!

What's the other big neuroscience discovery that affects all this?

The vast majority of our autonomic survival coping behaviors and reactions were automatically programmed before we were five or six years old!

That's the "Two-year Old" part.

Almost everything about how to fix this and change these subconscious coping behaviors can be explained with a metaphor about a young child.

The part of the brain that we are using to communicate, talk and think is incredibly complex. Yet, it may account for only 1% or 2% of the actual "computer" processing that is occurring in your non-cognitive, automatic body behaviors and metabolic processing!

Changing these deeply held patterns of behavior, especially if they are part of a survival coping response, would be like having to rewrite the binary code or programming language in your computer every time you wanted to use it! It just wouldn't be possible.

Fortunately, some brilliant programmers created "hacks" that allow them to go in and fix or update aberrant programming, and then, even more brilliant "hacks" that allow those of us whose computer skills are limited to clicking icons & a little typing (or dictation) to actually use our computers.

Guess what? Our amazing brains and neurology have a whole system of programming languages and neurological "hacks" (even some really cool "icons"!) that allow us to go in and change significant parts of our non-cognitive, subconscious behaviors and autonomic reactions, even if they were installed in early childhood or as a result of severe trauma or abuse.

These "hacks are the hidden secrets of habitual success!

As Judith Joy, an author, inspirational speaker, dream creation coach, and my colleague says: "One of the amazing hacks our bodies provide is body sensations. The body senses messages by using sensations. Think of a sensation as an incoming text message. You know when you have a text message because you hear a ding or a short musical phrase. The body sensation is the ding on an incoming message. From there you get to choose what you would like to be, have or do with it."

As Judith Joy, an author, inspirational speaker, Dream creation coach, and my colleague says: one of the amazing hacks our bodies provide its body sensations. The body senses messages by using sensations. Think of a sensation as an incoming text message. You know when you have a text message because you hear a ding or a short musical phrase. The body sensation is the ding on an incoming message. From there you get to choose what you would like to be, have or do with it."

That's what my Clarity and Creativity Coaching & Training programs are all about. My colleagues and I teach you, and, more importantly, coach you, to learn & master:

"Five Pillars of Childhood" that create powerful social & emotional resiliency

"Seven Hacks" that allow us to instantly shift non-cognitive coping behaviors and emotions

"Three Big Lies" that our social reality uses to keep us traumatized & sick

"Transitional Breath Model" to create instant physiology changes

Hidden Secrets to Spontaneous Creativity, even Dissolving "Writer's Block!"

ONE thing your Thinking Brain CAN do to instantly reverse unwanted behaviors and attitudes, even addictions!

"Four Languages" of the Body and Emotional Memories (Hint: None of them use words!)

The amazing secret that allows you to transform your traumatic memories into resiliency resources!

And much, much more.

As a wise man once said, "Healing is not an event, it is a process. It is actually the process of life optimized to the highest level." Hopefully we, and those whose lives we serve, can all work together to encourage more people to take advantage of the many resources at their disposal which can ultimately result in optimal health and life performance.

***

To contact DrRon:

For more information about DrRon & his trainings email us at drron@drronjahner.com

For support with developing optimal habits of health and dissolving issues with obesity, please go to:

https://coach.optavia.com/DrRon4Health

For personal transformational coaching in the Clarity & Creativity Coaching model, please contact Judith Joy, Dream Creation Coaching at

www.yeswithjoy.com

http://linkedin.com/in/drjahner

Robert M. Curran

Robert M. Curran is a business owner, Certified Life Coach, Mental Performance Coach, and creator of "The Curran Method." This is a one-of-a-kind 'mental skills' training unlike anything you have seen. Learn to unlock your personal potential and have, be or do whatever you desire.

Growing up, Curran had dreams of playing professional sports. He worked hard....just like you. He had successes and failures......just like you. But when his athletic career did not go as planned, and he felt as if he were climbing a mountain of sand, Curran decided to start his own landscape business. A friend introduced him to a book called *Psycho-Cybernetics* by Maxwell Maltz. This book sparked an interest in what the mind is capable of. In the mid 1990's, he began attending seminars, participating in workshops, and reading self-improvement books that dealt with increasing your mental performance in any area of life. As Curran continued to learn more and more in this realm, he decided that sharing this knowledge with people was what he really wanted to do.

Curran's passion for the 'mental skills' side of life has taken him on a journey through education and specialized training over the past 20 years—one that continues to grow and help him achieve his goals and dreams. Now, Curran has taken years of training, schooling and mentorships, and created 'The Curran Method!' This method will help you to have, be, or do whatever it is you desire in life.

How to Command What You Want... and Receive It!

By Robert M. Curran

Everything (and I mean everything) we do starts with our thinking. Whether it turns out for good or bad is up to you. I will show you how to do it. Remember the story you were told as a kid, about rubbing the Genie's magic lamp three times and being granted three wishes? Then, at some point, we were told that the story was not true. What if I told you that you can have, be or do anything you want, and it is as easy as rubbing a magic lamp? And what if your wishes were not just three, but limitless? I can show you how easy it is to use the power you have within you. You won't believe how easy it is.

The secret is, there is no secret. Yes, you heard me. I have heard people say, "This is the secret to wealth." But guess what, the only secret I have come up with over the last 25 years of studying, attending workshops and seminars, being mentored, reading books, listening to audios/videos, and learning from the past is that YOU ARE THE SECRET! The method I have to present to you is one that super successful people are using (whether they are aware of it or not) without exception.

If you are reading this, odds are this is not the first time you have sought out material on how to get what you want. I am sure you have listened to or read enough that you're at the point of giving up. Well, I am here to tell you to hold on to that horse. For 25 years I have worked to cut out all the garbage and leave you with the tools necessary to have, be or do whatever you want in life—period! I will not give you a bunch of homework or a plethora of charts to look at. What I will give you is 5 simple and easy steps to command what you want and allow it to come to you.

"You become what you think about."– Earl Nightingale

Have you ever heard this before? Well, it's true, and The Curran Method is a step-by-step menu of how to take your thinking process and have it help you to have, be or do whatever you desire. I would like to first touch on a few things you will need to know before beginning this process.

What is a Dream?

Do you have dreams? Do you know what a dream is? A dream is big—bigger than your lifetime. We normally do not talk about our dreams. Why? We think people will judge them as silly or unobtainable. Most do not know what a dream is; and if they think they do, why are they not achieving it? Dreams are different from goals. We have 'dreams at the top,' then a 'chief aim,' and finally there is the 'next logical step.' Odds are that the majority do not know what these steps are or how to use them to achieve their dreams, and that is why the successful people of the world are 1% of the population. Why not know what they know, or at least a little bit so you can start achieving your dreams and goals? The good news is there are two, and only two, reasons you do not have what you want. First, you are probably not putting out the right frequency with your thinking; you think you are, but you're not. Second, you are putting out the right frequency while simultaneously doing something to block it from coming in. That is where The Curran Method comes in. I will not only show you how to put out the right frequency, but to recognize if you are blocking your dreams and goals from coming in and how to fix it.

Success is a Decision Away.

What is the number one reason people don't succeed in their lives at the level they want to? It is not a lack of knowledge; people are just not very teachable when it comes to what they want out of life. We mostly run around thinking that what we are doing, or who we are listening to, is going to give us the secret to what we want. There are four reasons people fail: 1) We don't listen to the right people. 2) We are not very teachable, especially in the area of what we want specifically. 3) We spend too much time doing what we think is right to get what we want. 4) We don't spend enough time at a conscious competence level when learning how to get what we want.

"I'm going to do it, that's it, period!" When you get to this point in your life, things change. When you are sick and tired of being sick and tired, the universe around you changes; thus, your life changes. The hard part is that most don't know how to decide. You cannot decide because inside, you are afraid to change. I was once told that in order for your life to change, you need to change the things in your life. Easier said than done, I know. However, this is the area where decisions are made or not made. Sadly, most of us are unaware of how this works. There has probably been a situation in your life when the sign was right in front of you, but you weren't paying attention. The good news is, there are signs all day every day, and when I teach you how to change your thinking, you will not only see the signs but also learn to use them to your advantage. Your dreams and goals will start coming in to view and your life will change.

Correct Steps to Attracting What You Want.

This is also known as the Law of Attraction. There are a number of people out there teaching the Law of Attraction, and none of them are giving you the complete recipe for how it works or how you can use it for whatever you want. If your mom gave you the recipe for your favorite dish, but you didn't follow the instructions word-for-word, you wouldn't get the same results, would you? This same problem occurs with the Law of Attraction. The person presenting often adds their own words, changing the original recipe. Therefore, the results don't come out the same. I have the original recipe and will walk you through the simple (and I mean simple) step-by-step process.

Do you know what you want? I have a simple formula to share. There are three ways to define what you want: specifically (in great detail), in general, and just the feeling you get. None of these are better than the other, but if you want to get what's best you, I suggest getting what gives you the best feeling. Once you know what you want, you must know why you want it. Truly knowing the 'why' can be the most difficult part to uncover.

After you know what you want and why you want it, you must take massive action towards getting it. You can't sit at home, overthinking whether or not it is the right time—just get moving and act. Next, you need to ask yourself, "Is what I am doing getting me closer to want I want?" Finally, if the answer to that question is no, then you must change what you are doing until you get the results that will lead you in the right direction. Remember, the first sentence of this chapter? If not, go read it again.

99% of what is supposed to be in your life is floating around in the universe, out of sight and waiting for you to bring it in. Why isn't it in your life at this moment? Because we focus too heavily on the 'how.' We do not need to know how anything works; it just happens.

Getting the Law of Attraction to work for you begins with knowing what you want and believing you can have it. You must be obsessed with the idea of attaining it. The Law of Attraction will put everything in motion (people, places, events, etc.). Everything on your screen is affected by your thinking. So, when you consistently put out a vibrational frequency with lots of power behind it, everything outside your screen (that you cannot see) starts to move—slowly at first, then faster and faster the longer and more consistently you practice. The Law of Attraction then says that the vibration you put out will attract that same frequency back to you. The key is to have no doubt that you will get what you want. Most have difficulty believing because they want something that seems far out of reach. We can't help but leapfrog from where we are to something so big. You must be willing and able to take small steps; then the big ones will follow. FACT: 70% of lottery winners go bankrupt within a few years. This happens because their vibrational frequency has not changed—which was probably at the level of just making ends meet like over 90% of us are doing every day, week, month, and year of our lives.

"Clearly define your dream and get a burning desire for its achievement."– Napoleon Hill

Your thinking creates what you want, not how you will get it. You don't need to know the vehicle that is going to take you where you wish to go; just trust that it will. The universe will bring what you want into your life at the right time for you. Our thoughts effecting physical matter is proven scientifically, and you must believe this. Watch movie, "What the #$%& ! Do we know" to see. The universe brings people, events, things, situations, etc. into our lives every day that will bring you closer to what you desire. Your job is to look out for signs from the universe.

When you first start using my 5 steps method, you will have to use this information on a conscious level (conscious competence) in the beginning. If your level of belief is 3 out of 10, the process won't work for you—or it will work to some extent, but you will give into doubt and push away anything you had been attracting. At that point, you'd have to start over. My goal is to get you to where you can easily apply these steps to your life and can spend your time enjoying what you've created.

I have found that the best way to achieve your goals is to want things that make you feel good. You do this by letting the universe give you what is best for you. When you stop trying to figure out the 'how,' you are given things that make you feel good. When working through my method, use the words "I want" as much as you can. Do not put a time limit on how long it will take to achieve. Let the universe bring it when the time is right for you, not when you want it. Don't force things into your life by trying to figure out how; just let it happen. When you start to receive things, it means you are ready and have no doubt that it is coming in your life.

Develop a burning desire for what you want. This means putting what you want out into the universe with lots of power; the more power, the faster you will receive it. Transmit the frequency as much as possible and for as long as possible. It will take some time, and you will have to be patient. You must feel good when you are transmitting the signal of what you have fixed your thoughts on. Lastly, you must believe in what you want—have no doubt it is coming. All of this works much faster when you are in a state of 'feeling good.' Just remember, you cannot see 99% of what you're manifesting because it is off your radar screen. It is moving in relationship to you and the vibration you're transmitting.

When you believe it is on the way, you will feel great—despite not knowing how or when. You won't care because your belief will be vibrating at such a high level. Don't forget, success is just a decision away and when you use my procedure, have no doubt. Everything you have had, have now and will have in the future is because of your thoughts. You create everything in your life. When you take responsibility for that, your life will change.

The 5 Steps

Each of these steps has a lot of information within it. We will touch on the main part of each.

Who do you listen to?

Most of you are likely listening to someone who is giving guidance that will work up to a point. But soon, you will find yourself stuck, unable to get to the next level. Why? Most teachers have never actually done what they are teaching. They are just doing it for the money, not the satisfaction of helping others achieve what they want in life. You need to listen to people that have already obtained what you want.

Teachability Index

There are only two parts to this: the willingness to learn and the willingness to accept change. Most of you probably have a high level of willingness to learn; that will benefit you in life. The hang-up is an unwillingness to accept change. The tendency is to keep doing the same thing every day, over and over again, or to continue searching for 'the secret' when any new information out there is just being presented to you in a different way. Look at it this way. No one is making up new information. All the information out there has been passed down from generation to generation. The big difference is that individual teachers are filtering out and adding in their own thoughts. You may see some results, just not the results you are truly looking for.

Changing what you do each day, the people you listen to, and the way that you act overall needs to shift. Are you satisfied with what you have, or do you want more? You have to be willing to change something in your life to start anything new. To see where you are on the teachability scale, pick a number between 0 and 10 for both your willingness to learn and your willingness to accept change. Multiply them together and that will give you your teachability percentage. (i.e. Scoring a 10 on willingness to learn and a 5 on willingness to accept change makes you 50% teachable.)

Training Balance Scale

There are also two parts to the training balance scale. First, your thoughts. Remember the first sentence of this chapter? Yep, everything you do comes from your thinking. In order to get what you want you will need to change the way you are thinking. Remember what Earl Nightingale said? "You become what you think about."

There are a number of ways to change your thinking. During my coaching sessions, I go into greater detail, but start by giving yourself 69 seconds just to focus on what you want. It has been proven that after 69 seconds of doing this, your thoughts move into the universe and start shifting in your direction. Try it. Sit for 69 seconds and think of nothing other than what you want in life. Hard to do. Something other than what you want will most assuredly pop into your head. This is one of the major reasons you cannot get what you want. You can't think about it long enough to manifest it into your life.

Now, for the second part I have found to be very interesting and useful in everyday life. I taught this to my wife, and she got her dream job within a few months. The 'how' (as we've talked about before) is not to be known. I asked my wife one day, "What is your dream job?" I guided her by saying, "If you want it, just put out the feeling that you would get being at that job every day." A few months went by and she got a call from my sister that a job was opening up in the area that she might want to pursue. After telling me this, I just looked at her and said, "Remember, don't try to figure it out. Just keep the feeling you have about it and don't try to out-think the universe." She went to the interview, among 40 other applicants, and got the job hands-down. If she hadn't been relaxed, it probably wouldn't have worked out for her. She uses these techniques daily couldn't be happier.

Guys don't try to figure things out. There is so much out there available to us if we just relax and let it come.

4. 4 Steps in Learning

Anything we learn, we use a simple four-step process—one we were never taught in school. Learning and understanding these steps will help you obtain all your desires. First, unconscious incompetence—we don't know what we don't know. Second comes conscious incompetence. At this step, you become aware of what you don't know. Third is conscious competence, which is being aware that you are learning what is at hand. Finally, unconscious competence is being on autopilot. We do things automatically without thinking about them. It's like learning to tie your shoes. At first, you didn't know how to do it. When you became aware that you didn't know, you consciously learned, then after repetition and practice, you don't have to think about it anymore; you just do it. By learning these steps, you will be amazed at how much and how quickly you can learn.

5. Master the First 4 Steps

This is the easy one. You just need to go back through the first four steps until it becomes unconsciously competent to you. The hang-up is, over the years you have formed habits that are now ingrained into you, holding you back from learning new things. You must stay persistent and consistent with these 5 steps, and with practice, you will get better and better until it comes automatically to you, without much thought involved.

Above all, please remember that you create everything you have in your life. When you take responsibility, your life will change. Know what you want, why you want it and be willing to take massive action. Strive to see clearly whether or not what you are doing is getting you closer to achieving your dreams and goals. It is crucial that you know, realize and understand that everything you have is a direct result of your thinking.

You do in fact (whether you want to realize it or not) become what you think about all day long. If you would like to learn more, please feel free to contact me via any of the avenues below.

To your success,

Robert M. Curran

***

To contact Robert:

TheCurranMethod.com

1.630.514.9016

CurranMethod@gmail.com

Follow 'The Curran Method' on Facebook. Text or call with questions about his program and how to get started at 630.514.9016, or email him at CurranMethod@gmail.com.

Marc Kaschke

Marc Kaschke is the founder and CEO of Escaping Perfect and host of the Pursuing Perfect podcast. Kaschke is a lifelong entrepreneur and angel investor. He started his entrepreneurial journey selling sweet corn on the corner as a teenager in Nebraska. Kaschke later worked in the family John Deere dealership and owned a music store, a pizza restaurant and a float spa. He served as mayor of his hometown and on the boards for multiple local and regional organizations. He was a founding investor in technology startups that have raised hundreds of millions of dollars and achieved multibillion-dollar market capitalizations. He has played the role of co-founder, advisor, board member, and even temporary CFO for numerous startups. Kaschke currently works with high-performing individuals and companies to help them escape perfect, grow themselves and their businesses. He is an avid history buff and passionate college football fan.

Progress Over Perfect Will Transform Your Life

By Marc Kaschke

I slumped into the kitchen chair and collapsed my head into my hands. Thoughts were racing in a loop in my head.

How could I be so stupid?

Maybe I really wasn't good enough?

Why was I avoiding important issues and procrastinating all the time?

Why was I constantly comparing myself to others?

How did I start doing things that just weren't me?

Would I ever be able to recover from this set of failures?

I was 28 years old at the time. The previous eighteen months had been a rollercoaster. I'd turned $25,000 into $50 million only to lose it all. My firm had acquired half of the world's largest used jet dealership and made the largest sale on eBay. Then the FBI discovered my partners were committing bank fraud on a massive scale. My girlfriend died in a car accident.

I was in total despair. I felt like an absolute failure. I reached a breaking point. I knew I was not living the life I wanted to live. I knew something had to change. I couldn't keep going down the path I was on.

It started a 15-year journey of discovery filled with many painful mistakes, soaring successes and much trial-and-error.

But I finally figured it out. I was trying too hard to be perfect.

I didn't understand perfectionism. I was familiar with the OCD version of perfectionism. The need for organization all the time or having everything in alignment.

I didn't think I was a perfectionist. I'm not the best dresser (thank goodness for my wife), I'm a bit overweight, and my desk is a perpetual mess. But like a tiger stalking its prey, perfectionism was waiting to pounce at the most inopportune times.

I didn't realize perfectionism could present itself as:

All-or-nothing thinking

Procrastination

Avoiding new challenges because you might fail

Seeking the constant approval of others

Setting unrealistic expectations so you don't have to try

Fixating on failures instead of successes

Self-sabotage

If any of these points sound like you, then you might be a perfectionist to some degree.

Looking back, I'd been searching for perfect my entire life. I wanted to have the perfect life, the perfect job, the perfect body, the perfect wife and the perfect family. But didn't everybody. Perfect was my destination. I didn't realize I was doing it and I certainly didn't understand the negative impact it was having on my life.

We are bombarded daily with images of perfection often not realizing the photo we see in the magazine has been photo-shopped. We unfairly compare ourselves to ideals and others that don't represent reality.

It is easy to create in our minds what "perfect" looks like. It can also limit our options in the world. I would never have met my wife if I hadn't let go of my perception of perfection.

That may sound harsh, but in my mind, I knew what a perfect wife would look like. I knew every detail. It was a ridiculous teenage ideal. No wonder I was still single at 33 years old.

I first saw my future wife at a luncheon meeting. She was helping bring a Boys & Girls club to my hometown. My first thought was, "Wow! She's cute and smart and cares about our community. I wonder if she is single?" As she continued talking, she mentioned she had five children. I was bummed. Clearly, she was married. If not, she had children and that was a deal killer for me.

Luckily, as she was finalizing the project, she called me up with a few questions. As we got to talking, we realized we had a lot in common. I decided to break one of my "perfect" rules and I asked her out on a date. It was one of the best decisions of my life. I soon went from hard-core single to uber-dad in a moment. I ended up with a great wife, amazing children and a richness to my life I didn't even know I was missing. It never would have happened if I hadn't been willing to adjust my thinking on what "perfect" meant.

Perfect isn't always packaged as we envision it.

I once heard a story about Neil Armstrong. He explained how a trip to the moon worked. He said something like, "If you're off an inch on landing, it's really no big deal. You will safely land on the moon. If you're off an inch on takeoff, you'll miss the moon by a million miles."

The good news is our lives are not moonshots. We don't have to get everything exactly right at launch. In fact, if we think that way, we will likely over-analyze . . . end up paralyzed . . . and do nothing. Striving for perfection is the easiest excuse to do nothing because perfect isn't possible. Striving for progress should be the goal.

What if there was a way…

To get your life or business back on track?

To find a way to put aside your doubts and fears?

To find success from failure?

To begin living the true life you were meant to live?

Maybe you already know you are a perfectionist or perhaps you're simply exploring the idea. Either way, the lessons below are tools that will help if you find yourself stuck, frustrated or overwhelmed. These are lessons on:

Not beating yourself up

Making failure your friend

Making progress over perfection your goal

Letting go of ego

Taking immediate, dramatic and powerful action

DON'T BEAT YOURSELF UP

It was a little after 2 AM. My friend Heather opened the door to her rental home. She dropped her purse and screamed. Sprawled out on the floor at the bottom of the stairs was her roommate Scott. Stripped, bruised and bloody, with ragged breathing. He was clearly in severe pain. She rushed to his side to help him up onto the couch.

"What happened?" she asked.

"Someone broke in and robbed us. They beat me up and stole your cash from the kitchen."

Devastation sank in. Heather worked as a waitress in a bar and kept all her tips at home. The $3,000 she had stashed away was gone.

"Let's get you to the emergency room," Heather advised.

Grabbing a blanket to wrap around Scott, Heather assisted Scott out to her car. Arriving at the hospital, Scott was rushed back to a room. After a thorough checkup, the doctor indicated he had two broken ribs and a broken wrist. He was wrapped up and sent home.

Arriving back at the house, Heather helped settle Scott back on the couch. She felt horrible for her roommate. As she cleaned up some of the broken items lying around, something didn't feel right. First, she noticed the TV. Then the stereo. As she glanced at Scott, she noticed he was still wearing his expensive watch.

"Scott, we need to talk."

She settled into the chair next to him. "How is it that someone broke in, stole your clothes and my money yet left the watch on your wrist and didn't steal any of our electronics?"

Scott was squeamish but also a little loopy from the drugs he'd been given at the hospital. He struggled to think clearly. His well-planned story was crumbling.

Heather became more adamant, "What happened Scott?"

Unable to resist, Scott mumbled. "Heather, I took your money and drove to the casinos. I thought I could win some easy money and return your cash before you got home this morning."

"Who beat you up, then?" she asked.

"I did," Scott replied.

I remember when Heather first told me this story. I thought it was crazy. Who would beat themselves up by throwing themselves down the stairs? Who would hurt themselves bad enough to break bones to create a cover story? It was silly and bordered on the ridiculous.

And yet, looking back, I realized I had done the same thing many times. Maybe I didn't throw myself down a staircase, but I certainly would beat myself up with my negative thoughts over mistakes I made in my life.

I'd ask myself, "Why would someone want to work with me or help me develop my ideas? I've had many failures. I don't have the right degree or background or skills to launch a new company."

I beat myself up over it relentlessly. I thought I needed everything perfect before getting started on a new project. I became an angel investor partly because it allowed me to piggyback off others' success. It kept me from feeling the daily failures that are necessary to create a thriving company. I focused only on my failures and mistakes. I did not recognize the strengths and abilities I possessed.

The stories you tell yourself are powerful. Make sure you are telling yourself the right ones.

For me to move on, I had to throw away all those negative emotions.

I am reminded of when I got married and we were preparing to merge households. We ordered a large dumpster and started filling it with all the items that wouldn't make it to our new home. When I got the bill I nearly fainted. We had thrown out eight tons of trash.

Similarly, we let emotional junk build up inside of us until it can become overwhelming. Maybe we've let toxic friends or co-workers bring us down. Maybe we've let past mistakes rule our lives. Just like moving provides an opportunity to throw out all the things you no longer need, embarking on change requires that we forgive ourselves, throw away all that is no longer serving us and start with a clean slate.

What negative thoughts can you begin to remove from your life today?

MAKE FAILURE YOUR FRIEND

As a proud new grandpa, I enjoy watching our grandbaby explore. He looks at the world as a fresh new adventure. Every piece of furniture is a new mountain to climb and anything on the floor is something to touch, feel . . . and try to eat.

He is unconcerned with failure. If he falls. He gets up again. It doesn't seem to cross his mind that there is anything wrong with repeatedly falling flat on his face. He wants to learn how to stand. He wants to learn how to walk. And he is not going to stop trying until he is successful.

Yet something happens as we age. We lose our fearlessness. We develop an inner critic that echoes endlessly in our head. We feel people are judging us and, to protect ourselves, we start judging ourselves first.

Before my grandson was born, I thought of all the new things I could teach him. It turns out I am learning from him. Learning that it's okay not to know the answer, it's okay to fall if I get back up. We need not fear failure but embrace it as a wonderful tool to learn from.

Don't focus on what happens if you fail. Focus on what happens if you succeed.

Fear that comes from failure may originate from more primitive times when there was a real threat of being eaten by a wild creature. Today, we still have those same instincts, but they are misplaced. If we don't create the perfect PowerPoint at work, we're going to be okay.

As a perfectionist, failure is to be avoided. Yet, avoiding tackling a problem or taking on a new project is the surest way to mediocrity.

I challenge you this week to find a fearless little human to watch for a while. What lessons do *you* see?

PROGRESS OVER PERFECT

Change has a way of happening slowly. We often don't notice the incremental changes that can add up over time.

When I first moved out on my own after college I lived in a tiny cabin.

I'd look in the bathroom mirror each morning and think, "I look about the same as I did yesterday."

I continued doing that for months. Then I saw a photo of myself with some friends. My first thought was, "Who is that guy? That is not the person I saw in the mirror."

I was fat.

I realized I needed to fix my diet and begin exercising again. I found a personal trainer and we got to work. But the same thing happened again. I would wake up and look in the mirror and say to myself, "You look about the same as you did yesterday." I was losing weight, but it was a slow process.

Once I lost 15 pounds, my trainer pulled out an odd contraption for me to strap on. He pulled out a bowling ball to place in it. He wanted to show me that even though I didn't feel I was making progress that I actually was. I didn't believe 15 pounds was that significant. But wow. That workout was brutal. Every movement was more challenging. Every step more difficult. I was making massive progress even if I didn't realize it.

Pursuing perfection can impact every area of our lives. We can fall into the mindset of all-or-nothing thinking. If we can't get in an hour workout then we don't do the workout at all when getting in 15 minutes would still be helpful. We can also get tempted by a plate of cookies and eat one and think, "Well, I ruined my diet today. I might as well eat the whole plate."

Tiny daily changes make a huge difference over time. We can expect instant gratification and instant results.

Remember that transformation takes time. Don't let yourself get frustrated when things aren't moving as fast as you'd like. Keep making the small gains. Over time, you will be shocked at what you can achieve.

What small step can you take today to move you closer to your goals and dreams?

LET GO OF EGO

In my experience, company founders and entrepreneurs also struggle with perfection. Many assume they know what the perfect solution to a problem looks like. They spend immense resources to bring this ideal to life...but find no one willing to buy.

I had a front-row seat to the development of a digital product that seemed amazing. The founder was an expert in the field and had spent significant resources on development. Finally, the founder had his moment in the sun, a meeting with a buyer from a large, national corporation with a very well-matched need. However, in sitting down for the sale, the buyer indicated an interest in a slightly modified version of the product. This did not fit the original vision of the founder who was set on implementing his "ideal" version of the product. A sale was not made that day and the company struggled to gain traction.

In contrast, another digital company I worked with had no actual product created. What they did have was a great vision and a mockup of a basic product. They used both and approached a potential customer to gauge interest. The customer liked the concept but made suggestions on what they would like changed. The founders made the changes and worked overtime to complete the programming so they could make the sale and start generating revenue.

We see here a clear contrast between a perfection and a progress mindset. Perfect wasn't necessary. Waiting to build the ideal product, and not letting go of "perfect", caused significant damage to one company while the opposite approach has proven fruitful for the other. Let go of ego, of personal definitions of perfection, and be willing to learn from those around you.

There are times along my own path where I would have found more success by thinking more like that second start-up. I often thought everything needed to be perfect before beginning a new project. I let my own ego take control. I wasn't willing to take on partners or play a secondary role. It didn't fit my vision of perfection. I needed to get out of my own way.

Good enough beats perfect every time.

Think of a time you let ego get in your way. What could you have done differently?

TAKE THE LEAP

I was standing on a cliff in Rio de Janeiro and preparing to hang glide for the first time. At the time, I was a large man at around 245 lbs. Only one guy was willing to tandem with someone my size. He was tiny (and very brave). He first walked me to the edge of the cliff and showed me the long, steep drop-off. He explained that once we got hooked into the hang glider and started running that I could not change my mind. At that point, he would be unable to stop someone my size and we would plummet to our death. I looked over the edge again. Doubt was creeping into my mind.

This was a stupid idea.

What if I tripped? What if I didn't run fast enough? What if I ran too fast? I could do it another time. We walked back to the hang-glider. I wanted to call it off but didn't. We started running. I am not even sure when we went airborne. My legs didn't stop moving. At some point, well beyond take-off, my tandem partner politely told me I could stop running and place my feet back in the strap. I was flying.

The feeling of freedom and exhilaration was amazing, I was soaring like I never had before.

Likewise, when you decide to take the leap to overcome perfection, get your life back on track and begin achieving your dream life. Don't stop. Start running. Take the leap. And you, too, can begin to fly.

It's OK to experience fear and doubt.

It's OK to not have a perfect plan in place.

It's OK to make mistakes.

Remember making progress over waiting for perfection will transform your life.

And if you need a tandem partner . . . I am here to help.

***

To contact Marc:

LinkedIn: linkedin.com/in/kaschke

Website: kaschke.com

Facebook: facebook.com/EscapingPerfect

Twitter: @marckaschke

Podcast: Pursuing Perfect

Mato Gatnik

Mato Gatnik is a European exponential mentor, consultant, coach, author, investor, entrepreneur, networker, business matchmaker, and developer. Since his early years, he has been involved in marketing, sales, branding, and business development which took him from Slovenia to Italy, Croatia, USA and back to homeland Europe returning with enriched global experience.

As a constant learner, he continues enrolling in ongoing intensive studies of leadership, lean 6s, efficiency and management. Recently he expanded his education with studies in psychology, coaching, and neuro linguistic programming (NLP). His work also includes innovations and improvements in print, packaging, direct sales, and network marketing.

Mato's passion, mentoring and helping motivated top performers to achieve exponential results, to which he is fully committed. He obtains his knowledge by researching the broken focus syndrome, combining it with lean, kaizen, and other efficiency sciences. His methods and results are combined in the art of Lardiology, science dealing with obtaining results and achieving more with less. He is also a philanthropist, renowned author of several brands, articles, books, and courses.

He lives in Adriatic (among Italy and Croatia) and operates globally. He is available for mentorships, public appearances, advisory, and board positions, as well as for networking, business matchmaking, and joint ventures.

If you need some guidance, a piece of advice or a second opinion from someone who is a firm believer in good value and fair play, experienced, future orientated, sharp minded, efficient, practical, and "no box" thinker, you cannot afford to miss getting his insight.

The 7 Simple Phases to Balanced Path Toward Any Big Goal, Lasting Success and Fulfilment

By Mato Gatnik

How it all began

The question was born in a local restaurant, just on the Italian border, in the mid-eighties and it followed and challenged me over several decades of my life and career. It originated from the observation that the brightest, best educated, and most hard-working people rarely win the jackpot or thrive.

For example, have you ever experienced the feeling, when your mind is focused on your goals every second of the day, when you constantly learn, develop, and implement new practices and genuinely see how your offer is invaluable in comparison to the others, yet the results do not seem to come. Many others seem to prosper while your business struggles. You keep pushing yourself into new, different approaches, paying attention and importance to one, then another development idea and yet, all your efforts do not bring the results you expect. You start asking yourself why this is happening.

This was my story for near a quarter of a century. It may as well be a classic entrepreneur's tale. I dropped out of University to pursue a business idea of mine. I travelled the world, left my impact in the media, generated millions in sales, created some successful advertising campaigns and brands. Bought and sold companies. Experienced the taste of success and failure learning from both. I went back to the university, got first child, graduated while establishing a million-dollar business which I eventually lost. I restarted and started raising again, while dealing with health, addictions and trouble. Yet I succeeded to the top again. But I was not fulfilled and soon began disliking it. So, I decided to go "solo", depending on myself only. I am now collaborating with teams but relying on and reporting to the toughest of bosses only, my consciousness. And all the way - I love(d) my life.

It was through these ups and downs that I slowly found out what really matters, although it took a while and came at a high price. The biggest assets were **discovering the importance of balances, focused knowledge, mental liberation, goals, habits, and effective steps toward "spinning and rolling", magnetic attraction, and deeper individual fulfillment.**

So, to rewind back to my initial question as to why some win the jackpot (succeed with less), while others struggle and at one point most probably quit in despair?

If I put my answer into the simplest form; the less you grasp for the furthest, the more obtainable the nearest is. By using pure logic, it means that the simpler something is, the easier is to achieve. This fact, however, is most often overlooked. So, if we split a goal into 7 essential topics of achievement and fulfilment, we only need to resolve one simple task at a time and move to the next one. When all 7 parts are completed and we arrange them in the circle as a flywheel, this is easily reproducible by "rotating" it. The faster this circle spins, the bigger and greater the results are, and we can move on further. The set of our steps to the major goal is essentially a flywheel. I named it Mag's balanced fulfillment flywheel which is my single most important tool for any achievement. It involves magnetism, fulfillment, action, steps, and balance. And a bit of myself as well.

The Mag's balanced fulfillment flywheel model. Why it is so useful and important

As a real success never comes at a discount and you always need to pay the full price, the flywheel helps you determine overall cost and benefits. But by using leverages you can make certain result pivots, so the whole process of fulfillment is faster, smoother, and more efficient. It also helps you to avoid procrastination, since it calls for a start. The most important thing to keep achieving the "big picture" results is to evenly balance all fulfillment steps.

Let me give you an example. You cannot build a vila the same way as you would build a doghouse. You need to trade in something more, more material, planning, energy, and money. But the wealth, impact, and legacy that you obtain out from your construction project, is highly different when you build villas or dog houses. Yet, some doghouse constructors made it all the way to the Shark Tank show and achieved international success (Innovation Pet). This is still more than most of the entrepreneurs will ever succeed. The important thing is what is your aspiration that starts the whole thing and the balance, that keeps it going.

Planning your operations by following the balanced flywheel steps can start at any stage and helps you carefully plan all remaining phases. This is, without a doubt, profoundly important because it determines everything needed, in proportions to start "rolling" and shows you, how to multiply it. Then you only need to keep it controlled, constantly moving, and in balance. This, for sure, will generate and attract success!

So, what are the 7 stages of my fulfillment balanced flywheel?

1) **Mindset**

"Begin by always expecting good things to happen." -Tom Hopkins

The mindset is the mother of it all. This includes our knowledge, beliefs, desire to learn and improve and finally, progress. Without a proper mindset, it is hard if not impossible, to progress and prosper.

Do not forget to nourish your mindset. This can be done in various ways with each aimed at the different segments. Mindset includes taking good care of our body, mind (soul), and stomach (energy, needs), keeping us in good physical and mental shape. Some practice yoga, meditate, go swimming or hiking. Others enjoy music, movies, or books. You can figure out your own ways, just do it.

Possible leverage to increase this phase efficiency: Pick three life philosophies that represent you, one for each of the three mentioned fragments. Plan actions.

Pivot, to gain more: Find a mentor, a coach, or you may want to do short daily reading. Practice gratefulness. Avoid transactional thinking.

2) **Trade** - Nothing happens without a trade. To move forward, we need to put in some energy and our will. We trade our time, knowledge, energy, property, ideas, and plenty more. Never forget that for each of your trades, you need to make two sales. The first one is, to make someone listen to you and make it worthwhile. The second is to actually trade (sell) your product to get the desired return. This is creating relationships and increasing your chances to succeed. So, in short and simple explanation, learning how to be a good seller, and knowing what it takes to become one, helps us in being efficient, taking us to the next phase.

Keep in mind that cooperation leverages results but winning the market is competition. Select your partners carefully, so you do not drop out of the game.

Possible leverage to increase this phase efficiency: Create the relations and trust. Use technology, cooperation, endeavour to profit from recommendations and referral power. Profit from bundling and subscription models and first give, then ask.

Pivot, to gain more: Offer what you genuinely believe others need, want or will benefit from. The value you show is your gain.

3) **Efficiency** - All our effort is in vain if we trade with poor efficiency. Productivity also goes hand in hand with efficiency and always strives to achieve more with less. There are several factors that influence efficiency, but the basic is simple - stick to order, organization, and lean methodology. Whatever is not profitable, it is a loss. If the loss is higher than the outcome, we do not generate sufficient results, which represents our next phase in the form of profit.

Possible leverage to increase this phase efficiency: Inspiration is an efficiency booster since it raises motivation. Always respect the Pareto rule that 20% of actions brings you 80% of results; so keep the focus on the 20.

Pivot, to gain more. Let us be productive and do more with the same. In this way you are not taking away, deducting or reducing, which may have a negative impact. This is a more positive approach to efficiency.

4) **Prosperity** - Efficient trading generates prosperity, the profit, the wealth. This can be in various forms. Wealth is a state of mind, it does not absolutely mean "materially rich". Building massive wealth rarely happens unless you have a firm belief that you can achieve it and "publish" that mindset to the world. Profit itself cannot bring long-term fulfillment but is essential to keep the flywheel balanced and going.

Having all the money, all the free time, fulfilled material dreams, and desires may soon get an inquisitive mind bored. We can use part of generated wealth and trade it again. However, we will need to take all the following steps to complete the flywheel process and avoid jumping back and forth between 2 stages which would eventually make us lose the momentum.

Possible leverage to increase this phase efficiency: Pay attention. Be nice to everyone. Show people you care, and you will get better results. Still, do not listen to the majority and traditional beliefs. Pivot to gain more. It does not take much money to live a good life. The true wealth is in freedom to choose the commitments. Use wealth to work for you.

5) **Influence** - We can soon make an impact through an efficient trading that generates wealth and an influential mindset. It is on us, how to use our influence. After all you now completed over half of the flywheel. Why don't you publish your success? The art of attracting, charming, and influencing people is called charisma. It is the result of living rightly, in harmony with your values and beliefs. It is an inevitable attribute of anyone confident in their actions.

If we aim toward higher, focused goals, the best way is to take advantage of it in spinning our flywheel faster. So, increase actions and results without further efforts. If this sounds complicated think about it openly. We discussed earlier that "simple can take you there farthest".

Possible leverage to increase this phase efficiency: You are only making an impact when you're out of your comfort zone. You cannot influence a change if you are not changing. So, lead to a change in solving everyday problems and making an impact. To be better at it, use priming.

Pivot, to gain more: Use success and wealth to instruct others. They can be part of your change too and profit from it no matter how uncomfortable it may appear. Going after great things is uncomfortable, yet the only way to achieve and have strong impact on others. The best way? Write a book.

A moment of vulnerability and authenticity is more powerful than an hour of flattery and false charm. – Anthony Moore

6) **Purpose** - You will always have opinions and thoughts that are influenced by the environment no matter how unbiased you think you are. We are a product of everyone and everything around us. In order to find your true purpose and greatness do not focus on goals, focus on humanity, your community, on your tribe. Become a lasting star in it.

Possible leverage to increase this phase efficiency: Make your "manifesto" to pursue your created life, a life created by you, according to your beliefs, instead of the world "happening" to you. Though, keep in mind, what H.S. Thompson wrote in 1958 and is today more true than any time before: "Every man is the sum total of his reactions to experience. As your experiences differ and multiply, you become a different man, and hence your perspective changes. This goes on and on. Every reaction is a learning process; every significant experience alters your perspective." Think of changes, that COVID-19 brought to your purpose.

Pivot, to gain more: Take responsibility to find, promote, and implement solutions to the problems of nowadays.

7) **Fulfillment** – Your core satisfaction and meaning of your existence. The phase, that makes you get up at five o'clock in the morning and work till late at night yet keep you happy and energized. The satisfaction that you experience from inspiring others

and the gratefulness to those, who inspire you. The joy of small things, the peace of your mind and the moment when everything is perfect. Ability to see the steps made and hills climbed and feeling proud about it. Your Ikigai, your reason for being, and your ability to lift others to the same stage.

Possible leverage to increase this phase efficiency: Do, what you believe and love. Start by being thankful, that striving for fulfillment is even an option. Advantage from your benefits and pass them on. There is no better feeling than being genuinely thanked and praised.

Pivot, to gain more: Keep in mind: *"The journey matters more than the destination. If you want to go fast, go alone. If you want to go far, go together."*

Another ingenious thing about the whole flywheel concept is that you can start at any stage, and it remains your guideline for the rest of it. It can help you predict the inputs toward the desired goal - remember - balance is everything. Whatever your idea, plan or phase, this concept can make it work for you. Most important is that it sets your steps toward achievement, it distributes a bigger goal into smaller steps and shows you how to multiply the initial goal to exponential results. Or, putting it to "riches" language; get the idea, plan how to make it work to earn the first thousand, and spin the wheel 1000x to have the first million. Plain and simple.

The new approach to focus and efficiency - use lardiology for results

Although the above sounds almost too simple to be true, it usually does not get much more complicated if we do not make it that way.

Enters lardiology. Lardiology is all about achieving results and keeping the focus, going step by step, one thing after another. It basically shows how to avoid chasing glitters instead of sticking to focus and communicating it efficiently.

I discovered that keeping the focus and following the plan consistently determines efficiency of achieved results. How to remain on the path and avoid all temptations and distractions while including possible improvements? It is quite simple, like 1-2-3.

The **first step** is to reduce the impact of our mind and trust more to our instincts and reason. The mind is a storage of all kind of information, and the majority of it was placed there by others. They represent other people's opinions and experiences, mostly obtained in different circumstances. Our reason is our personal logic and can direct us more genuinely, leaving us more open to accepting opportunities when they arise, yet follow our path. It is also helpful at "out of the box" thinking or even enabling us to *"think like there is no box"*. In other words, anything is possible.

The **second step** - To be successful, we need to efficiently communicate our ideas. This is done, when others not only understand, but also memorize (and accept) it. We can achieve this, by presenting our message using a combination of all three sensory learning (understanding) modalities: visual, auditory (reading), and kinesthetic and combine them into communication. Use an image - preferably infographic; text, speech – sound; and making the receptor jot down the main idea to engage his activity.

This is extremely powerful and works best at online (video) presentations. I named it lardiography. We see proof of its efficiency in ever-increasing online video usage in all fields. By using the so-called lardiography method, we incrementally increase the chances that our message is acknowledged and accepted. Such acceptance positively influences your determination and persistence.

The **third step** - Make it permanent. Whatever brings you the initial result, make it last. Do not lose focus and jump on the train taking you out of the way. Keep improving, keep upgrading until it makes sense, and brings better results. So, stick to actions that bring the desired outcome and repeat them daily. Make them a habit, a lifestyle. There are many useful methods and tools that help us in being efficient - from the "Don't break the chain" table to different time planners or Simpleology. Find the one that suits you most and make it a daily routine. By doing this, also success becomes a daily constant in your life.

I really admire one of Steve Jobs / Apple anecdotes:

When the first iPhone came out and a reporter complained about how it was too hard to type on a touchscreen, Steve Jobs replied: "Your thumbs will learn".

That is Apple. Apple often knows the users more than the users know themselves. They achieve this by lengthy and careful research and focusing on providing good and consistent UX and evergreen solutions.

What we can learn from it is that consistency makes everything simpler, faster, and longer lasting. It attracts.

"We are what we repeatedly do. Excellence, this is not an act, but a habit." – Aristotle, around 350 BC

Along your road, do not forget about yourself.

Just like goal achievement needs a certain balance of flywheel stages, the same is with your life. Organize events in your life as a set of balanced flywheels and balance them among themselves. So, for mindset, complete the entire flywheel keeping all phases balanced. Liberate mind. Invest just the right amount of money, energy, and time. Make the upgrading and learning most efficient (remember 1-2-3). Profit from the wealth of your new knowledge and use it to increase your influence (respecting the time investment). Ask yourself, what was the purpose of everything and if it shows your greatness to future generations. Does this make you fulfilled and gives you energy to work even harder, to spin it faster?

Great. But remember to learn to relax, pause and recharge. Do not get chained into one of the goals but flywheel and prioritize it, keep them in balance. That means having a truly rich life.

If you want to crack the rich code, you do not need to innovate a lot. Think of your idea, that will make your life fulfilled while helping others enough, that they would follow you. Having problems? Read more. Sooner or later, you will find the right information. Then put it in the right flywheel stage. Complete other stages and find a target audience. Spin the action. Attract and fulfill. The expectations, sales, others, you.

How many different flywheels did you make to achieve ultimate fulfillment? Does it make you rich? What is rich for you?

Elevate your mindset. Be consistent. Restart when you are surely not fulfilled anymore.

This is my way of cracking the code. Need some help?

You can download the worksheet of balanced flywheel on my website.

***

To contact Mato:

Email: me@mag.consulting,

www.mag.consulting, www.linkedin.com/in/matogat

OrcID: 0000-0002-9813-7018, ISNI: 0000 0004 8513 3725

Afterword

Life and business are always a series of transitions… people, places, and things that shape who we are as individuals. Often, you never know that the next catalyst for improving your business and life is around the corner, in the next person you meet, next mentor you hire or the next book you read.

Jim Britt and Kevin Harrington have spent decades influencing individuals and entrepreneurs with strategies to grow their business, developing the right mindset and mental toughness to thrive in today's business environment and to live a better life.

Allow all you have read in this book to create a new you, to reinvent yourself and your business model if required, because every business and life level requires a different you. It is your journey to craft.

Cracking the Rich Code is a series that offers much more than a book. It is a community of like-minded influencers from around the world. A global movement. Each chapter is like opening a surprise gift, that just may contain the one idea that changes everything for you. Watch for future releases and add them to your collection. If you know of anyone who would like to be considered as a co-author for a future volume, have them email our offices at support@jimbritt.com

The individual and combined works of Jim Britt and Kevin Harrington have filled seminar rooms to maximum capacity and created a worldwide demand. If you get the opportunity to attend one of their live events, jump at the chance. You'll be glad you did.

If you are a coach, speaker, consultant of entrepreneur and would like to get the details about becoming a coauthor in the next Cracking the Rich Code book in the series, contact Jim Britt at support@jimbritt.com or watch this video and schedule a time to speak with Jim: https://www.richcode.club/beacoauthor/

To Schedule Jim Britt or Kevin Harrington as a featured speaker at your next convention or special event, online or live, email: support@jimbritt.com

Master each moment as they become hours that become days.

Make it a great life!

Your legacy awaits.

STAY IN TOUCH

www.JimBritt.com

www.JimBrittCoaching.com

www.CrackingTheRichCode.com

www.KevinHarrington.tv

https://www.richcode.club/beacoauthor/

For daily strategies and insights from top coaches,

speakers and entrepreneurs, join us at:

THE RICH CODE CLUB---FREE members site.

www.TheRichCodeClub.com

www.ingramcontent.com/pod-product-compliance
Lightning Source LLC
Chambersburg PA
CBHW071333210326
41597CB00015B/1442